Nourishing the Inner Life Clinicians and Humanitar

For Lindy,
With all my best wishes!
Donna Orange
1~10 - 16

Nourishing the Inner Life of Clinicians and Humanitarians: The Ethical Turn in Psychoanalysis demonstrates the demanding, clinical, and humanitarian work that psychotherapists often undertake with fragile and devastated people, those degraded by violence and discrimination. In spite of this, Donna M. Orange argues that there is more to human nature than a relentlessly negative view. Drawing on psychoanalytic and philosophical resources, as well as stories from history and literature, she explores ethical narratives that ground hope in human goodness and shows how these voices, personal to each analyst, can become sources of courage, warning, and support, of prophetic challenge and humility, which can inform and guide their work. Over the course of a lifetime, the sources change, with new ones emerging into importance, others receding into the background.

Orange uses examples from ancient Rome (Marcus Aurelius), from twentieth-century Europe (Primo Levi, Emmanuel Levinas, Dietrich Bonhoeffer), from South Africa (Nelson Mandela), and from nineteenth-century Russia (Fyodor Dostoevsky). She shows not only how their words and examples, like those of our personal mentors, inspire and warn us, but also how they show us the daily discipline of spiritual self-care. Though these examples rely heavily on the discipline of spiritual reading, other practitioners will find inspiration in music, visual arts, or elsewhere and replenish the resources regularly.

Nourishing the Inner Life of Clinicians and Humanitarians will help psychoanalysts to develop a language with which to converse about ethics and the responsibility of the therapist/analyst. This exceptional contribution is highly suitable for both practitioners and students of psychoanalysis and psychotherapy.

Donna M. Orange teaches, consults, and offers study groups for psychoanalysts and gestalt therapists. She seeks to integrate contemporary psychoanalysis with radically relational ethics. Her recent books include *Thinking for Clinicians: Philosophical Resources for Contemporary Psychoanalysis and the Humanistic Psychotherapies* (2010) and *The Suffering Stranger: Hermeneutics for Everyday Clinical Practice* (2011), both published by Routledge.

Nourishing the Inner Life of Clinicians and Humanitarians

The Ethical Turn in Psychoanalysis

Donna M. Orange

Routledge
Taylor & Francis Group

LONDON AND NEW YORK

First published 2016
by Routledge
2 Park Square, Milton Park, Abingdon, Oxon, OX14 4RN

and by Routledge
711 Third Avenue, New York, NY 10017

Routledge is an imprint of the Taylor & Francis Group, an informa business

© 2016 Donna M. Orange

British Library Cataloguing in Publication Data
A catalogue record for this book is available from the British Library

Library of Congress Cataloging in Publication Data
Orange, Donna M.
 Nourishing the inner life of clinicians and humanitarians : the ethical
 turn in psychoanalysis / Donna M. Orange.
  pages cm
 Includes bibliographical references and index.
 1. Psychotherapists—Psychology. 2. Psychotherapist and patient.
 3. Psychic trauma. 4. Intersubjectivity. 5. Humanitarianism—
 Psychological aspects. I. Title.
 RC451.4.P79O73 2016
 616.89′14—dc23
                                                      2015020090

ISBN: 978-0-415-85610-2 (hbk)
ISBN: 978-0-415-85611-9 (pbk)
ISBN: 978-1-315-67681-4 (ebk)

Typeset in Sabon
by Keystroke, Station Road, Codsall, Wolverhampton
Printed in Great Britain by Ashford Colour Press ltd

For Natalie Gannon, CND
And in memory of Frances Madden, SNJM

[O]ne must yield to the other the first place in everything, from the *après vous* before an open door right up to the disposition—hardly possible but holiness demands it—to die for the other.

(Emmanuel Levinas, *Is It Righteous to Be?*)

Contents

Contents

Preface

Non basta. It is not enough. I am not enough. My previous two books, *Thinking for Clinicians* and *The Suffering Stranger*, made available some resources from my chief intellectual traditions—philosophy and psychoanalysis—for describing my psychotherapeutic sensibility. These books attempted to show significant convergence between dialogic attitudes and radical post-holocaust[1] ethics with "ethical-turn" trends emerging in recent psychoanalysis. But these books left the struggling clinician, including their writer, in a painful gap between infinite responsibilities to the suffering others and the worker's all-too-finite human capacities.

Each book answered an appeal from psychotherapist colleagues. The first, *Thinking for Clinicians* (Orange, 2010), responded to clinicians who asked for help reading philosophy, using its concepts and questions to help them read psychoanalytic literature. *The Suffering Stranger* (Orange, 2011) answered those who for many years had requested a book on hermeneutics, the study of interpretation and meaning, for those who work with the devastated, with those whose suffering seems beyond meaning. Now I am responding to two more requests.

Sometimes colleagues have asked me to produce something more personal, even a memoir. A combination of personal reticence and ethical sincerity—intended, at least—prevents me. My life is not about me, but for the other. And yet, biography haunts us all: how much fate and how much choice brings us where we find ourselves today? Born a Roman Catholic in the Pacific Northwest, I took a radical turn in early midlife to New York, studied at Yeshiva University, and have since lived and worked in a mostly Jewish world. While embracing psychoanalytic culture, I also learned German (allegedly to read philosophy and Freud) and married into a German-American family. While I have studied the German Lutherans' enthusiastic support for National Socialism—as the reader will see in Chapter 6—I have avoided looking much into the Catholics' complicity and energetic participation, which were probably worse. Similarly, I have avoided biography and memoir, hoping to tackle the works of "mourning and moral psychology" (Lear, 2014), of internalization, integration and integrity, other-wise. "Other-wise" refers to living for-the-other (Levinas,[2] 1981), as well as to the hope that we can learn to do so wisely.

The second query, however, I cannot evade: what forms of responsibility plague us all, including clinicians, and how do we keep responding? What personal, spiritual, and communal resources nourish us as we try to keep responding and living humanly? Each book of this trilogy attempts, in as dialogic a spirit as possible, to reply to a question, but this third one, in particular, will end with questions with which each reader can engage. No formula emerges to fit each one's need.

So, this third volume responds to those who keep asking how anyone—clinician or humanitarian worker—can continue to live an ethic that never allows us to say that we have done enough. Beyond training or formation, serious, deep, non-dogmatic, dialogic, and non-abusive; beyond profound personal desire rooted in a sense of vocation as well as in relational history; beyond the ongoing intellectual and supportive resources of our professional communities; what do we need to keep responding, to keep working with the devastated? Given our vulnerabilities to the emotional hazards of humanitarian work, given our human exposure to illness and aging, given our personal and human limitations, given the isolating character of much ethical, humanitarian, and therapeutic work, how do we go on healing, teaching, and restoring dignity to others?

This book will primarily describe the practice of philosophy (in the ancient sense) and will attempt to relate it to an "ethical turn" (Baraitser, 2008) in contemporary psychoanalysis. Claire Elise Katz explains that "this turn—to put the Other first—needs to become the *guiding condition* of our lives" (Katz, 2013, p. 72; original emphasis). Emmanuel Levinas, she goes on,

> describes this humility in terms of the one who has no time to turn back to self. It is not a question of "denying" the self—as in an asceticism, for the self is not yet of concern. It is not the choice between me and the Other, for that choice is not yet possible. Rather the self is turned toward the Other.
>
> (Katz, 2013, pp. 72–73)

Thus this book will encourage the practicing clinician or humanitarian, also a practicing philosopher, to internalize the crucial resources needed to nourish and sustain the kind of practice that clinical work in the best of the psychoanalytic tradition, including the ethical turn, requires. The required capacities and attitudes involve not only wisdom and compassion, but also vulnerability and fallibilism, courage and humility. Given that we clinicians have human frailties, how are we to sustain the burdens, loneliness, and attacks? This book attempts a partial response to this question.

To avoid abstractions, each book has chosen exemplary—though more-than-imperfect—interlocutors. First, instead of talking about philosophy in general, we spoke with Martin Buber, Hans-Georg Gadamer, Maurice Merleau-Ponty, Ludwig Wittgenstein, and Emmanuel Levinas. To bring the hermeneutics of trust to life, we studied Sandor Ferenczi, D. W. Winnicott, Frieda Fromm-Reichmann, Heinz Kohut, and Bernard Brandchaft. Along the way, however, something more personal has occurred, something that Sandra Buechler (1998), writing of the psychoanalyst's experience of loneliness, calls the use of an "internal chorus." In her view,

> The internal chorus we bring into our offices every day must be of comfort, and must be sufficiently stimulating, to encourage the creative use of aloneness. The feeling the chorus must give us is that whatever may go on today, with this particular patient, does not define us as analysts, for we have already been defined and have defined ourselves through our analytic identifications and identity formation. We are not personally and professionally at stake with each new interaction with a patient.
>
> (Buechler, 1998, p. 111)

So, my internal chorus keeps me stable and responding to the other, even when I feel besieged, persecuted, exhausted, or, in Winnicott's words, in danger of retaliating (Winnicott and the Institute of Psycho-Analysis (Great Britain), 1975). When I fail, as I have so often done, it helps me to resume my work with less self-recrimination than I could do without these voices. Buechler continues:

> With this foundation, we can experience aloneness with a patient as information, rather than as judgment. We can turn the aloneness over in our minds, wonder what it is about, become curious about it, see it as meaningful, as something to understand, but not as an obstacle or an indictment. An aloneness that doesn't cost us a good connection with ourselves, with our chorus, or with the patient can be used creatively.
>
> (Buechler, 1998, p. 111)

My philosophers and psychoanalysts from the previous two books are all indispensable members of my internal chorus,[3] upon whom I can call when needed. They speak to me, separately and together, both to reproach and to warn me—like the *daimon* of Socrates, and like Sandra Buechler's supportive choristers, who remind me that my very being is not at stake in every session. Those appearing prominently here give me the further experience, not particularly comforting or comfortable, of "*being enjoined* as a reader," as Jonathan Lear (2012, p. 169; original emphasis) writes. My choir also includes people whose names few would recognize: my best teachers who helped me to imagine that women could be leaders but never became "names" themselves; my training analyst and two early supervisors who believed in me long before I had any sense of my own capacities; many unpretentious craftspeople, outside the clinical and humanitarian worlds, who work hard and faithfully at whatever they do.

Each of us assembles our nourishing resources in whatever way we can: through meditation, imitation, various forms of spiritual journeying. For me, probably due to a discipline learned young in my convent years, my best path runs through a period of meditative reading, pursued daily and early in the day before other concerns crowd it out. Each of the authors who appears in this book, and some of those in the previous two, can be read as objects of study, as dialogic interlocutors, and as spiritual guides. They help to form that inner ethical voice that Socrates called his *daimon*, keeping me prepared for the face and voice of the stranger to whom I am called to respond.

Buechler (1998) appeals to the image of the long-distance runner. In my younger years as a marathoner, I remember needing both to pace myself and to find internal and external resources to keep me going. For me, the idea and the reality of the internal chorus continue to develop. Some members recede into the background, while others gain prominence. Even during the writing of this book, some shifts have occurred, as I learned disappointing news of some figures I had long admired, and came to know and treasure others more. Some come from within my professional world, and some from a larger cultural sphere, as I suspect they do for psychotherapists and humanitarian workers of all persuasions.

This book focuses special attention on some chorus members from beyond my world of psychotherapy practiced in the psychoanalytic tradition. It also brings them into conversation with each other, so that the book's outcome surprised me more than a little. They have become characters in my internal dialogue, as if this were a work of fiction, so readers will find my impressions, not a scholarly treatment. But I suspect that readers who engage their own internal choruses in conversation will also find both sustenance and revelations. "Know thyself," admonished the ancient Greeks. To know more intimately those who influence us, and whose voices nourish and support us—not only the so-called "bad objects"—can help to maintain the ethical response. Otherwise our work simply becomes too hard and lonely.

First, however, why is our work so lonely, and why do we need this help so much? My first chapter indicates the traumatic origins that make our work so demanding, within the situation of a "burning world" (Cushman, 2007; Richardson and Zeddies, 2004). Relying on recent work on testimony and realization, I explain why working with the seriously traumatized demands so much from the clinician, requiring such internal choral resources to be endlessly nourished and replenished. Without reviewing the scholarly and scientific trauma literature at length, we consider trauma, along with the condition of "traumatism" it evokes in calling forth ethical response, to make it clearer why such personal, communal, and spiritual resources become indispensable to clinical and humanitarian workers.[4]

The second chapter describes the developmental ethics of personal responsibility in Hans Loewald's psychoanalysis, and asks what is added by an ethics of hospitality (Orange, 2012), clinical generosity (Butler, 2004; Corpt, 2009), and vulnerability (Aron and Starr, 2012; Butler, 2004) with which so many of us have been trying to confront both the elitism of traditional psychoanalysis and the indifference to suffering people whom we seem unable to see and hear or to allow to disturb us. Some will ask: why should I have to feel guilty all the time? Well, it depends on what we mean by "guilty" and by "ethics." I suggest that there are several versions of ethics with which we psychotherapists, individually and as a community of scholars in dialogue, need to concern ourselves.

The third chapter addresses a question that explodes into the conversation as soon as I mention the ethical ideas of Dostoevsky and Levinas. Are they talking about Freud's moral masochism? Putting the other first, will I not lose myself? Are we not trying to help our patients to move past just such self-lessness? We walk through the history of these questions, and consider the constitution of the ethical subject, not as someone who *wants* to suffer, but as someone *willing* to do so when faced with the suffering of others. I explain that surrender, in Emmanuel Ghent's terms, to the ethical task is no automatic submission, no false selfhood, but what Winnicott called the "not less than everything." It is not trivial. The ethical life acts by undergoing pain, suffering, or persecution for the other. It is lived other-wise.

In the fourth chapter, beginning to exemplify the "internal chorus," I turn to the historian of ancient philosophy Pierre Hadot, who showed clearly that for Socrates, Plato, the Stoics, and the Epicureans, philosophy was primarily a therapeutic way of life, practiced within a community of scholars, each of whose ethical theories was intended to support each group's chosen path. Hadot's books have become daily companions in my chorus. Together with A. A. Long (2002), who taught me to read Epictetus, Hadot opened for me the sense that one could live for the human community every day without so much worry about the results. Knowing that we are small in the universe, realizing that we are always preparing to die, differentiating between what belongs to us (our choices and attitudes) and what does not (fame, money, the choices and opinions of others, even health) liberate us from many worries. Hadot's own favorite, a teacher of just these attitudes, Marcus Aurelius has been a longtime companion for me in times of trouble.

Chapter 5 takes us directly to hell. The young Torino (Turin) chemist Primo Levi, determined that the immediate experience of those "drowned and saved" in Auschwitz must be told and known, began writing his "ghastly tale" on his lunch hours as soon as he was able to return to work after his liberation. His insistent voice for human dignity, always refusing equivocation and evasion, ultimately costing him his life, haunts and challenges me. It accords with those of Dostoevsky and Levinas, who insist that we must never be indifferent to the death of the other. We return to him in Chapter 8, on the prophetic quality of clinical and humanitarian work.

In Chapter 6 we follow Nelson Mandela and Dietrich Bonhoeffer. The latter, a Christian theologian who seems to have understood non-indifference to the fate of the other from a very young age, and lived it out to the end, was imprisoned and hanged for his part in the plot to assassinate Hitler. His sense of community as crucial to the ethical or religious life made it all the more difficult for him to bear years of isolation in prison. Mandela, a revolutionary who grew into a world symbol of quiet human dignity, remained in prison for 27 years rather than compromise the full equality of his people. Mandela and Bonhoeffer, like Hadot, both understood philosophy as a way of life. Each managed to do "spiritual exercises" in prison every day, and to develop personally for the service of the human community.

Dostoevsky's Russia, alongside Jewish texts and phenomenology, formed the first of the three great influences on the ethics of Emmanuel Levinas. In the seventh chapter we study his great masterpiece, *The Brothers Karamazov*—albeit not in the depth it deserves, of course—but for some of what it contributes to the chorus. (I must remind the reader already and again that each clinician or humanitarian worker must find, assemble, and sort out her or his own choir. No one can take mine. But, for a related literary figure, one might choose Dickens, Dostoevsky's favorite English novelist, for his similar ethical sensibilities and narrative capacities.) Even though others lived more recently, because of his prophetic voice, expressed both in his own writing and in his love for Pushkin's poem *The Prophet*, I consider Dostoevsky last.

The book closes with meditations on prophecy and on humility, in particular clinical humility. From the Hebrew prophets, through many of the texts read here, to the prophetic phenomenology of Emmanuel Levinas, I have been learning to understand clinical and humanitarian work as prophetic word and action. From such prophetic word, once heard, there is no turning away, only attempting to hear better, to respond even before fully hearing. But because the call comes from infinity to finite me, vulnerability and repeated failure require many kinds of humility, of surrender to fallibility, to aging, to the other. Authenticity, self-definition, my place in the sun become unimportant; instead, unobtrusively, comes a life lived for the other.

The astute reader will already have noticed that this book has a more personal cast than the previous two: these choristers are *my special people.* They had serious flaws, just as I do: Dostoevsky was a gambler and an anti-Semite (this did not stop Levinas from adoring his work); Bonhoeffer's attitudes toward women and marriage were ante-diluvian, to my mind, and though he died for his efforts to interrupt the holocaust, he still believed Jews were less evolved Christians; Mandela's personal courage and statesmanship outstripped his treatment of his own family, reputedly;

Levinas thought Europe the center of the universe, and made problematic use of gender concepts in his theorizing. Like them, I have biases that only others can see, though I keep trying to see better by listening with my remaining ear, and by reading my critics.

My love for languages has probably attuned me to some members of my chorus: to Primo Levi's Italian; to Levinas's, Merleau-Ponty's, and Hadot's French; to the German of Freud, Gadamer, Wittgenstein, Bonhoeffer, Loewald, and Bach. Almost before I could speak English, I was hearing the church Latin still returning to me in Gregorian chant, and in the music of Bach.[5] It has only recently struck me that the central and most stunning incident in Levi's book of testimony, *If This Is a Man*, comes when his French companion in Auschwitz asks for Italian lessons, and Levi begins explaining Dante to him. We will return to this incident, but my point here is that, for me, languages, and my fascination with them, have been an ongoing internal resource. Languages link us not only to others, but also to their very otherness. Studying them constantly diminishes any remaining sense of my self-centrality. I trust that readers will find other such nourishing reserves.

This book's unifying theme, apparent in every chapter, will be ethics: not the social contract ethics envisioning a plurality of independent individuals negotiating rights, duties, and properties, but the pre-primordial ethics of infinite responsibility to the other person (Levinas, 1979, 1998) studied in my two previous books. Clinicians and humanitarian workers need internal and external support because their work demands courageous ethical response every day, and never lets up. For an easier life, this book would be irrelevant, a waste of time.

Careful readers will further notice that this book, more than the others, addresses younger and mid-journey clinicians from an aging view. To shift into more familiar psychoanalytic language, it speaks of internalizing the voices and example of those we need to sustain us if we are to do this work over many years. It introduces readers to some of those whom, in my later years, I have deeply admired. All these people, I repeat, had major flaws. All bore sorrows. Levi died by suicide, Bonhoeffer by hanging in a Nazi concentration camp. Most spent extended time in prison or prison camps, and all suffered multiple and serious personal losses. Still, all managed to contribute something significant to human culture, and their voices have interwoven to support me in ways I will try to describe. You will also see that most of them rightly cause me significant discomfort. In particular, they charge me with the problem of my love for the riches of European culture—in particular, German culture, the site of the most calculated massacre in recorded history of another people with whom I have also come to feel deeply identified. So, my choristers support me and comfort me, but they also keep me worried.

They do not impose on me, as I will explain in the chapter on clinical humility, the obligation of surviving in a particular way, or even of surviving.

Indeed, writing this book has itself been a humbling experience: I have learned that I undervalued some of those who have influenced me, and overvalued others, such as Bonhoeffer. As Simon Critchley writes, "The fabrication of a book is like the growth of a cancer, where a cell departs from its usual metabolism, connecting with and infecting other cells, interconnecting to form the sentences on a page" (Critchley, 1999, p. 33). This dark metaphor describes for me the gradual emergence of a complex ethical accusation, infection, and persecution you will find interwoven in the pages to come, a syndrome I could not envisage when I set out. What I do hear clearly from all my choristers is the responsibility to live for the other, not for myself. Paradoxically, their very insistent conviction sustains me.

Though Sandra Buechler's "internal chorus" inspires this work, those whom I read for sustenance do not always comfort, as Franz Kafka wrote to his friend Oskar Pollak:

> I think we ought to read only books that bite and sting us. If the book we are reading doesn't shake us awake like a blow on the skull, why bother reading it in first place . . . what we need are books that hit us like almost painful misfortune, like the death of someone we loved more than we love ourselves, that make us feel as though we had been banished to the woods, far from any human presence, like a suicide. A book must be the axe for the frozen sea within us.
>
> (Quoted in Malone, 2003, pp. 117–118)

Though my aesthetic is less austere than Kafka's, readers will find some chapters here more challenging than comforting, but still, I hope, sustaining to their ethical core.

Above all, I hope to start a conversation among younger colleagues about their own intellectual, cultural, and spiritual resources. In addition to one's early teachers, in addition to bodily care, hobbies, family, and well-nourished friendships, in addition to continuing professional growth, each clinician, I believe, needs to find personal inner voices over time—living and dead people who inspire and admonish and sustain in times of trouble. This chorus will change over time, as influences fade and new ones step up, but it must never be neglected.

Mine provides examples that have become important to me in my later years, though some have endured over a long period of time. Those discussed here are not the formative voices; many of those were the significant women of my years in education and academia.[6] Others function as what baroque musicians call *continuo* or ground bass: they accompany all my internal conversation. Examples of these include Socrates, who argued that it is better to suffer than to do evil, and that death does not threaten a good human being; and, no matter what religious people have made of him, the

Jesus of the Sermon on the Mount, preaching "Blessed are the poor, those who mourn, and those who suffer persecution for justice's sake."

This very conversation, however, might become a resource beyond the usual shop talk, whether clinical or theoretical, that stocks our conferences. We might even become choristers for each other.

Meanwhile, despite the impression I may be creating, some of my best choral supporters are still living, and many—directly or indirectly—have helped me to create this book. These include George Atwood, Doris Brothers, Sandra Buechler, Elizabeth Corpt, Shelley Doctors, Bob Fiore, Jackie Gotthold, Janice Gump, Judith Lewis Herman, Lynne Jacobs, Dan Perlitz, Warren Poland, Mike Reison, Peter Shabad, Dan Shaw, Leonard Shengold, Ellen Shumsky, and Bob Stolorow, as well as members of my study groups. Both Lynne Jacobs and Don Braue read the full manuscript and offered usable suggestions when I could no longer see my work. Pilgrim Place in Claremont, California, full of people who exemplify the values in this book, has fortunately been my home during the last months of its preparation. They arrive here after lives of often heroic service to live in intentional community, caring for each other and continuing to serve impoverished people near by, as well as the endangered earth. My husband Don Braue has not only supported my "infinitely demanding" (Critchley, 2007) clinical life but bears my concentration which silences him too often, and edits my writing with an ear attuned to the non-academic philosopher and the non-psychoanalyst. My gratitude to him surpasses categories. My major intellectual debts I hope to acknowledge along the way, though one never does this enough. Thinking of these good people, I remember Winnicott (1945), and his note that he never knew what he had stolen.

Notes

1 For an explanation of the decision not to capitalize this term, see note 3 in Chapter 6.
2 Levinas's name is sometimes spelled "Lévinas" in his published work. However, to avoid confusion, the accent has been omitted from all citations in this book.
3 Readers familiar with my earlier resistance to dualism (Orange, 2002) may find the language of inner life, internalization, and internal chorus surprising. Internalization provides the key, by which what has been external becomes personally owned, as if carried around internally, available and sustaining in times of trouble. Internalization, understood psychoanalytically (Loewald, 2000), explains the development of a spiritual life that is truly neither inside nor outside, but both.
4 Frank's *The Renewal of Generosity* (2004) similarly provides philosophical and ethical resources for both patients and medical workers who face extreme and prolonged suffering.
5 Johann Sebastian Bach deserves a chapter in this book. Composer and conductor of the chorus, he outstrips my capacity to describe either his achievements or his influence on me. His portrait, as the old composer of the *St. Matthew Passion* and the *B Minor Mass*, hangs in my study. The conductor John Eliot Gardiner (Gardiner, 2013) comes close to capturing his spirit for me.

6 Unfortunately, as in my last two books, most of my prominent interlocutors here will be male, with a resulting loss for which I apologize in advance to all readers. Whether the disparity between my strong personal attachments to female colleagues and my major use of male intellectual and cultural resources has a particular meaning, I do not know. An increasingly important counterexample is the tremendous though unassuming voice of Judith Lewis Herman, a pioneer devoted to restoring human dignity to those shattered by human rights violations like sexual abuse.

References

Aron, L., and Starr, K. (2012). *A Psychotherapy for the People: Toward a Progressive Psychoanalysis*. Hove and New York: Routledge.

Baraitser, L. (2008). Mum's the Word: Intersubjectivity, Alterity, and the Maternal Subject. *Studies in Gender and Sexuality*, 9, 86–110.

Buechler, S. (1998). The Analyst's Experience of Loneliness. *Contemporary Psychoanalysis*, 34, 91–113.

Butler, J. (2004). *Precarious Life: The Powers of Mourning and Violence*. London and New York: Verso.

Corpt, E. (2009). The Importance of Analytic Generosity in the Treatment of Inter-generational Trauma. Paper presented at the Conference on Intergenerational Trauma, Dublin/London.

Critchley, S. (1999). *Ethics—Politics—Subjectivity: Essays on Derrida, Levinas and Contemporary French Thought*. London: Verso.

Critchley, S. (2007). *Infinitely Demanding: Ethics of Commitment, Politics of Resistance*. London and New York: Verso.

Cushman, P. (2007). A Burning World, an Absent God: Midrash, Hermeneutics, and Relational Psychoanalysis. *Contemporary Psychoanalysis*, 43, 47–88.

Frank, A. (2004). *The Renewal of Generosity: Illness, Medicine, and How to Live*. Chicago, IL and London: University of Chicago Press.

Gardiner, J. (2013). *Bach: Music in the Castle of Heaven*. New York: Alfred A. Knopf.

Katz, C. (2013). *Levinas and the Crisis of Humanism*. Bloomington, IN: Indiana University Press.

Lear, J. (2012). The Thought of Hans W. Loewald. *International Journal of Psycho-analysis*, 93, 167–179.

Lear, J. (2014). Mourning and Moral Psychology. *Psychoanalytic Psychology*, 31, 470–481.

Levinas, E. (1979). *Totality and Infinity: An Essay on Exteriority*. The Hague and Boston Hingham, MA: M. Nijhoff and Kluwer Boston.

Levinas, E. (1981). *Otherwise than Being, or, Beyond Essence*. The Hague and Boston Hingham, MA: M. Nijhoff and Kluwer Boston.

Levinas, E. (1998). *Otherwise than Being, or, Beyond Essence*. Pittsburgh, PA: Duquesne University Press.

Loewald, H. (2000). *The Essential Loewald: Collected Papers and Monographs*. Hagerstown, MD: University Publishing Group.

Long, A. A. (2002). *Epictetus: A Stoic and Socratic Guide to Life*. Oxford and New York: Clarendon Press and Oxford University Press.

Malone, N. (2003). *Walking a Literary Labyrinth: A Spirituality of Reading*. New York: Riverhead Books.

Orange, D. (2002). There is No Outside. *Psychoanalytic Psychology*, 19, 686–700.

Orange, D. (2010). *Thinking for Clinicians: Philosophical Resources for Contemporary Psychoanalysis and the Humanistic Psychotherapies*. New York: Routledge.

Orange, D. (2011). *The Suffering Stranger: Hermeneutics for Everyday Clinical Practice*. New York: Routledge.

Orange, D. (2012). Clinical Hospitality: Welcoming the Face of the Devastated Other. Keynote address presented at the New Zealand Association of Psychotherapy, Wellington.

Richardson, F., and Zeddies, T. (2004). Psychoanalysis and the Good Life. *Contemporary Psychoanalysis*, 40, 617–657.

Winnicott, D. W. (1945). Primitive Emotional Development. *International Journal of Psychoanalysis*, 26, 137–143.

Winnicott, D. W., and the Institute of Psycho-Analysis (Great Britain) (1975). *Through Paediatrics to Psycho-Analysis*. London: Hogarth Press and the Institute of Psycho-Analysis.

Acknowledgments

Besides my personal thanks expressed at the end of the preface, I owe special gratitude to Kate Hawes, editor at Routledge, who has supported me from start to finish with this project, even in my most grumpy moments. Her understated British faith in me kept me going. Sue Wickenden has gracefully seen the project through to the end, despite her mountains of work, despite my forgetting details. The production team at Routledge, from covers to content, works devotedly, skillfully, and invisibly. Thank you all.

Parts of this book appear recently or simultaneously elsewhere, though revised to work here:

Chapter 2: (2014). What Kind of Ethics? Loewald on Responsibility and Atonement. *Psychoanalytic Psychology*, 31, 560–569.
Chapter 3: (forthcoming). Is Ethics Masochism? Or Infinite Ethical Responsibility and Finite Human Capacity. In David Goodman and Eric Severson (Eds.), *The Ethical Turn: Otherness and Subjectivity in Contemporary Psychoanalysis*. New York: Routledge.
Chapter 6: (2015). Foreword: Reconciliation without Magic: Preface Honouring Nelson Mandela. In Pumla Gobodo-Madikizela (Ed.), *Breaking Cycles of Repetition: A Global Dialogue on Historical Trauma and Memory*. Leverkusen: Budrich.

Chapter I

Trauma and traumatism

"Burnout"—jargon but evocative—suffered its moment of fame some years ago among my psychoanalytic colleagues (Brothers, 2008; Buechler, 2000; Cooper, 1986). We wondered what we were doing wrong: working too hard, being too kind, ignoring aggression, neglecting self-care? Many of us, however, suspected much more serious reasons for our breaking down. Among the "suffering strangers" (Orange, 2011) who arrived at our doors, we had received the soul-murdered (Shengold, 1999, 2000), the all-but-drowned (Levi, 1989; Levi and Woolf, 2008), the left-for-dead, and found ourselves called "to empty oneself anew of oneself . . . like in a hemophiliac's hemorrhage" (Levinas, 1981, p. 92). How were we ourselves to survive?

In the psychoanalytic world, Ferenczi was the first to acknowledge this question seriously. Many would argue that he provides a bad example, but I am not so sure. Working with those destroyed in early childhood, he found that their rage evoked his own wounds, his own capacity to hurt and even to do harm. Whether he died young from pernicious anemia (today so easily treated with vitamin B12), from exhaustion, or from both, he showed us how to give what Winnicott would later call "not less than everything" (quoted in Kahr, 1996, p. 125). These two pioneers, however, showed me both courage and human limits.[1] They did not leave the other to die alone even at the risk of their own death.

Staying with the traumatized demands all our capacity. The spectacular event mesmerizes us for the proverbial fifteen minutes. Victims, of clergy, of football coaches, of war, of genocide, and of child abuse command our attention just as long as they remain on the front pages and on television news; in other words, not for long. Somewhat better, our hospitals' trauma centers attend to the wounds of the raped and those almost dead from gunshot wounds or war injuries. If they can get help from the Veterans' Administration at all, soldiers receive drugs and brief cognitive therapies, while survivors of more private, familial violence are consigned to the indignities of managed care. At best, the traumatized become the "subjects" of scientific studies of their brains. This familiar story scarcely needs retelling here, except for the profound sorrow and helpless shame (see Chapter 5 on

Primo Levi) that it creates in me; and, I imagine, in you. Responding to these abandoned ones, the biblical widows, orphans, and strangers, requires that we nourish ourselves from without and within—that is, taking the outer riches within.

This chapter will follow a thread: through trauma itself, through the need for testimony and witness, to the demands that work with extreme trauma places on those who witness and mourn, to the intersubjectively configured experience of shame embedded in trauma. It prepares the ground for the two chapters that follow on responsibility and its shadow, masochism.

Trauma itself

Others have extensively studied the nature and treatment of extreme traumatic experience. Thus, without detail, and with apologies to those neglected, let me mention a few of the courageous pioneers whose work has most affected me: Judith Lewis Herman, whose relentless devotion to human dignity keeps her always in the front of my internal chorus; Dori Laub and Shoshana Felman, who have reverently and persistently collected testimony from shoah survivors; George Atwood, who taught me and many others to regard psychotic people as trauma survivors; Robert Stolorow, whose indispensable work I consider in more detail below; others who work with those who suffer from complex dissociations created to survive violence (Chefetz, 2009; Chefetz and Bromberg, 2004); and many more (Brown et al., 2007). In addition, there are the researchers who have given their lives to the organized study of trauma—too many dedicated people to count, and too much research to summarize here.

The worst traumatic states result, I believe, from human cruelty, often organized by schemes that seem unquestionable: slavery (Gump, 2010), discrimination, racism, sexism, childism (Young-Bruehl, 2012). These arrangements are often invisible to the participants in the systems, especially to those who benefit from them, but are nonetheless violent and leave transmitted scars, infecting "to the third and fourth generation" (Numbers 14:18).

What I want to revisit now, from several angles, results in part from this societal maltreatment, and can be variously described in what I might call a hermeneutics of trauma and madness.[2] Trauma's first phase arrives as a shocking, disorganizing event: a bomb, an earthquake, the loss of a child, parent, or other dear one, the loss of one's own functioning, a threatening diagnosis. Still, as many have observed (Atwood, 2011; Carr, 2011; Davoine and Gaudillière, 2004; Orange, 2011; Stolorow, 2007), albeit few have truly listened, trauma becomes intractable suffering in the absence of relational holding and even more so in the presence of relational contempt and devaluation. Psychological trauma's essence, according to Stolorow and Atwood (1992, pp. 52–53), lies in "the experience of unbearable affect," absent the "requisite attuned responsiveness [needed] from the surround to assist in its tolerance, containment, modulation and alleviation." Let us first listen to the voices of those who have already developed this point before I expand on it.

Robert Stolorow (2007), from some twenty years of reflection on his own traumatic experience and on his engagement with Heidegger's philosophy, has developed a phenomenology of traumatic experience that emphasizes at least three important elements. First, trauma disrupts temporality; that is, it destroys our experience of the threefold dimensionality of past, present, and future. The traumatic event is always now, and always impending. Nothing firmly recedes into the past—whatever that may mean—where it no longer threatens. Second, trauma creates a profound sense of personal alienation, in which the traumatized person does not belong to the human world of others, but always walks around as a ghost or a stranger, with a permanent sense of weirdness. Third, trauma destroys what Stolorow calls "the absolutisms of everyday life," the familiar sense that others will be there in the morning, and so on. The only hope for the traumatized to continue at all is that they find, in the second phase after the initial shock, what Stolorow calls a "relational home" in which the traumatic experience, with all its disorganizing consequences, can be welcomed and held, and thus find a "sibling in the same darkness" (2007, p. 47).

Military psychiatrist Russell Carr (2011) has brilliantly applied and expanded Stolorow's work by creating a short-term therapy for soldiers who return from combat. He speaks of the necessity of the therapist's engaging his own experience in finding an "intersubjective key" to the soldier's traumatic experience, and of the absolute necessity that this key, like a "portkey" in *Harry Potter* (Rowling and Dale, 2000; Stolorow, 2011), be carefully understood together in the "relational home."

The lifework of George Atwood illustrates the indissoluble link between trauma and madness. Like Harry Stack Sullivan, Frieda Fromm-Reichmann, and Donald Winnicott ("we are poor indeed if we are only sane" (Winnicott, 1945, p. 140)), Atwood has always seen the so-called psychotic or schizophrenic as one of us, and all of us as their brothers and sisters. Traumatized others abandoned in the second phase, siblings in the darkness whose hand no one ever took, they appear so strange that we avoid them. Atwood hears Daniel Paul Schreber,[3] like his own patients, no matter how confused or deluded, as telling their own stories of soul murder in the only way they can. He reminds us that trauma cannot be cured. It has befallen us:

> The traumatic events we are speaking of will affect the person down to the moment of his or her last breath. There is, however, hope for the person, for his or her life and future . . . The role of the analyst is to work, in concert with the patient, to establish a setting that will come to include the unbearable and unsayable. The patient will fall, sometimes devastatingly, into despair in the course of this process, feeling there is no

hope for survival at all. At such times the analyst must connect to the despair and reflect his or her developing understanding of its original and contemporary emotional contexts. In this way, he or she contradicts the patient's expectation that there is no place for the suffering that is felt, and a new context gradually comes into being wherein the unbearable can begin to be borne and the unsayable can begin to be said. This is the pathway toward wholeness, and it can be a very long one.

(Atwood, 2010, pp. 118–119)

Atwood's open-hearted hospitality (Orange, 2011) toward unspeakable suffering, his relentless search for the meaning in every form of human psychological suffering—creating what Stolorow (2007) calls a "relational home" for traumatic experience, inspiring generations of students and colleagues like me—demands tremendous faithfulness from both therapist and patient.

Thus far, American voices with European inflections—from phenomenology, hermeneutics, and ethics: that is, from Husserl and Heidegger, from Gadamer and Levinas—have filled our account. Let us turn to French voices (Davoine and Gaudillière, 2004), themselves informed by many years of American dialogues through Austen Riggs Hospital, but profoundly rooted in the violent world of twentieth-century Europe. Every mad/traumatized patient Davoine and Gaudillière describe carries the stigma of some unspeakable, unspoken other or others gone missing, in war or genocide. In each "case" (*casus*, we are informed, in Latin means falling, as if into a common human befallenness), the "intersubjective key," to borrow Carr's felicitous phrase, consists in the analyst's moment of recognition of a profound common fate, a "social link" between patient and analyst. Davoine and Gaudillière (2004, p. 136) generalize:

Like it or not, analytic discourse can be established when speech emanates from a locus without a subject or from someone who experiences himself as a reject . . . In the proximity of combat and risk, this speech can be addressed only to a therapist who is familiar with the same field . . . the intersection of two trajectories allows for a triangulation. Only in this way can essential facts, expelled from transmission [of trauma], sometimes be located. Their existence becomes possible once again, after having been annulled, because an other attests to them, from an independent source, on the basis of his experience.

The analyst must be listening most attentively, both to the patient and to herself, to catch these moments of intersection. My own patients taught me well.

Jeb, close to my age, who grew up in the same part of North Dakota where my own grandfather—whom I met only once—had lived, arrived for his first consultation with a specific plan for suicide by gunshot. Brought up as a more or less proper psychoanalyst, and long before I had learned to be more easily self-disclosing in my practice, I instinctively told him in that first session that like him, I was a transplant in New York and that my grandfather came from North Dakota. I then asked him if he would get rid of the gun so that we could work together. He did, and we worked together for seven years until he died from lung cancer.

Meanwhile, he told me that when he was eight, his father, a troubled but larger-than-life figure whom he had adored, threw himself in front of an approaching train. His older brothers, he remembered, wanted nothing to do with his grief, so he wandered the streets of his town alone. His mother, who did speak to him, he remembered only from her back as she worked in the house. He was her audience from behind.

Probably I was able to work with Jeb, despite his horror of my politics, which he inferred from catching me with the *New York Times* on my desk, because the "intersubjective key" involved not only the North Dakota link to a missing history still unknown to me, but even more to the faceless mother endlessly talking at me, but never with me. At the time I did not know this well enough to make use of it directly—no matter, perhaps—but it probably formed the "intersubjective key" or the "social link" (Davoine and Gaudillière, 2004). This link allowed me to be Jeb's witness.

Trauma and witness[4]

Several years ago, having encountered a disturbing error message on my computer, I called technical support. The competent helper, whose accent I recognized as Indian, managed in a half-hour or so to solve my problem. During a pause, I asked where he was located, and he named an area of southern India. "Were you close to the tsunami?" I asked. "Oh yes, but we are all safe here, and all my family too, some of whom were much more exposed. Thank you for asking." Then he began to repeat, almost singsong style, "It was so unexpected. We didn't expect it. It was so unexpected. We didn't expect it." We returned to our task, but as soon as there was another pause, the refrain returned. "It was so unexpected. We didn't expect it. Thank you for your concern. Thank you for asking," and so on. Even when our task was successfully completed, it was difficult to end the call.

This incident illustrates several aspects of the phenomenology of traumatic experience, familiar to all clinicians and humanitarian workers: emotional freezing, the violation of expectancy, the destruction of temporality, the need for witnessing, the selective disorganization of experience, and mourning. For now, let us focus on witnessing, with its potential to release traumatic experience from freezing and partially restore human dignity. Next we will briefly explore the effect of this witnessing on those supporting the sufferers. This radical passivity, vulnerability, or receptivity we might rename the ethical formation of subjectivity or, in short, *traumatism*, an ethical condition of what Levinas called persecution, or useful suffering, and a concept to which we will return.

To begin, let us assume that trauma is both event and experience. Something terrible has occurred: an earthquake, a rape, the death of a child, torture, genocide, a cancer diagnosis. Nothing can be as it was before, nor trusted to be as we assumed it to be. One's world is just deranged (Stolorow, 2007), and even when gradually reorganized around the tornado's devastation or the dictator's dictates, this reality is always haunted by the sense that terrible things might happen at any moment. The psycho-analytic witness, as Warren Poland (2000) has so clearly and eloquently written, is the one who "gets it," and thus allows the patient to get it, exactly as my question to my computer consultant released his traumatic experience.

Another impressive body of work has emerged—at the last moment, so to speak—from the dying-out community of holocaust survivors. Invited to speak by interested psychoanalysts (Laub and Auerhahn, 1993), archivists, and indeed their own children and grandchildren, they are unfreezing their stories and, sometimes, beginning to die more peacefully. Repeatedly they say, "I thought I should not burden you with these memories. I didn't know that you would want them, no matter how gruesome, no matter how ugly and confusing." When the child or grandchild says, "But I wanted to know *you*," some bit of humanity, stolen long ago, begins to return. Something similar, as Poland (2000, p. 20) explains so clearly, occurs in the clinical exchange:

> For a patient's testimony to come to life and extend beyond simple conscious access, a comprehending witness is required. Catalyst to the patient's capacity for self-knowledge and self-definition as a unique individual among others, witnessing makes personal testimony most fully possible and meaningful.

The therapeutic function of witnessing invites, catalyzes, and dignifies the testifying of the patient. Judith Lewis Herman, daughter of shame theorist Helen Block Lewis, and indefatigable advocate for those most degraded by violence, further explains:

> In this slow and laborious process, a fragmented set of wordless, static images is gradually transformed into a narrative with motion, feeling, and meaning. The therapist's role is not to act as a detective, jury or judge, not to extract confessions or impose interpretations on the patient's experience, but rather to bear witness as the patient discovers her own truth. This is both our duty and our privilege.
>
> (Herman, 2009, p. 135[5])

Probably Poland means something similar when he reflects: "it seemed to matter that an other know. My place was not then to hold; my place was to be alongside him" (2000, p. 24). The clinical witness does not take over the other's suffering; but she or he does make it more possible for the other to realize it[6] with integrity, dignity, and some measure of restored inclusion in human community.

Still, no one can take away the rape or the torture, the neglect or the abandonment. No one can make up for the soul murder (Shengold, 1989). The clinical witness treats the traumatized one as a fellow human being who in no way should have been so mistreated. Yes, we analyze with the patient the ways in which she or he continues to live out the traumatic situation. But we refuse to blame the victim. Instead we steadfastly insist that we are *both and together* more human than otherwise, included in the human community. This insistence, mostly implicit, potentially undermines some of the shame that ordinarily accompanies traumatic shock. "It was so unexpected. Thank you for asking." Inclusion gradually works against humiliation.

This may be a good place to note that the work of witnessing and inclusion does not usually look heroic. I did not drop everything and join an organization for tsunami relief. All I did was to ask a simple question that recognized that I was not talking with a machine. Perhaps Martin Buber would say that I shifted from the I–It to the I–You (Buber and Kaufmann, 1970). Emmanuel Levinas might say that I spoke a word of welcome to the other (Levinas and Nemo, 1985). I might say that traumatic experience awaits and requires intersubjective witness for its realization, in the sense of taking on reality.

Colleagues who work with victims of torture remind us that the most traumatic aspect afterwards is the community's disavowal (Cordal, 2005; Viñar, 2005), as we will see when studying Primo Levi. Samuel Gerson (2009) describes with his "dead third" the situation in which not only those who could provide witness are dead, but those who still should fill this need are as good as dead because they are unable or unwilling to do so. He cites the story of Helen Bamber, founder of the Medical Foundation for Victims of Torture in London, who at 20 arrived as a volunteer at just-liberated Bergen-Belsen, an experience she describes:

> People were in very difficult situations, sitting on the floor, they would hold on to you and dig their fingers into your flesh and they would rock and they would rock and they would rock and we would rock together. You saw people rocking, but the act of rocking together and receiving their pain without recoil was essential. The reason people are so humiliated by terrible assaults on their body and mind is that they have a sense of contamination and the realization I had was that one had to receive everything without recoil. It was one of the important

lessons I had in Belsen. I remember saying to one person, who I didn't think would live very long, that I would hold her story and her story would be told.

(From an interview with Doron Levene, quoted in
Gerson, 2009, p. 1353)[7]

Witnessing, obviously, means more than reporting from a distance. It ranges from my simple question to a tech support worker to Helen Bamber's fully embodied "without recoil" emotional availability. Created—as Dori Laub (1992) explains—as an event without possibility of witness, calculated—as Primo Levi recounted—to destroy all such possibility, the shoah requires more than ordinary response, and even today we can barely begin to speak its reality.

In another instance, last year when I arrived in Santiago to do some teaching, two colleagues who had lived through the Pinochet dictatorship took me to the recently opened Museo de la Memoria, which shows and tells this history in detail. My friends told me that they had been unable to visit this museum before then, but had told themselves, "When Donna comes, we will go," as if, it seemed, I could be a witness, and allow them to suffer this history. Before traveling to Chile, I had read several books and accounts of this period, from various points of view, so was well acquainted, I thought, with the "facts" and knew that to this day people in Chile see the period of the dictatorship from different perspectives.

So, my husband and I accompanied these two colleagues—whom I already knew from meetings in New York and Madrid, and from two days in Santiago—to the museum. First, we entered an installation displaying, in darkness, the photos of the disappeared, who then again disappeared. As I remember it, we then all went our separate ways, looking and reading at our own pace, but I met each colleague, who showed me things that had special significance for her. The place where we three women met, unexpectedly, in silence, was the torture room. The instruments of torture are displayed and explained, and videos of torture victims telling their stories run continuously. We stood in tears together. I do not remember much else, except that I subsequently got lost and could not find my way out of the museum to meet the others. But they told me that my interest in their history, and going there with them, was very important for them.

Some have called this intersubjective witnessing process the *realization* of trauma—that is, making it real. In its frozen state as trauma, it inhabits a ghostly state. Hans Loewald (1960) would have said that we clinicians invite it into transference, where it can live in the daylight and interrupt the most destructive forms of recycling, or at least bring them into the dialogic situation. Dori Laub, however, acknowledges that testimony remains a "ceaseless struggle" and writes of the receiver of testimony much as of a therapist who helps a patient to mourn unbearable losses:

It is the realization that the lost ones are not coming back; the realization that what life is all about is precisely living with an unfulfilled hope; only this time with the sense that you are not alone any longer—that someone can be there as your companion—knowing you, living with you through the unfulfilled hope, someone saying: "I'll be with you in the very process of your losing me. I am your witness."

(Felman and Laub, 1991, p. 90)

Others (for example, Goodman, 2012) find that witnessing, either as one who testifies or as one who accompanies, possesses the power to speak for those deprived of voice, for those who are gone, for human dignity itself: "Each and every act of witnessing is vitalizing as it breaks through a wall of traumatic helplessness and silence" (p. 11). Testimony, alongside the willingness to hear it reverently, matters. Witnessing says that your suffering matters to others. In the words of Robert Louis Jackson (1993, p. 67), "The price of seeing and knowing all may be, for the witness, darkness and despair. Yet the act of witnessing, the act of suffering, may be the only way the darkness can be redeemed."

Mourning

Unfortunately, however, we have no shortcut to any of this; mourning, a thread that runs through most chapters of this book, seems to be the only road. The best of traditional psychoanalytic theory—the work of Loewald on the waning of the Oedipus complex,[8] for example—teaches us murdering and mourning our parents as the royal road to psychological maturity via internalization. But how do we mourn enough, not just for inadequate parents—the fate of most of us—but for massive psychological trauma, including for trauma in which we fear we have somehow inadequately resisted, from rapes accepted for fear of even greater violence, to walking without a fight into ghettoes and camps? How do we adequately mourn the holocaust, the disappearances and tortures and the living in fear for year after year under dictatorships, the childhoods lived in constant fear and violence, often followed by adulthoods of domestic violence? How is it possible to mourn memories of rape and torture enough? How do we mourn the memory of standing by, of averting our eyes while others suffered, or the knowledge we too might have stood by in the face of atrocity? These are the questions that confront us as clinicians as we hear Jean Améry: once tortured, always tortured. These are the questions that confront us as we hear the insistence of Améry, Primo Levi, and the poet Paul Celan, determined to testify, determined to find witnesses, but for whom the mourning evidently was not enough.

We humanitarians and clinicians are confronted with our own mourning: perhaps our work will not be enough for some people. We witness as best we can; we stand or sit alongside, implicitly saying that no human being should ever be treated as you were treated, no matter what you have done before or since. But we know that it may not be enough. We may not be enough. The other is other. Poland (2000, p. 24) slips into his essay (at a moment of anticipated honesty between him and a patient), "the prophet in Ecclesiastes tells us that he who increases knowledge increases sorrow." This perhaps has wide applicability to our work with survivors of massive psychological trauma.

What of the witness?

Poland notes that in each instance where he experienced himself as a genuine witness for the patient, an extraordinary reversal occurred. He observed:

> a shift in my sense of the relationship between my patient and me . . . At such times I feel myself engaged with the other person experienced as somehow more in that person's own right. It is not that I am unaware that the patient's turmoil is eliciting reactions in me. Rather, it is as if I am not as involved as usual with sorting out for myself how my own engagements are part of the developing process. Despite the presence of other emotional reactions to the patient, I feel at these moments an awareness, generally comfortable though often new, of the patient's intact otherness even as we are together. I am more aware of the patient's distinct integrity.
>
> (Poland, 2000, p. 25)

Poland goes on to theorize about this experience,[9] but for now, let us take the experiential description on its own so that we can explore the Levinasian idea of traumatism.

The traumatism of persecution

"What does it mean," asks Simon Critchley (1999, p. 188), "to think the meaning of the unconscious in terms of the traumatism of persecution? What does it mean to think the subject—the subject of the unconscious—as trauma?"

Notable in Poland's description, and picked up in commentary by Alfred Margulies (2000), comes a move from reacting to the patient to responding to an other. Margulies writes: "In loosening the grip of a hermeneutics of suspicion, Poland is moving from *trying to figure someone out* toward *trying to be with an Other*" (2000, p. 76; original emphasis). I would amend Margulies's formulation slightly but perhaps importantly: Poland *finds himself* alongside the other. This may be the consequence of a more fundamental shift in attitude that he has already made: he often writes of working in the service of the patient. But "trauma" and "persecution"?

The clinician, like other humanitarian workers, lives in a double asymmetry. From a surface point of view, we have all the power in the clinical relationship. We set the time, the place, and the fee, and decide whether to see this troubled person at all. On the other side, once we are involved, we are besieged and persecuted by the face of the other, just as Emmanuel Levinas wrote. One expression he used for this condition of infinite responsibility, when we are so finite, was traumatism.[10] Critchley (2007, pp. 60–61) explains that, for Levinas, "my relation to the other is not some benign benevolence, compassionate care or respect for the other's autonomy, but is the obsessive experience of a responsibility that persecutes me with its sheer weight." He continues: "The ethical demand is a traumatic demand, it is something that comes from outside the subject from a heteronomous source, but which leaves imprint within the subject" (2007, p. 61). The condition of the subject persecuted by pre-original responsibility, traumatism never ends. Of course, we hear Levinas in two registers, as insomniac himself for whom the murders never end and the dead never return,[11] and as philosopher of subjectivity beyond and before ego.

Let us listen: "It is from subjectivity understood as a self, from . . . the dispossession of contraction, whereby the Ego does not appear but immolates itself, that the relationship with the other is possible as communication and transcendence" (Levinas et al., 1996, p. 92). The Levinasian subject, far from being an expansive or agentic ego,[12] is subjected, more passive than all passivity, persecuted, taken hostage, responsible for the other in a pre-original traumatism. This subject's receptive capacity makes possible its relationship with the other as communication and transcendence "on the hither side," before anything can be said. The subject is constituted as a subject in a "*traumatisme originel*," as subject of persecution and suffering. In Critchley's (1997, p. 231) words, "He thinks the subject as trauma—ethics is a traumatism." What might this mean?

From Levinas's earliest post-captivity writings onwards, we find the theme of the "*il y a*" ("there is"), the rumbling horror that keeps the insomniac awake endlessly, a traumatic symptom if ever there was one. Levinas spoke of "*traumatisme assourdissant*" ("deafening traumatism"), and reminds me of soldiers who return from Iraq and Afghanistan, and of my patients whose families were like war zones, always filled with screaming. But he gave this insomnia a philosophical meaning, further transforming it in his later work into the endless sense of responsibility for the other. This ethical subject, a sentient self who hears the cries of suffering and sees the face of the other long before it becomes the thinking thing, suffers herself from this deafening traumatism.[13]

Further, like the victims of violence themselves, their therapists may suffer from "too much contrast." Photographers know that too much contrast in lighting conditions ruins an image, making it impossible to render anything comprehensible. A smart and experienced photographer, even one with the best equipment, avoids these situations, and seeks those that will cooperate with the art and craft available. Similarly, the victim of traumatic shock finds it impossible to organize or make sense of the contrasts between a former or surrounding world of reason and harmony, and the experience of total destruction (physical or psychological or both). Presidents and governors who visit tornado-ravaged towns attempt to comfort by witnessing this unbearable contrast, but they seldom stay long.

Similarly, for many profoundly traumatized patients, too much contrast between their experiential worlds and those that seem to surround them confuses and confounds. A child whose nighttime experience of sexual abuse by the same parent who creates the "perfect family" image for her and in the community cannot bear the contrast, and survives by dissociation or by other forms of escape, perhaps by a very fragile but massive accommodation. Adolescents and adults devastated by loss, abuse, usurpation, and complex interpersonal mistreatment, perhaps beginning in the earliest weeks of life, often become easily overwhelmed by the requirements of "normal" social life, with its small talk. So, compassionate clinicians tell them that they recognize the impossibility, just as the camera cannot accommodate such lighting conditions. This very respect for impossibility creates a minimal witness, opening a crack of inclusion to those who will always feel they could never again belong with humans. Similarly, supervisors and consultants who work with humanitarian clinicians can recognize and mitigate this shock.

But the path to inclusion is hard, dark, and rocky. In a small memorial piece for his friend the Swiss psychotherapist Hans Trüb (1952), Martin Buber wrote that "a soul is never sick alone, but there is always a between-ness also, a situation between it and another existing being" (Buber and Buber Agassi, 1999, p. 21). Even though one feels so alone,

> in the immediacy of one human confronting another, the encapsulation must and can be broken through, and a transformed, healed relationship must and can be opened to the person who is sick in his relations to otherness . . . this way of frightened pause, of unfrightened reflection, of personal involvement, of rejection of security, or unreserved stepping into relationship . . . this way of vision and of risk is that which Hans Trüb trod.
> (Buber and Buber Agassi, 1999, p. 21)

Explaining to Buber why, despite many positive experiences, he could not write his book, Trüb described himself as having the "tunnel disease" of people who always work underground:

> I have under great renunciation of the spiritual general context, reached the lonely and hidden place of the isolated persons—hoping for the best,

if I ever find my way back—and now that I really can communicate with
the single, isolated individual, I don't find my way back. I am afraid of
indiscretion. I avoid the light of day and am frightened of my own word.
(Quoted in Buber and Buber Agassi, 1999, p. 171)

Healing through meeting, as both Buber and Trüb called it, or working in
the interhuman, is perilous for both healer (see Jaenicke, 2008) and patient.
In Buber's words, "It is a cruelly hazardous enterprise, this becoming a
whole" (Buber and Buber Agassi, 1999, p. 26).[14]

Levinas often disparaged psychoanalysis, hearing only that consciousness
and the thinking ego should rule, but understood with many contemporary
psychoanalysts that the responsible and responsive worker inevitably suffers,
traumatized by the sufferer welcomed hospitably and non-indifferently
(Marcus, 2006). In Critchley's (1999, pp. 239–240) words,

> a subject lacerated by contact with an original traumatism that produces
> a scarred interiority inaccessible to consciousness and reflection, a
> subject that wants to repeat compulsively the origin of the trauma . . . a
> subject of melancholia, then. But this is a good thing.

How is this "a good thing"? Levinas believed that the condition for the
possibility of ethics, for responsibility for the other that would not permit
catastrophes like those he had seen and lived, was a non-evasive capacity to
put oneself radically at the disposal and service of the other. Only when
we are thus capable are goodness, generosity, courtesy, substitution, even
holiness, possible. This was his argument. Others might explain goodness,
and selfishness, with competing theories of evolution. According to Robert
Bernasconi (2002), Levinas asked—our central question in this book, too—
what are the conditions for the possibility of ethics? In other words,
what kinds of human beings must we be, and be supported in remaining,
to make substitution possible, one life for another? To work without
retaliation, as Winnicott (1969) and Racker (1966) challenged psychoanalysts to do, can often amount to Levinasian substitution, at least for a
while. How does one remain vulnerable enough to hear and feel the suffering
of the other, and robust enough to survive this work with those bound
to mistrust us?[15]

What I did not see in the Museo de la Memoria in Santiago, lacking time
to read everything, and lacking much Spanish, were the stories of people
who risked their own lives to save others under the dictatorship. But I have
heard and read these stories, just as they exist in the holocaust museums, in
South Africa, and in the civil rights struggle in the United States. In every
horror they are too few, but we need these stories, as well as the stories of
small gratuitous kindnesses that remind us of our common humanity.
Believing their very possibility meant that human subjectivity could not be

constituted egoistically, but that selfishness was a deformation, Levinas named these accounts "stories of holiness."

His work, I believe—a philosophy both of trauma and of mourning—reminds us that mourning will go on for ever, but that we can smile through our tears, because the traumatism is the condition for the possibility of welcoming and accompanying the other.

Trauma and shame

Judith Lewis Herman, whose pioneering work connected war trauma with incest for clinicians years ago and relentlessly, has now turned her attention to another link. Returning to her mother's pioneering work on shame (Lewis, 1974, 1987), she now sees post-traumatic stress as a problem of shame. What does she mean? And how does this shame come to infect the clinician so deeply that it creates what Levinas called traumatism? Nikki Giovanni (2002, p. 106) expresses the effect on one who can feel the impact of the other's abject poverty:

> I cried for The Little Match Girl. I hate people who tried to make that a cute story. She was poor. Her family was poor. She froze to death because of the indifference of the people inside with a fireplace and food and drink. And that was that. This is not a musical. This is not fun.

We are meant to be ashamed in the face of abject poverty.

Perhaps the crucial importance of testimony, and of the clinician's witnessing, discussed above, lies in the area of shame and the restoration of dignity. Shoshana Felman (1995, p. 53) writes:

> What constitutes the outrage of the Holocaust—the very essence of erasure and annihilation—is not so much death in itself, as the more obscene fact that death itself does not make any difference, the fact that death is radically indifferent: everyone is leveled off, people die as numbers, not as proper names. In contrast to this leveling, to testify is to engage, precisely, in the process of re-finding one's own proper name, one's signature.

Primo Levi (1989) wrote that the only real witnesses to trauma are those who just barely survived themselves, who did not quite reach the bottom. To allow ourselves to see, feel, and actually know what our patients suffer and have suffered, we survivor–clinicians must be ashamed (see also Chapter 7) to belong to a human race that perpetrates such crimes against humanity. Levi describes this feeling of shame as one of the first indications that some minimal humanity was returning to the survivors. We will return to this theme, scarcely touched on here, in later chapters.

Trauma and the life of non-indifference

Without the possibility of evasion, without escape from scraping on our own traumatic wounds, without nearly adequate words to express the little we do understand, psychotherapists face traumatic devastation daily, just as humanitarian workers do. So, psychotherapists may retreat into distancing, diagnosis, cynicism, or even into blatant ethical violations, leaving their patients more confused and self-blaming than when they arrived. To work long days, weeks, years in the service of the other who comes to us destroyed, in one way or another,[16] clinicians need external and internal supports. Continuing education, peer-supervision groups and study groups (i.e., community), hobbies, the arts, family, friendships, physical exercise—everyone knows about these external things, though many of us neglect them as we become overconfident or overwhelmed.

After two chapters on responsibility and its false friend masochism, I focus for the rest of this book on what clinicians and humanitarian workers rarely discuss: the need to nurture, continually to replenish, an internal life. To sustain and challenge a life of non-indifference to the suffering of others, a life lived other-wise, we need nourishing voices to help us. The middle chapters study some members of my current internal chorus, only to exemplify, to help readers imagine and develop their own. It will become obvious along the way that some indispensable voices for me do not have whole chapters in this book: for example, Emmanuel Levinas, Hans Loewald, and Judith Lewis Herman. In the final chapters, we will address values, those most profound attitudes that orient a life, and make a life for-the-other sustainable. Horror forces us to consult these values, and to face our vulnerabilities in the face of overwhelming evils. We ask often what truly matters—protecting myself or keeping myself available and responsive? Once Levi's words have been carved into my heart (Hatley, 2000), can I ever live in peace? And where are the limits of all of us, especially of those who live non-indifferent? The next two chapters address such questions.

Notes

1 I have come to respect the clinical wisdom of Judith Lewis Herman, tireless worker and spokesperson for the human dignity of the abused. She advocates working with them in groups and teamwork settings where the clinician has a lot of support. No one clinician can carry all the responsibility for these patients.
2 Hermeneutics is the study of understanding and interpretation. Originally a set of rules or principles for interpreting biblical texts, in the hands of Hans-Georg Gadamer it more recently became a general philosophy of dialogic understanding, based on listening to the voice of the other. For clinicians, this other often comes to us shattered, evoking whatever in us may be able to meet and respond (see Orange, 2012).
3 See also Schreber et al. (1955) and Orange (1993).

4 Parts of this section were presented at the IARPP's international meeting in Santiago, Chile, in November 2013.

5 In this same contribution Herman writes of the remembering, and the difficulties with witnessing to the remembering, by perpetrators.

6 Laub (1992, p. 10; original emphasis) notes the systematic deprivation of realization: "Not only, in effect, did the Nazis try to exterminate the physical witnesses of their crime; but the inherently incomprehensible *and* deceptive psychological structure of the event precluded its own witnessing, even by its very victims."

7 I would encourage readers of this account to seek out the YouTube film by Alfred Hitchcock, *Memories of the Camps*, for extensive video of the very days described by Helen Bamber.

8 Loewald (1979) referred, in his title "The Waning of the Oedipus Complex," both to its fate in the life of a person and to its decreasing centrality in psychoanalytic theorizing. This essay is his second masterpiece, after his "On the Therapeutic Action of Psycho-Analysis" (1960).

9 He likes to say that clinical work is the lab section for which philosophy is the lecture. I say that I hang out in the hallways.

10 I am extensively indebted to the magnificent essay by Simon Critchley (1997), who alone seems to have engaged deeply both the question of the traumatic in Levinas and the latter's treatment of psychoanalysis. One psychoanalytic essay (Bokanowski, 2005, p. 252) uses the word "traumatism," but very differently, to refer only to "a level of disorganization that has more to do with secondary processes—one that does not disrupt object relations or the binding of the instinctual drives." Trauma, for this writer, is a much more serious condition.

11 He began to write about insomnia during his years in a Nazi labor camp; I do not know whether he was literally an insomniac after the war.

12 Granted, there are other ways to understand the Freudian ego—for example, as the emergent related individual found in Loewald (1951)—but Levinas does not seem to have known them.

13 An extensive literature on vicarious trauma in psychotherapists and crisis workers attests to their widespread and profound problems living in incompatible worlds (for example, Herman, 1992; Pearlman et al., 2005).

14 I previously discussed Buber and Trüb in Orange (2010).

15 I am told (Robert Fiore, personal communication) that in the southern United States, Freud's repetition compulsion is called the "bound-tas", as "she was bound-ta marry that kinda guy," or "he was bound-ta get in trouble again."

16 My own favorite accounts, perhaps because of my own history, come from Ferenczi (Ferenczi, 1949; Ferenczi and Dupont, 1988), Fairbairn (1952), Brandchaft (Brandchaft et al., 2010), Shengold (1989), and Shaw (2014), but others may add their own.

References

Atwood, G. (2010). The Abyss of Madness: An Interview. *International Journal of Psychoanalytic Self Psychology*, 5, 334–356.

Atwood, G. E. (2011). *The Abyss of Madness*. New York: Routledge.

Bernasconi, R. (2002). What Is the Question to which "Substitution" Is the Answer? In S. Critchley and R. Bernasconi (Eds.), *The Cambridge Companion to Levinas* (pp. 234–251). Cambridge: Cambridge University Press.

Bokanowski, T. (2005). Variations on the Concept of Traumatism: Traumatism, Traumatic, Trauma. *International Journal of Psychoanalysis*, 86, 251–265.

Brandchaft, B., Doctors, S., and Sorter, D. (2010). *Toward an Emancipatory Psychoanalysis: Brandchaft's Intersubjective Vision*. New York: Routledge.

Brothers, D. (2008). *Toward a Psychology of Uncertainty: Trauma-Centered Psychoanalysis*. New York: The Analytic Press.

Brown, E., Laub, D., Loew, C., Richman, S., Itzkowitz, S., Sussillo, M. V., and Behm, A. (2007). Last Witnesses: Child Survivors of the Holocaust, Part I: A Roundtable Discussion. *Psychoanalytic Perspectives*, 4, 1–50.

Buber, M., and Buber Agassi, J. (1999). *Martin Buber on Psychology and Psychotherapy: Essays, Letters, and Dialogue*. New York: Syracuse University Press.

Buber, M., and Kaufmann, W. (1970). *I and Thou*. New York: Scribner.

Buechler, S. (2000). Necessary and Unnecessary Losses. *Contemporary Psychoanalysis*, 36, 77–90.

Carr, R. (2011). Combat and Human Existence: Toward an Intersubjective Approach to Combat-Related PTSD. *Psychoanalytic Psychology*, 28, 471–496.

Chefetz, R. (2009). Waking the Dead Therapist. *Psychoanalytic Dialogues*, 19, 393–404.

Chefetz, R., and Bromberg, P. (2004). Talking with "Me" and "Not-Me": A Dialogue. *Contemporary Psychoanalysis*, 40, 409–464.

Cooper, A. (1986). Some Limitations on Therapeutic Effectiveness: The "Burnout Syndrome" in Psychoanalysts. *Psychoanalytic Quarterly*, 55, 576–598.

Cordal, M. (2005). Traumatic Effects of Political Repression in Chile: A Clinical Experience. *International Journal of Psychoanalysis*, 86, 1317–1328.

Critchley, S. (1997). The Original Traumatism: Levinas and Psychoanalysis. In R. Kearney and M. Dooley (Eds.), *Questioning Ethics: Contemporary Debates in Philosophy* (pp. 230–242). London: Routledge.

Critchley, S. (1999). *Ethics—Politics—Subjectivity: Essays on Derrida, Levinas and Contemporary French Thought*. London: Verso.

Critchley, S. (2007). *Infinitely Demanding: Ethics of Commitment, Politics of Resistance*. London and New York: Verso.

Davoine, F., and Gaudillière, J.-M. (2004). *History beyond Trauma: Whereof One Cannot Speak, Thereof One Cannot Stay Silent*. New York: Other Press.

Fairbairn, W. (1952). *Psychoanalytic Studies of the Personality*. London: Tavistock.

Felman, S. (1995). Education and Crisis, or the Vicissitudes of Teaching. In C. Caruth (Ed.), *Trauma: Explorations in Memory* (pp. 13–60). Baltimore, MD: Johns Hopkins University Press.

Felman, S., and Laub, D. (Eds.) (1991). *Testimony: Crises of Witnessing in Literature, Psychoanalysis, and History*. New York: Routledge.

Ferenczi, S. (1949). Confusion of the Tongues between the Adults and the Child (the Language of Tenderness and of Passion). *International Journal of Psychoanalysis*, 30, 225–230.

Ferenczi, S., and Dupont, J. (1988). *The Clinical Diary of Sándor Ferenczi*. Cambridge, MA: Harvard University Press.

Gerson, S. (2009). When the Third is Dead: Memory, Mourning, and Witnessing in the Aftermath of the Holocaust. *International Journal of Psychoanalysis*, 90, 1341–1357.

Giovanni, N. (2002). *Quilting the Black-Eyed Pea: Poems and Not Quite Poems*. New York: William Morrow.

Goodman, D. (2012). *The Demanded Self: Levinasian Ethics and Identity in Psychology*. Pittsburgh, PA: Duquesne University Press.

Gump, J. (2010). Reality Matters: The Shadow of Trauma on African American Subjectivity. *Psychoanalytic Psychology*, 27, 42–54.

Hatley, J. (2000). *Suffering Witness: The Quandary of Responsibility after the Irreparable*. Albany, NY: State University of New York Press.

Herman, J. (1992). *Trauma and Recovery*. New York: Basic Books.

Herman, J. (2009). Crime and Memory. In K. Golden and B. Bergo (Eds.), *The Trauma Controversy: Philosophical and Interdisciplinary Dialogues* (pp. 127–141). Albany, NY: State University of New York Press.

Jackson, R. (1993). *Dialogues with Dostoevsky: The Overwhelming Questions*. Stanford, CA: Stanford University Press.

Jaenicke, C. (2008). *The Risk of Relatedness: Intersubjectivity Theory in Clinical Practice*. Lanham, MD: Jason Aronson.

Kahr, B. (1996). *D. W. Winnicott: A Biographical Portrai*. Madison, CN: International Universities Press.

Laub, D. (1992). An Event without a Witness: Truth, Testimony and Survival. In S. Felman and D. Laub (Eds.), *Testimony: Crises of Witnessing in Literature, Psychoanalysis, and History* (pp. 75–92). New York: Routledge.

Laub, D., and Auerhahn, N. C. (1993). Knowing and Not Knowing Massive Psychic Trauma: Forms of Traumatic Memory. *International Journal of Psychoanalysis*, 74, 287–302.

Levi, P. (1989). *The Drowned and the Saved*. New York: Vintage International.

Levi, P., and Woolf, S. (2008). *Survival in Auschwitz: If This Is a Man*. Thousand Oaks, CA: BN Publishing.

Levinas, E. (1981). *Otherwise than Being, or, Beyond Essence*. The Hague and Boston Hingham, MA: M. Nijhoff and Kluwer Boston.

Levinas, E., and Nemo, P. (1985). *Ethics and Infinity*. Pittsburgh, PA: Duquesne University Press.

Levinas, E., Peperzak, A., Critchley, S., and Bernasconi, R. (1996). *Emmanuel Levinas: Basic Philosophical Writings*. Bloomington, IN: Indiana University Press.

Lewis, H. (1974). *Shame and Guilt in Neurosis*. New York: International Universities Press.

Lewis, H. (1987). *The Role of Shame in Symptom Formation*. Hillsdale, NJ: Erlbaum Associates.

Loewald, H. (1951). Ego and Reality. *International Journal of Psychoanalysis*, 32, 10–18.

Loewald, H. (1960). On the Therapeutic Action of Psycho-Analysis. *International Journal of Psychoanalysis*, 41, 16–33.

Loewald, H. (1979). The Waning of the Oedipus Complex. *Journal of the American Psychoanalytic Association*, 27, 751–775.

Marcus, P. (2006). Religion without Promises: The Philosophy of Emmanuel Levinas and Psychoanalysis. *Psychoanalytic Review*, 93, 923–951.

Margulies, A. (2000). Commentary. *Journal of the American Psychoanalytic Association*, 48, 72–79.

Orange, D. (1993). The Restoration of Schreber's Stolen Self. In B. Magid (Ed.), *Freud's Case Studies* (pp. 135–156). London: Routledge.

Orange, D. (2010). *Thinking for Clinicians: Philsophical Resources for Contemporary Psychoanalysis and the Humanistic Psychotherapies*. New York: Routledge.

Orange, D. (2011). *The Suffering Stranger: Hermeneutics for Everyday Clinical Practice*. New York: Routledge.

Orange, D. (2012). Clinical Hospitality: Welcoming the Face of the Devastated Other. Keynote address presented at the New Zealand Association of Psychotherapy, Wellington.

Pearlman, L., Saakvitne, K., and Cavalcade Productions (2005). *Vicarious Traumatization* [video]. Nevada City, CA: Cavalcade Productions.

Poland, W. (2000). The Analyst's Witnessing and Otherness. *Journal of the American Psychoanalytic Association*, 48, 17–34.

Racker, H. (1966). Ethics and Psycho-Analysis and the Psycho-Analysis of Ethics. *International Journal of Psychoanalysis*, 47, 63–80.

Rowling, J., and Dale, J. (2000). *Harry Potter and the Goblet of Fire* [audio recording]. New York: Listening Library.

Schreber, D., Macalpine, I., and Hunter, R. (1955). *Memoirs of My Nervous Illness*. London: W. Dawson.

Shaw, D. (2014). *Traumatic Narcissism: Relational Systems of Subjugation*. New York: Routledge.

Shengold, L. (1989). *Soul Murder: The Effects of Childhood Abuse and Deprivation*. New Haven, CT: Yale University Press.

Shengold, L. (1999). *Soul Murder Revisited: Thoughts about Therapy, Hate, Love, and Memory*. New Haven, CT: Yale University Press.

Shengold, L. (2000). Soul Murder Reconsidered. *Canadian Journal of Psychoanalysis*, 8, 1–18.

Stolorow, R. (2007). *Trauma and Human Existence: Autobiographical, Psycho-Analytic, and Philosophical Reflections*. New York: The Analytic Press.

Stolorow, R. (2011). *World, Affectivity, Trauma: Heidegger and Post-Cartesian Psychoanalysis*. New York: Routledge.

Stolorow, R., and Atwood, G. (1992). *Contexts of Being: The Intersubjective Foundations of Psychological Life*. Hillsdale, NJ: The Analytic Press.

Trüb, H. (1952). *Heilung aus der Begegnung: Eine Auseinandersetzung mit der Psychologie C. G. Jungs*. Stuttgart: Ernst Klett Verlag.

Viñar, M. (2005). The Specificity of Torture as Trauma: The Human Wilderness when Words Fail. *International Journal of Psychoanalysis*, 86, 311–333.

Winnicott, D. (1945). Primitive Emotional Development. *International Journal of Psychoanalysis*, 26, 137–143.

Winnicott, D. (1969). The Use of an Object. *International Journal of Psychoanalysis*, 50, 711–716.

Young-Bruehl, E. (2012). *Childism: Confronting Prejudice against Children*. New Haven, CT: Yale University Press.

Chapter 2

Radical responsibility and clinical hospitality

> I am defined as a subjectivity, as a singular person, as an "I," precisely because I am exposed to the other. It is my inescapable and incontrovertible answerability to the other that makes me an individual "I." So that I become a responsible or ethical "I" to the extent that I agree to depose or dethrone myself—to abdicate my position of centrality—in favor of the vulnerable other.
>
> (Levinas quoted in Cohen, 1986, pp. 26–27)

To face soul-destroying trauma, as we attempted in the previous chapter, means—to me—to consider psychotherapeutics as a moral, a humanitarian, undertaking. What does this imply? Surely not the removal of practical considerations, for our concern remains always the suffering and embodied human being in social context. To see psychotherapeutics (and related humanitarian work) as a moral task, I believe, leads to a focus on the concept and practice of responsibility. The word "responsibility" carries, however, a history and a range of meanings, among which I will address chiefly three: responsibility to one's professional role; responsibility for one's own life and history; and responsibility to the other.

Responsibility to one's professional role

Patients place their souls in the hands of clinicians in moments of excessive suffering. Then responsibility implies not only fidelity to codes of professional ethics, but much more. We are enjoined to do no harm, but harm can result when intending to do good without enough wisdom. So, clinical and professional ethics concerns difficult dilemmas that contemporary clinicians face after the demise of "standard technique." Giants among psychoanalytic ethicists include Glen Gabbard and Andrea Celenza. Both have studied sexual misconduct among clinicians (Celenza, 1991, 1998, 2010; Gabbard, 1994, 2002), while Gabbard has, to my mind, sharpened our sensibilities about respect for patient dignity and privacy when we write about them (Gabbard, 1997, 2000; Gabbard and Williams, 2001). Though

I leave these topics in their capable hands, in no way do I mean to under-state their importance; work with the aftermath of ethical violations has formed the greater part of my life as psychoanalyst and consultant, and undoubtedly has shaped my sensibilities.

I give admittedly short shrift to professional ethics and responsibility in order to turn to the aspects that interest me for this book's purposes—that is, the ethics of non-indifference (Levinas, 1981), with the internal buttressing needed to live and work other-wise. First, however, let us consider, in the work of Hans Loewald, the best of what traditional psychoanalysis can offer those seeking to embrace the uttermost possible ethical non-indifference toward the fate and face of the other, to work other-wise.

Responsibility for one's own life and history: Loewald's contribution

To consider the topic of personal responsibility for what one makes of one's own history, I turn to Hans Loewald as an ethical thinker.[1] Though I find the word "ethical" only once in his writings, and "ethics" never, Martin Heidegger's massive ethical violation drove Loewald into psychoa-nalysis, by his own account and to our benefit. So let us compare Loewald's earlier, most celebrated, essay on therapeutic action with his mature "Waning of the Oedipus Complex," following him into his last work to see if we can discover what kinds of ethical thinking may emerge. Along the way remember Heidegger's *Sein und Zeit (Being and Time)* sitting on Loewald's desk, never abandoned. The betrayal was tremendous, but the tie never relinquished—again, to our benefit and perhaps also to our misfortune.

Hans Loewald's landmark 1960 paper, "On the Therapeutic Action of Psycho-Analysis," marks roughly a midpoint in the history of psychoanalysis, between *The Interpretation of Dreams* and today. In an elegant quartet he brought object relations, transference, the relations between instinctual drives and ego, and the function of the analyst in the analytic situation into a *tour de force* of just sufficiently deferential subversion, opening the sub-sequent history of our field for nearly everything that has followed in American psychoanalysis and in psychotherapies related to it.

So let us look first, briefly, at some aspects of this early Loewald work, and, second, consider him as an ethical thinker later rethinking responsi-bility and sublimation. Then, honoring him as he honored Freud, we may ask what remains to be done. What aspects of his thought may his use and reuse of both Freudian language and Heideggerian philosophy have illuminated and obscured? Where might a thinker of his stature be going next were he still with us?

Loewald gathered up the brilliant fragments of Freud's thinking, pieces Freud had left lying around as he inventively confronted new clinical and theoretical conundrums, then used what he learned from Heidegger to weave them into a whole. Loewald saw us always trying to refind our original unitary experience, to reconstitute our "primordial density," the same one Winnicott (1960) characterized as "no such thing as an infant," from which we later differentiate as we become ourselves in relation to others.[2] (Balint (1979) would have called it the "harmonious interpenetrating mixup.") Loewald reinterpreted drive theory much as contemporary evolutionary biology does—not as a theory of struggle, but as erotic (Lear, 1998), a striving to refind the original oneness. Instincts emerge from the integration of infant and environment. Basic concepts in psychoanalytic theory lose their strangeness in Loewald's hands. "Cathexis" becomes organizing activity, bonding, sometimes even love. "Primary process" becomes the richness of our ongoing access to our earliest and embodied mother–infant experience, constantly alternating with the differentiated, more organized, and linguistic life. "Secondary" in his view gains the connotation of secondary as coming later in the process of psychological organization and integration of experience. "Primary process" completely loses its shamefulness and turns out to be the rich resource of imaginative, cultural, and even, perhaps, transcendent life. A close reader of Freud who never left the American Psychoanalytic Association and never founded a school of thought, Loewald recognized the baby-watchers and Winnicott as his kindred spirits.

No wonder. As a phenomenologist, Loewald had profoundly rethought temporality. Past, present, and future interpenetrate so much that he could welcome primary process as the source of our creativity and of religious life. (He later repeatedly expressed regret that Freud could see so little constructive use for religion.)

How did Loewald accomplish all this rethinking? *Nachträglich*—that is, backwards. He took a late text of Freud, a piece from *Civilization and Its Discontents*, and used it to read everything that came before, as if to say, "Here is the deeper meaning in Freud that he would have developed, if he had had the time." Freud wrote:

> An infant at the breast does not as yet distinguish his ego from the external world as the source of the sensations flowing in upon him. He gradually learns to do so, in response to various promptings . . . In this way, then, the ego detaches itself from the external world. Or, to put it more correctly, originally the ego includes everything, later it separates off an external world from itself.
>
> (Freud and Strachey, 2005, pp. 66–68)

With this text in hand, Loewald (1960) relationalized Freud and argued in his most famous paper that the therapeutic power of psychoanalysis resulted from the relational—that is, transferential—transformation of old miseries. Analysts, unlike the detached and distant mirrors of stereotypical psychoanalysis, make themselves available to the patient for transferences. Loewald (2000, p. 250) wrote:

> Without such transference—of the intensity of the unconscious, of the infantile ways of experiencing life which have no language and little organization, but the indestructibility and power of the origins of life—to the preconscious and to present-day life and contemporary objects—without such transference, or to the extent to which such transference miscarries, human life becomes sterile and an empty shell. On the other hand, the unconscious needs present-day external reality (objects) and present-day psychic reality (the preconscious) for its own continuity, lest it be condemned to live the shadow-life of ghosts or to destroy life.

The most famous passage in this paper is always worth rereading:

> The transference neurosis, in the technical sense of the establishment and resolution of it in the analytic process, is due to the blood of recognition which the patient's unconscious is given to taste—so that the old ghosts may reawaken to life. Those who know ghosts tell us that they long to be released from their ghost-life and led to rest as ancestors. As ancestors they live forth in the present generation, while as ghosts they are compelled to haunt the present generation with their shadow-life. Transference is pathological in so far as the unconscious is a crowd of ghosts,[3] and this is the beginning of the transference neurosis in analysis: ghosts of the unconscious, imprisoned by defenses but haunting the patient in the dark of his defenses and symptoms, are allowed to taste blood, are let loose. In the daylight of analysis the ghosts of the unconscious are laid and led to rest as ancestors whose power is taken over and transformed into the newer intensity of present life, of the secondary process and contemporary objects.
>
> (Loewald, 2000, pp. 248–249)

Often forgotten is that this famous passage is the work of a relatively young Loewald, much of whose best work came later—even on therapeutic action. Did transference remain the cure for what ails us? Is the kind of psychoanalysis Loewald eloquently described in 1960, and that many of us recognize gratefully from our own experience, really possible as a "psychotherapy for the people," so named originally by Freud, and newly evoked by Lew Aron and Karen Starr (2012)? Let us see what more Loewald offered.

First, like the infant researchers, particularly Daniel Stern (1985), Loewald believed in our capacities for self-organizing and self-healing through "internalization" or superego development. In other words, no longer compelled like an automaton, the growing child or adult makes the moral values her or his own: "A sense of self begins to emerge with increasing internalization, leading to the development of a sense of self-responsibility with the formation of the superego and the shouldering of guilt" (Loewald, 1985, p. 437). In analysis, he believed, the work of mourning closely linked up with resuming the processes of internalization:

> The relinquishment of external objects and their internalization involves a process of separation, of loss and of restitution in many ways similar to mourning. During analysis, problems of separation and mourning come to the fore in a specific way at times of interruption and most particularly in the terminal phases of treatment.
>
> (Loewald, 2007, p. 1114)

Mourning internalizes what must be relinquished, integrating a personal life, a moral life, as Loewald would later say.

Mourning

In perhaps his second most significant paper, "The Waning of the Oedipus Complex," Loewald developed Freud's mourner into his vision of the ethical human being. To take on responsibility for our own lives, we must absorb the guilt for our very own *Vatertötung* (murder of the father). That is, to take on authority over our own lives and live responsibly, we must break something that can feel not only like letting our parents (or analysts) go, but destroying them. (I am reminded of Winnicott's destruction-leading-to-use discourse.) In Loewald's (2000, p. 387) words,

> It is a parental authority that is murdered; by that, whatever is sacred about the bond between child and parent is violated . . . it is the bringing forth, nourishing, providing for, and protecting of the child by the parents that constitute their parenthood, authority, and render sacred the child's ties with the parents.

So, claimed Loewald, the process of becoming ourselves, developmentally and in analysis, constitutes a developmental task from which we cannot escape. This heavy task involves bearing the burden of guilt for the sorrow we inflict on those who give us life: "We are usurping their power, their competence, their responsibility for us, and we are abnegating, rejecting, them as libidinal objects . . . we destroy them in regard to some of their qualities hitherto most vital to us" (2000, p. 390). Along the way, we "appropriate"— he asks us to note his use of the same word he used for taking on parental authority—our needs and impulses. So, the responsible, authoritative self has not only agency but needs. Moreover, we begin "to experience ourselves as agents, notwithstanding the fact that we were born without our informed consent and did not pick our parents" (p. 392). Never have I heard a clearer statement of Heideggerian "thrownness" (*Geworfenheit*).

If things go well, Loewald noted, the residues include tenderness, mutual trust, and respect. But the path, as he also warned us, runs through tremendous mourning, also a task of the ethical life that we may never evade. Though he said little about mourning here, he ended with his stunning redefinition of self, "in its autonomy, as an atonement structure, a structure of reconciliation, and as such a supreme achievement" (2000, p. 394). What can he possibly have meant by this? Perhaps the Oedipus complex, instead of waning, self-destructs, or maybe not. Then he posted a warning: "If I were to go deeper into these matters, issues such as mourning, remorse, repentance, would have to be considered" (2000, p. 394). No atonement structure of selfhood, no self-responsibility, no full assumption of guilt for one's crimes, no repentance arrives without mourning.

He did return to this subject. In one of his last published papers, "Termination Analyzable and Unanalyzable," Loewald (1988, pp. 156–157) suggested that mourning, in a sense, undoes the work of separation:

> Mourning in its full sense involves the gradual relinquishment of a cherished relationship with another person, and its internalization. By internalization I do not simply mean remembering the person and the relationship in thoughts, images, and fantasies. I mean an increasing dissolution of the relationship as one with an external object—whether present or imagined—leading to an absorption into the very fabric of the subject.

With this understanding in hand, Loewald saw this work of mourning as pervading every analysis from the beginning, but variously configured depending on the patient's trouble. Today we might frame these differences in attachment terms. One patient may resist—that is, fear being in treatment at all, or continuing with it, dread closeness and dependency. Another may resist ending treatment, for fear of unbearable loss. But the end will in any case haunt the work from the beginning (Heideggerian finitude). My colleague Elizabeth Corpt (2013) speaks of the door that opens—in every treatment and every session—as the door that also closes.

We must note a curious contrast between Loewald's notion of mental health as it emerges from a good analysis and that of the predominant ego psychology of his era. "Being more individuated," he wrote in this same late article, "means experiencing the loneliness and vulnerability, and the richness and freedom of individual existence" (Loewald, 1988, p. 161). So individuation, paradoxically, brings us less individuation, less self-sufficiency, more loneliness, and more vulnerability. What happened to the resoluteness (*Entschlossenheit*) of his beloved Heidegger? Perhaps here we have a hint of his realization about the sources of the betrayal, but Loewald never told us directly. Below we will find, however, vulnerability linked to a kind of ethics that Loewald was not quite able to consider.

Sublimation

Besides internalization and fluid linking between primary and secondary process, Loewald transformed the psychoanalytic concept of sublimation from a defense into a creative transformation of one's personal history. Earlier the unconscious was a crowd of ghosts, to be laid to rest as ancestors in the analytic process as the past is mourned. Now the life accepted and taken up anew as one's own life participates in eternity, even in the *nunc stans* (abiding now) of the mystics. It participates in something much larger than ourselves. Loewald pictures for us a human life restored to an integration with losses mourned, and possibilities embraced, far beyond resentment, by way of engagement in transference and through a drama that relationalists might today call "enactment." His patient at the end of analysis knows that her life is her life, her dreams are her dreams, her projects are her own. She takes responsibility for her life:

> our basic needs, in such transformation, are not relinquished, nor are traumatic and distorting childhood experiences made conscious in order to be deplored and undone—even if that were possible. These are part of the stuff our lives are made of. What is possible is to engage in the task of actively reorganizing, reworking, creatively transforming those early experiences which, painful as many of them have been, first give meaning to our lives. The more we know what it is that we are working with, the better we are able to weave our history which, when all is said and done, is recreating, in ever-changing modes and transformations, our childhood. To be an adult means that: it does not mean leaving the child in us behind.
>
> (Loewald, 2000, p. 545)

To me, this represents not a claim to cure trauma, to exorcize the ghosts of the unconscious, but an intent to welcome the wounded, even the soul-murdered (Shengold, 1989), so that the patient can gradually own his or her personal history. His patients (Hurwitz, 1986; S. Stern, 2009) remember Loewald as an analyst of few words, but those words often captured closely their younger emotional situation.

Loewald took Freud's language, and used it to surpass Freud in a relational, humanistic, and existentialist direction. Explicitly refusing claims that Freud's "science" belonged with biology among the hard sciences, he claimed that psychoanalysis, whether theorizing or treatment, considered human beings as moral agents:

We have only to think of the role played in psychoanalysis by such problems and concepts as inner conflict, anxiety, guilt and shame, the superego, and the antagonism between the exigencies of societal and instinctual life. At the same time psychoanalysis deals prominently with man's love life; think of its emphasis on sexuality and of the central importance of transference in its various meanings and ramifications. Religious life, although viewed by Freud from a narrow and biased standpoint, has been another important subject of psychoanalytic research.

(Loewald, 2000, pp. 534–535)

Above all, as we have seen, he thought moral the appropriating of responsibility. As in most psychotherapeutic discourse, responsibility for Loewald tended to mean responsibility for one's own life, even unconscious life. In his words:

The movement from unconscious to conscious experience, from the instinctual life of the id to the reflective, purposeful life of the ego, means taking responsibility for one's own history, the history that has been lived and the history in the making . . . that mass of past living and experiencing, which took place without self-awareness, and often—and this is more important—without the ego's mediation. The idea of responsibility, in its most basic sense . . . refers to that inner responsiveness to raw experience which is the hallmark of the ego and transposes experience onto a different plane.

(Loewald, 2000, pp. 538–539)

In other words, I take on my original situation—all that has happened to me without my choice—and integrate it as *my life*. I stop attributing my life to fate, or to my situation; I will take on mourning and become a responsible human being. We can hear the resonances of Heidegger: temporality, finitude, and resoluteness.

In his later work, however, I also hear the hints of overwhelming and endless mourning. The self is an atonement structure.[4] "Sublimation is a kind of reconciliation of the subject–object dichotomy—an atonement for that polarization" (Loewald, 2000, p. 460). Individuation and internalizing mean realizing vulnerability. Yes, he speaks explicitly of mourning for our Oedipal crimes, but what of the six million? The hints and nuances lurk just below the surface, and in every footnote where he mourns the loss of reading and teaching Freud in the original German.

It is possible—though of course I cannot know—that Loewald could not take the next steps toward radical ethics because, as a relatively privileged refugee, he could not speak—like many of his generation (Kuriloff, 2014)—of his own traumatic losses when others had suffered so much more. For those of us who study philosophy, however, the one hint he did provide always haunts:

> Philosophy has been my first love. I gladly affirm its influence on my way of thinking while being wary of the peculiar excesses a philosophical bent tends to entail. My teacher in the field was Martin Heidegger, and I am deeply grateful for what I learned from him, despite his most hurtful betrayal in the Nazi era, which alienated me from him permanently.
>
> (Loewald, 2000, p. xliii)

Another of Heidegger's Jewish students, who spent five years in Nazi labor camps, simply wrote: "It [my life] has been dominated by the presentiment and the memory of the Nazi horror" (Levinas, 1990a, p. 291).

But Loewald, as we have learned from Jonathan Lear (1998), supported by his love for Freud's original German and his understanding of Heidegger's great work, gave us the discourse of mourning and responsibility, fluid and creative linking of primary and secondary process, of Eros which binds up that which seems disparate, and finally sublimation.

As mentioned at the outset, there are also forms of responsibility concerning us in our professional lives—duties to protect our patients and clients from many forms of harm, exposure, and misuse of power—so that our work of cure, care, or healing may continue. But beyond responsibility for our own lives and professional responsibility, a third type needs to concern us.

In popular culture, unfortunately, the lingo of responsibility sounds far less nuanced than even the two mentioned thus far. Listen to the cabinet secretaries who testify before congressional committees. "Yes, I take full responsibility for that; don't ask me any more questions." "I will even resign from my position." "Yes, I am responsible for that area; you don't need to worry about it." Everything is clear. Even in the voices of women, responsibility sounds strong, agentic, masculine, white, intellectual, capable, no-nonsense. Vulnerability and receptivity place you among the needy, the feminine or those of uncertain gender, the darker skinned, irrational, irresponsible, takers, those who may need public healthcare. These must be shunned at all costs.

But there have always been people who elude these dichotomizing concepts, not because they are binaries, but because such categories can never encompass human beings. What if the work that Loewald described so well—laying the ghosts of the unconscious to rest as ancestors so that we may take up our own lives responsibly—is only a prelude? What if— enigmatically and as I suspect he also felt—it is preliminary to what makes our work, and life in a fractured and "burning world" (Cushman, 2007), an ethical task?

For me, the strongest hint that Loewald understood a kind of responsibility that I have never found in Heidegger—a responsibility not only for one's own life but for the other—emerges in his descriptions of parenting:

> the recognizing-caring activities of primary caretakers crucially contribute to the development of the child's psychic life by the fact of their being ahead of his present stage of organization. Parental caring, knowing, understanding, embedded in their interaction with the child, take place in the context and perspective of the child's overall requirements and future course of development, as perceived and misperceived by the parents.
>
> (Loewald, 2000, p. 540)

Here we can hear both Heidegger, who warns against leaping ahead, and the developmentalists' zone of proximal development. But we can also hear Heinz Kohut, who substituted for the family rivalry, Odysseus, who protected his son, as well as Erik Erikson, who thought generativity natural. But Loewald (2000, p. 242) continued to describe the ways in which the mother's "acts of organizing the infant's activities and experiences within an envisioned temporal-spatial totality of his being" allow the infant to come into being. The mother, like the analyst Loewald had described in 1960 as holding an image of what the patient could become, ethically provides for the other. As Loewald had so many times re-translated where id (undifferentiated) was, there ego shall come into being (*Wo Es war, soll Ich werden*). But we may need more.

Responsibility to the other: the ethical turn

Trauma exposes vulnerability. More aware of this link, we find something changing in contemporary psychoanalysis, something we might characterize as an "ethical turn" (Baraitser, 2008), a turn in a direction beyond psychoanalysis itself, and everyday talk of the ethical. In 2011 two interdisciplinary conferences, attended by many psychoanalysts, occurred: Psychology and the Other (Cambridge, MA)[5] and Bystanders No More (New York). Psychoanalysts and others, many inspired by Neil Altman's pioneering work (2010), are involving themselves and their writing with Palestinian–Israeli troubles, with transgender people, with the undocumented, with whiteness and gross inequalities, with class differences understood from below. Other examples have followed. We have begun to allow ourselves to be made increasingly uncomfortable. We are starting to know that it matters little whether we are recognized or not.

But we have left now the discourses, or language-games, of psychoanalysis itself and have entered the world of the ethical. Let us listen to a few voices from this sphere to take the measure of its sensibility: Emmanuel Levinas, Simon Critchley, and Judith Butler.

Because we will revisit him on the question of subjectivity, Levinas can appear briefly here. A five-year Nazi labor camp survivor who lost all his Lithuanian family, he wrote:

> that face facing me, in its expression—in its mortality—summons me, demands me, requires me: as if the invisible death faced by the face of the other—pure alterity, separate, somehow, from any whole—were "my business." [As if I were, always already, my brother's and sister's keeper.][6] As if, unknown by the other whom already, in the nakedness of its face, it concerns, it "regarded me" before its confrontation with me, before being the death that stares me, myself, in the face. The death of the other man puts me on the spot, calls me into question, as if I, by my possible indifference, became the accomplice of that death, invisible to the other who is exposed to it; and as if, even before being condemned to it myself, I had to answer for that death of the other, and not leave the other alone to his deathly solitude. It is precisely in that recalling of me to my responsibility by the face that summons me, that demands me, that requires me—it is in that calling into question—that the other is my neighbor.
>
> (Levinas, 1999, pp. 24–25)

The miserable other *interpellates* (calls on me) me, traumatizing me, taking me hostage, calling me to subjection, to substitution (Levinas, 1981), to the only kind of meaningful suffering, that taken on for the sake of the other. Levinas used "interpellate" in its precise philosophical meaning of "to bring into being or give identity to," as well as "to command." Precisely in responding to the command that the other's suffering imposes on me I am brought to subjectivity, constituted as subject, in his view. There is no masochism here, no pleasure in this suffering. But of course no one can live up to the infinite demand, the endless responsibility, so like Dostoevsky (see Chapter 7), I am forever guilty for all, before all. Daily the unexpected stranger comes before me, welcomed into the queue before me, helped up the subway steps by thousands of unexpectedly courteous New Yorkers, allowed into the expressway lane. She need not show her identity card if she needs help. When someone calls her a "dirty Jew," I will know to say that I'm Jewish too, or to protect her from pogroms. If Palestinian, she is *my* sister. Refugee children, from Latin America or Syria, are *my* children—this is non-indifference. Though the ethic of responsibility—framed in response to extreme situations, and full of traumatic memory—often sounds extreme, it grounds itself in everyday proximity to those unexpected interpellations, situations that ethically call us out. "Without ever having done anything, I *have always been* under accusation, I am persecuted" (Levinas et al., 1996, p. 89; emphasis added).

Critchley (2007) comments that infinite responsibility to the other creates what Levinas liked to call "the curvature of intersubjective space" (Levinas,

1969, p. 291) in which the other always occupies the high point. All theories of intersubjectivity that emphasize mutuality and reciprocity and dialectic— namely those of "*les trois H*" (Hegel, Husserl, and Heidegger)—miss this radical asymmetry. "When I am within the relation, then other is not my equal, and my responsibility towards [the other] is infinite" (Critchley, 2007, p. 60). Critchley (pp. 60–61) continues:

> Levinas makes the extreme claim that my relation to the other is not some benign benevolence, compassionate care or respect for the other's autonomy, but is the obsessive experience of responsibility that perse- cutes me with its sheer weight. I am the other's hostage, taken by them and prepared to substitute myself for any suffering and humiliation that they may undergo. I am responsible for the persecution I undergo and even for my persecutor; a claim that, given the experience of Levinas's family and people during the Second World War, is nothing less than extraordinary.

Critchley will go on to claim, as did Derrida (1999), that this ethical subjectivity must be a split one.

Meanwhile, the discourse of responsibility—often dismissed by feminists because of Levinas's admittedly unwise use of gender categories, and because, perhaps, women have long enough borne the care of others—returns in the voice of Judith Butler. She hears the ethical call in the affirmation of the precarious, the vulnerable, and the traumatized:

> if they [the unnameable and ungrievable lives] do not appear in their precariousness and their destruction, we will not be moved. We will not return to a sense of ethical outrage that is distinctively for an Other, in the name of an Other. We cannot, under contemporary conditions of representation, hear the agonized cry or be compelled or commanded by the face.
>
> (Butler, 2004, p. 150)

She worries that our ethical subjectivity becomes systematically occluded by media manipulation.

The ethical constitution of subjectivity

Suppose we grant to developmental and intersubjective psychoanalysts that subjectivity, or a sense of selfhood, originally emerges—absent significant developmental trauma—from the harmonious interpenetrating mixup (Balint, 1979); maternal care (Winnicott, 1965); self–selfobject relatedness (Kohut, 1977); primordial density (Loewald, 1980); the intersubjective field (Stolorow et al., 1987); or relationality (Mitchell, 2000). The daily work of psychotherapists involves understanding and responding to the many in our world whose early and later trauma and other trouble bring them to our doors.

But what constitutes our own subjectivity, our own moral center or *hegimonikon*, as the ancient Greeks and Romans would have called it? Where do we hear the voice of the *daimon*, of conscience, of responsibility? Butler, in a lecture given at the Nobel Museum in Sweden (Butler, 2011), suggested that the precarious face of the suffering other faces us daily on television, in our newspapers, and on our handheld devices, infinitely close and infinitely distant.

How does one respond? Some join Doctors Without Borders, surely a life without recognition. In 1939, the theologian Dietrich Bonhoeffer returned to Germany to rejoin other German Christians in the plot against Hitler's life—his twin sister had married a Jew so he had intimate knowledge of what was happening—instead of remaining in New York, as colleagues advised him to do (see Chapter 6). He spent much of the war in prison, and was hanged before its end. Witold Pilecki (2012), as we now know from his newly available account, volunteered to be a prisoner in Auschwitz, where he remained for three years, attempting to organize resistance and to communicate to the outside world about the nature of the place. He tried to keep his name unknown to protect others. He was tortured, tried, and executed by the Communist government of Poland in March 1948. Likewise many journalists have died in their recent efforts to tell stories of oppression and violence.

But many serve humbly, scarcely knowing themselves that they are simply doing what they must. A dear colleague objects to thinking of herself as ethical or Levinasian as she faithfully accompanies and cares for dying friends while continuing all her own work. But I believe that her very subjectivity—whatever that may mean—emerges in this response to the other. I am grateful for the following words from the French theorist Gilles Deleuze:

> To say something in one's own name is very strange, for it is not at all when we consider ourselves as selves, persons or subjects that we speak in our own name. On the contrary, an individual acquires a true proper name as the result of the most severe operations of depersonalization, when he opens himself to the multiplicities that pervade him and the intensities which run through his whole being.
>
> (Quoted in Baraitser, 2008, p. 86)

So, to begin with, we must never expect to be recognized in our own name. Multiplicities run us through. Moreover, as Dostoevsky understood once he had been imprisoned in Siberia, morality is no abstraction. The other—possibly ugly, disgusting, demanding, and grotesque, at least in need of my care—is my sister or brother. The colicky infant who can give me nothing requires me to respond. Responsibility replaces recognition in the world of the ethical. Recognition, sought as an end in itself, may collapse into the world that the social contract philosopher Thomas Hobbes believed natural to humans: solitary, poor, nasty, brutish, and short. When recognition arrives by chance, it seems to me a gift to be humbly received and passed on to others.

Subjectivity constituted by response to the other will look quite unpretentious.[7] Years ago, as a young philosophy graduate student and a stranger in New York, I was a guest for some weeks at a convent while I looked for a place to stay near the university where I would be studying. Remarkably, it took me two weeks to find out which of the sisters was the local superior. Her attitude of service to the others made her indistinguishable from the rest. Retired now, she also worked for many years as a contemporary Freudian psychoanalyst, and became an important influence on my decision to study psychology and psychoanalysis. Unsurprisingly, we have been close friends for 35 years.

To serve the other, without much recognition, without self-promotion, is to allow ourselves to be interpellated (commanded, and thus brought into being) every day, both at home and far away. Many will call this an impossible life, and surely for any one of us, on any given day, it has its limits. Granted, but we see simple, extraordinary goodness around us every day. Shall we settle for less?

Responsibility as clinical hospitality[8]

We never had guests in our family home. My mother, orphaned herself and overwhelmed by her ten children (of whom I am the eldest), made it clear to all of us that we were not ever to bring other children into the house. Ashamed, she had no idea how to make them welcome in the chaos, nor had she much experience as a guest herself. I do remember one exception, when I was six and there were only five children. The parish priest came to dinner, we children sat silently, and the adults talked. I, as usual, was seated between two toddlers, to cut up their food, and also jumped up now and then to see to the baby's needs. Apart from this one instance, I had no opportunity to learn the spirit or skills of hospitality. But I have often, as the playwright says, "depended on the kindness of strangers."

Today, in the United States, we live in a culture where hospitality usually forms part of the expression "the hospitality industry." Public discourse about immigration primarily concerns fences, incarceration, and deportation, not hospitality and welcome. The Emma Lazarus poem engraved on our Statue of Liberty at the entrance to New York Harbor—"Give me your tired, your poor, your huddled masses longing to breathe free"—seems a distant memory of a spirit that we can barely recall. Thus my personal and family history joins with a cultural impoverishment. Now I want to retrieve the "hospitality" whose relatives are compassion, generosity, kindness, welcome, and humanism, a word that belongs in a rich interdisciplinary discourse: anthropological, literary, historical, theological, philosophical, and psychological—that is to say, in the human sciences. From my own readings in philosophy and psychoanalysis, with a few excursions, I want to join hospitality with the work of clinicians of every humanistic and humanitarian spirit, and to speak of clinical hospitality.

To structure this thinking about clinical hospitality, let us turn to the work of three twentieth-century French philosophers, mining each for clinical inspiration. First, Emmanuel Levinas provided his radical challenge to welcome our ethical responsibility for the suffering other arriving, unexpected and uninvited, at our door. Next emerged his younger colleague Jacques Derrida, reminding us that the same word in the Romance languages denotes host and guest, bringing us all the linguistic and conceptual ambiguity and complexity we clinicians confront in attempting to fulfill the ethical demand. He explained how the Levinasian host becomes a guest in her own home, or even a hostage. Finally comes the apparently gentler voice of hermeneut Paul Ricoeur, also a friend of Levinas, whose late work on translation spoke of linguistic hospitality, inviting us to dialogue and mourning. Each of these invites a clinical reflection.

Levinas, a Lithuanian Jew, never forgot that French nuns had hidden his wife and daughter while he spent five years in a Nazi labor camp. He knew what hospitality could be worth. Still, to describe his meaning, he returned in his Talmudic lectures to Abraham, the ancestor, not only of those belonging to the three monotheistic faiths, but of every fully human person. He wrote:

> Father of believers? Certainly. But above all the one who knew how to receive and feed men: the one whose tent was wide open on all sides. Through all these openings he looked out for passersby in order to receive them. The meal offered by Abraham? We know especially of one meal, the one he offered to the three angels—without suspecting their condition as angels ... Abraham must have taken the three passersby for three Bedouins, for three nomads from the Negev Desert—three Arabs, in other words! He runs toward them. He calls them "your Lordships." The heirs of Abraham—men to whom their ancestor bequeathed a difficult tradition of duties toward the other man, which one is never done with, an order in which one is never free. In this order above all else, duty takes the form of obligation toward the body, the obligation of feeding and sheltering. So defined, the heirs of Abraham are of all nations: any man truly man is no doubt of the line of Abraham.
>
> (Levinas, 1990b, p. 99)

Here Levinas refers, in a Talmudic and biblical context, to his philosophical and ethical claim that the other has an infinite claim on my protection and care, that, as he often said, there exists a "curvature of intersubjective space" (Levinas, 1969, p. 291) in which the stranger transcends my need for comfort absolutely. "Abraham was the one whose tent remained open day and night, the one who fed his guests without asking who they were beforehand" (Chalier, 2002, p. 107).

Immediately, however, he goes on to confront the difficulty in which the question about Abraham had arisen: the rabbi's son has hired some workers, and agreed to feed them. The rabbi says:

> My son, even if you prepared a meal for them equal to the one King Solomon served, you would not have fulfilled your obligation toward them, for they are the descendants of Abraham, Isaac, and Jacob. As long as they have not begun the work, go and specify: you are only entitled to bread and dry vegetables.[9]
>
> (Talmud Tractate *Baba Metsia*, quoted in Levinas, 1990b, p. 94)

Levinas commented that the rabbi is so frightened because he understands that his son has committed himself to infinite hospitality, to an infinite ethical obligation that will be well understood by these descendants of Abraham, Isaac, and Jacob, who know about the tent that is open on all sides. Levinas (1990b, p. 99) went on to recall the words of a famous Lithuanian rabbi, Israel Salanter: "The material needs of my neighbor are my spiritual needs." So, the father counsels his son immediately to set limits and conditions on his obligation. "What is truly human," Levinas continued, "is beyond human strength" (1990b, p. 100). But the subject of limits already arises in the Talmudic context.

In his philosophical work, Levinas, student of Heidegger and Lithuanian survivor of five years in Nazi labor camps, who lived and worked in France until he died in 1995, propounded one big philosophical idea: namely, that before everything comes "a radically asymmetrical relation of infinite responsibility to the other person" (Critchley and Bernasconi, 2002). In his great work, *Totality and Infinity*, he contrasted what he called "totalizing"— treating others as something to be studied, categorized, or comprehended— with responding to the suffering "visage" of the other.

This other, no alter-ego that resembles me, bursts the bounds of the pheno-menology Levinas had learned from Edmund Husserl and Heidegger. As David Ross Fryer (2007, p. 582) puts it, "Husserl discovered the other ego as an other ego like myself, but Levinas discovered the other person as also a radical other beyond my capability and capacity to know." This irreducible "face" always transcends our concepts, representations, catego-ries, and ideas. The human other presents me with an infinite demand for protection and care, just as the Talmudic rabbi understood his son's responsibility. Each face says, "You shall not kill. You shall not allow me to die alone." Hearing and seeing means living other-wise, for-the-other.

Let us listen to the formulation in his essay entitled "Substitution" (Levinas et al., 1996, p. 91): "It is through the condition of being a hostage that there can be pity, compassion, pardon, and proximity in the world—even the little there is, even the simple 'after you sir.'" Responsibility for the other, said Lévinas, "is the essential structure of subjectivity" (Levinas and Nemo, 1985, p. 95).

Subjectivity transforms in Levinas. Only in the suffering of the other, and in my response, do I (a *moi*, not an ego) come into being, "*me voici*," called into being by the other's naked and vulnerable face. The sovereign self, with its "place in the sun," always trying to have more, would be indifferent to the plight of the other. What minimal subjectivity remains to me, instead, comes about via my response to the widow, the orphan, and the stranger. Again, in the instance of a gift, "the other can be said to dispossess me on occasion so that giving is not an act, but an ethical event whereby I lose my sense of mine in the face of the other" (Critchley and Bernasconi, 2002, p. 240). Though this would not be Levinas's own formulation, something happens to me in the face of the other's need so that my giving has the quality of participating. My background role becomes habitual. Derrida (1999, p. 46) later paraphrased Levinas: "the relation to the other is deference."

What can the working clinician make of all this? Where is *our* discourse of hospitality and welcome? Though only recently have words like "compassion" (Orange, 2006), "kindness," and "generosity" (Corpt, 2009) found their way into psychoanalytic literature, if we look carefully, we can find their forebears. Sandor Ferenczi wrote to Freud about tact: "I merely think that one must from the outset place oneself in—feel oneself into—the patient's situation" (Ferenczi, 1949, p. 248; see also Poland, 1975). Ian Suttie (1935) wrote of tenderness, Winnicott (Winnicott and the Institute of Psycho-Analysis (Great Britain), 1975) of maternal care. Hospitable spirits have also existed in the other humanistic psychotherapies, with which I am less familiar.

Oddly, however, psychoanalytic reticence has combined with the worship of efficiency and cost-effectiveness to render invisible, and even disparaged, clinical warmth and unhurried welcome, but it remains an indispensable need. Such emotional availability (Orange, 1995) involves being prepared for whatever openhearted empathic stretching the other may need of me.

Elisabeth Young-Bruehl (quoted in Fox, 2011) redescribed empathy when she wrote of the work of the biographer: "The usual, indeed, the clichéd way of describing empathy as 'putting yourself in another's place' seems to me quite wrong ... empathizing involves, rather, putting another person in yourself, becoming another person's habitat." She continued, crucially: "But this depends upon your ability to tell the difference between the subject and yourself." Empathy has nothing to do with merger: it requires separated otherness, in Levinasian terms, or, in Hans-Georg Gadamer's words, "It is the other who breaks my self-centeredness by giving me something to understand" (Gadamer, 1985, p. 9; my translation). With this Levinasian caveat— clearly applicable beyond biographers—empathy or clinical hospitality might mean, as wholeheartedly as possible for me, making a space for the patient in my own homeless heart, so that the devastated other may have a developmental second chance (Orange, 1995).

But the question of endless responsibility to and for the other troubles us clinicians (thus Chapter 3 on the masochism question), as we can see from the Talmudic lectures that it troubled Levinas too. Catherine Chalier (2002, p. 108) writes:

> In his Talmudic reading, Levinas insists [that] . . . the descendant of Abraham knows that there is no limit on his obligations towards the worker. The contract thus comes to limit my obligations toward the worker and not, as one might assume, to institute a minimum of obligation toward him. [This is a fine distinction!] This means, very precisely, that obligations towards the other are infinite and do not depend on good will or choice. They precede freedom and consecrate the descendant of Abraham [every good human being] to an infinite service, to a responsibility that is greater than the commitments that have actively been taken on . . . contracts and customs attempt in fact to introduce some limit to this initial or more exactly, immemorial, limitlessness.

In his philosophical writings, Levinas addressed this problem by saying that as long as there are only two, the other's need transcends me utterly. My hospitality transforms me into a hostage (these two words have the same root in the Romance languages). But as soon as there are three or more, the question of justice arises. Then we need laws and contracts and agreements— all those structures that manage limits.

So, can we simply say to the shattered sufferer who arrives at our door that we offer only bread and vegetables? Forty-five minutes, and see you next week? No, of course not. Long ago a patient, brilliant but always hovering on the edges of madness, protested to me that everything about psychotherapy and psychoanalysis was arranged for the protection and convenience of the clinician, and had nothing to do with the needs of patients. Only after I invited him to help me design something that might better meet his needs, and to try things out for a while—now I might say I opened at least two sides of my tent—did we settle into fairly conventional treatment for many years. Before then, we walked on the nearby beach, sat in coffee shops—anything to reduce his sense of weirdness.

But because there are many patients, each with special needs of his or her own, and since I am a limited human being myself, ever more so each month and year, I must, like the rabbi's son, set contracts in advance for time, place, and payment, and work out the rest as best and hospitably as possible in a spirit of welcome, a tent-open spirit. Otherwise they too may notice the closed-off spirit, and turn away in despair once more.

Derrida, who saw clearly what Levinasian ethics would politically require—open borders, the tent open on all sides—also saw the impossibility. He grew up much exposed to anti-Semitism in Algeria, and thus knew exclusion well. His graveside oration "Adieu to Emmanuel Levinas" is published with a long and longing essay on hospitality, entitled "A Word of Welcome." He explained that welcoming the other with an open door means submitting oneself to the other, making oneself receptive and teachable.

Soon, however, the complications and ambiguities begin to emerge. If only we could simply open our door and heart to all in need as the Abrahamic "law of hospitality" commands. But the conditional *laws* of hospitality always conflict with, and indeed radically oppose, the unconditional *law* of hospitality. According to these conditional laws, you may enter only when invited; and you must behave well according to local customs when you are inside. You must accept just what is provided, not asking for more. You must already speak, or quickly learn, the local language, and not expect yours to be learned or understood by your hosts. You must contribute to the local economy, and keep a low profile, disappearing into the local culture. And so on. Above all, you must not be other, or have needs that might call on the unconditional hospitality. The conditional hospitality is a system that maintains itself in a tenuous balance prior to the arrival of the uninvited foreigner, the Levinasian widow, orphan, or stranger.

Derrida, however, invited us to consider that both types of hospitality may be inextricably linked. In his inimitable style, he started by drawing our attention to the linguistic ambiguities, beginning with the use, in Romance languages, of the same word for guest and host:

> we must be reminded of this implacable law of hospitality: the *hôte* who receives (the host), the one who welcomes the invited *hôte* (the guest), the welcoming *hôte* who considers himself the owner of the place, is in truth a *hôte* received in his own home. He receives the hospitality that he offers *in* his own home; he receives it *from* his own home—which, in the end, does not belong to him. The *hôte* as host is a guest . . . The one who welcomes is first welcomed in his own home. The one who invites is invited by the one whom he invites.
>
> (Derrida, 1999, p. 41; original emphasis)

Let us consider this paradox in our everyday clinical work. A suffering person, new or not, arrives to my welcome. Immediately the tables are turned. Nothing happens unless I surrender the leading role, and allow the patient to lead me, to teach me, to take me hostage, to inhabit me (as Elisabeth Young-Bruehl reformulates empathy). My welcome creates the possibility that the other may welcome me into her world of loss, confusion, devastation. The welcomer becomes the one who may be welcomed as a lost and wandering stranger. The home I thought I owned was only a way-station, a tent to be opened toward the other who then might in turn share something, some bread of suffering, with me. Derrida quotes Levinas on the strange welcome of the home:

> The home . . . is not a possession in the same sense as the movable goods it can collect and keep. It is possessed because it already and henceforth is hospitable for its owner. This refers us to its essential interiority, and to the inhabitant that inhabits it before every inhabitant, the welcoming one par excellence, welcoming in itself.
>
> (Levinas quoted in Derrida, 1999, p. 43)

So, the hospitable one is dispossessed not only of agentic subjectivity—subjectivity becomes subjection and receptivity—but also of possession in the sense that he is king of the castle. Likewise the hospitable clinician, the more "clinical wisdom" she accumulates, will live with an ever-diminished sense of control. Like my wise old mother-in-law, who told me she was "learning how to be ninety-eight," not-knowing and not-having will be good enough. It will keep the sides of the tent open for the hungry and strangers.

A third philosopher, this one from the Christian tradition but also long incarcerated during the Second World War, turned his attention to problems of translation in his later years. Paul Ricoeur (1913–2005) brings a generous and hospitable hermeneutic to the problem of translation. It has always seemed to me that translation and therapeutics are kindred forms of work, and my intuition finds philosophical articulation in Ricoeur's *On Translation* (Ricoeur, 2006). According to an old proverb in at least French and Italian, to translate is to betray: "*Traduire, c'est trahir*"/"*Traduttore, traditore.*" In other words, when I translate your words into my own meaning, even within the same language, I have already betrayed you. This commonplace shows up in almost every book review of a translation, especially when it involves poetry. Any one of us familiar with more than one language, or who does any clinical work, understands the truth of this proverb, and Ricoeur gives it its due.

But he does more: he points out that the violence of translation goes both ways. Not only do I do violence to an Italian text when I try to translate it into English, or to a patient's words or gestures when I try to read them through my own contexts, but the Italian speaker, as I feel it, pounds nails into my head by forcing me to think and feel and verbalize otherwise, as does my patient. (Some psychoanalytic theories would claim that the patient intends to do this—to let me feel his suffering. I am not so sure.) Now we are back in the territory marked out by Levinas and Derrida, where we are both devastated strangers walking uninvited into each other's house, disrupting each other's sense of being at home. Now we can imagine how unsurprisingly so many clinical misunderstandings and impasses, enactments in some psychoanalytic discourses, come about.

But translation attempts to bring linguistic and personal worlds together, and sometimes succeeds, albeit with great difficulty. To find our way, Ricoeur advocates what he calls "linguistic hospitality." What does this strange idea involve? It first requires us to reject the Chomskian suggestion of a basic universal underlying language, as well as the Jungian Ur-image, and to embrace instead the idea of genuine otherness, of real plurality (James, 1977). We cannot drill down into our language, into our own unconsciousness, if you will, to find the other. The others, with their languages, cultures, histories, religions, and all that these mean to them, are truly others.

Rejecting Chomsky's (1968) universalizing, and accepting true plurality, also means embracing complexity (Coburn, 2009, 2014; Galatzer-Levy, 2002) and giving up any search for context-free simplicity. We should expect the languages into and from which we translate, like human life generally, to be "unruly and imprecise" (Taylor, 2011, p. 2). Ricoeur (2006, p. 33; original emphasis) wrote:

> As regards the perfect language . . ., besides the fact that no one has *written it down*, the difference between the supposed artificial language and the natural languages with their idiosyncrasy, their peculiarities, proves to be insurmountable, as there is no fulfillment of the preliminary condition of an exhaustive enumeration of simple ideas and of a unique universal procedure of derivation.

So, the translator, like the clinician, needs to abandon the search for simplicity, and for the perfect translation (or the analyzable patient), and begin to look for the meanings of fidelity and trust. Both the translator's reader and the therapist's patient arrive at our door needing hospitality, needing our faithful care. Without apparently thinking of clinicians, James Taylor (2011, p. 4) wrote of our task: "Without recourse to a third, artificial language, the translator must work, patiently and carefully, from within the resources offered by her own language in her attempt to accommodate the foreign language." Without recourse to our theoretical shop talk, we must work from the resources offered by our personal experience to open our tent to the stranger. Often, as Davoine and Gaudillière (2004) remind us, these resources will come from our traumatic past.

In other words, the work of hospitable clinical translation, or what I am calling clinical hospitality, will normally involve what Ricoeur named "work of remembering" and "work of mourning." The translator/clinician constantly faces her own limitations, created by the incapacity of her language to understand and express what the other wants and needs to say. My first Italian teacher, asked by a student how one might say a certain expression in Italian, responded, "You don't. An Italian would never say that." Then we were faced with a kind of mourning for the loss of our own idiom, and a resistance to accepting the limitations of both languages. I am neither allowed to force my idiom on the other, nor to feel that mine is superior. On the contrary, I must mourn my loss of my beloved at-homeness in my own language, open the flaps of my tent, and invite Italians to explain to me what they might say in such a situation.

Similarly, when I believe I have understood my patient's experience (when I think I have done the work of remembering)—even when it seems to resemble mine—and she reacts to my response with withdrawal or anger, I must mourn my foreignness, and notice my resistance to acceptance of not-knowing, and embrace our shared search. This means, again, opening the tent flaps, so that the other—however unfamiliar and unwashed, by my standards—may begin to teach me. But the seductive hope for the common language is a hard resistance to overcome, even by "linguistic hospitality." In Ricoeur's (2006, p. 9) words,

> the dream of the perfect translation amounts to the wish that translation would gain, gain without losing. It is this very same gain without loss that we must mourn until we reach an acceptance of the impassable difference of the peculiar and the foreign.

Ricoeur made it clear, I think, that not only the patient but also the hospitable clinician must engage in the works of remembrance and mourning. But he also outlined the rewards, in terms we rarely find in the clinical literature:

> [It] is this mourning for the [perfect] translation that produces the happiness associated with translating. The happiness associated with translating is a gain when, tied to the loss of the linguistic absolute, it acknowledges the difference between adequacy and equivalence, equivalence without adequacy. There is its happiness. When the translator acknowledges and assumes the irreducibility of the pair, the peculiar and the foreign, he finds his reward in the recognition of the impassible status of the dialogicality of the act of translating as the reasonable horizon of the desire to translate. In spite of the agonistics that make a drama of the translator's task, he can find his happiness in what I would like to call *linguistic hospitality*.
>
> (Ricoeur, 2006, p. 10; original emphasis)

For me, this statement eloquently states the worth of a moderate conception of the translator's and the clinician's vocation. When we open our tent flaps to the suffering other, without too many preconceptions about what will come in or what will be given or taken, we can take some satisfaction in being used, in surrendering to the otherness of the other. We need not worry about doing it perfectly, understanding perfectly, or any of that.[10] Winnicott would have spoken of good-enough hospitality, and I believe Ricoeur would have understood him.

We began with a Levinasian story of Abraham, who kept his tent open on all sides, though the later rabbis understood that no one could really do this. We went on to Derrida's story of the inevitable complexity of hospitality, in which the tables are so quickly turned, as we clinicians know so well. Finally, we have begun a Ricoeur-inspired reflection on the double challenge, and the double work, of linguistic hospitality. Each of these philosophers deserves much more reflection, but I commend them to your reading, and hope to continue my own.

Meanwhile, we take up the question most frequently addressed to the ethics of radical responsibility: the fear of masochism.

Notes

1 Born in Germany, refugee from Nazi Europe, Hans Loewald (1906–1993) spent most of his professional life in New Haven, Connecticut, where he became, in the eyes of many, the greatest psychoanalytic theorist after Freud as well as a bridge to relational thinking. His understated personal style has kept him less well known than he deserves to be.

2 Winnicott's famous saying included the idea that there is only an infant in the context of maternal care. In the situation of good-enough caregiving provision, the infant emerges as a person in her own right.

3 My favorite definition of unconsciousness.

4 "[T]he word 'atone,' literally and in many contexts, means to become or cause to become at one, to reconcile, to bring to concord or harmony" (Loewald, 2000, p. 390).

5 This conference reconvened in 2013, with almost double the attendance of the original event.

6 In this passage Levinas, as often throughout his work, alludes to the story of Cain in Genesis 4:9 ("am I my brother's keeper?") to emphasize the problems of bystandership and indifference to the plight and fate of the threatened other.

7 In his second great work, *Otherwise than Being, or, Beyond Essence* (1981), Levinas contrasted "saying" (ethical subjectivity, response to, or even substitution for the other) with "the said" (the reduction of the other to generalities, objects of knowledge, categories). Here, unlike the earlier and apparently more radical contrast between murderous totalizing and infinity of responsibility, the saying and the said mutually evoke each other. Still, however, one side of the duality leans toward holiness. Saying still says "*hineni*," "take and eat," "take and drink." Unsurprisingly, world hunger preoccupied Levinas.

8 An earlier version of this section was presented as the keynote speech "Clinical Hospitality: Welcoming the Face of the Devastated Other" to the New Zealand

Association of Psychotherapists, Te Rōpū Whakaora Hinengaro, Wellington, February 2012.
9 At least, he says, the text does not say "bread of dried vegetables," "like the [bread] we ate during the war" (Levinas, 1990b, p. 100)—that is, when he was in captivity.
10 Thomas Ogden's masterful essay on Fairbairn (Ogden, 2010) reminds me of Ricoeur's point.

References

Altman, N. (2010). *The Analyst in the Inner City: Race, Class, and Culture through a Psychoanalytic Lens* (2nd edn.). New York: Routledge.
Aron, L., and Starr, K. (2012). *A Psychotherapy for the People: Toward a Progressive Psychoanalysis*: New York: Routledge.
Balint, M. (1979). *The Basic Fault: Therapeutic Aspects of Regression*. New York: Brunner/Mazel.
Baraitser, L. (2008). Mum's the Word: Intersubjectivity, Alterity, and the Maternal Subject. *Studies in Gender and Sexuality*, 9, 86–110.
Butler, J. (2004). *Precarious Life: The Powers of Mourning and Violence*. London and New York: Verso.
Butler, J. (2011). Precarious Life: The Obligations of Proximity. Lecture given at the Nobel Museum, Sweden. Retrieved from www.youtube.com/watch?v=KJT69AQtDtg, (accessed September 5, 2015).
Celenza, A. (1991). The Misuse of Countertransference Love in Sexual Intimacies between Therapists and Patients. *Psychoanalytic Psychology*, 8, 501–509.
Celenza, A. (1998). Precursors to Therapist Sexual Misconduct. *Psychoanalytic Psychology*, 15, 378–395.
Celenza, A. (2010). The Analyst's Need and Desire. *Psychoanalytic Dialogues*, 20, 60–69.
Chalier, C. (2002). Levinas and the Talmud. In S. Critchley and R. Bernasconi (Eds.), *The Cambridge Companion to Levinas* (pp. 100–118). Cambridge and New York: Cambridge University Press.
Chomsky, N. (1968). *Syntactic Structures*. The Hague: Mouton.
Coburn, W. (2009). Attitudes in Psychoanalytic Complexity. In R. Frie and D. Orange (Eds.), *Beyond Postmodernism: New Dimensions in Clinical Theory and Practice* (pp. 183–200). New York: Routledge.
Coburn, W. J. (2014). *Psychoanalytic Complexity: Clinical Attitudes for Therapeutic Change*. New York: Routledge.
Cohen, R. A. (1986). *Face to Face with Lévinas*. Albany, NY: State University of New York Press.
Corpt, E. (2009). The Importance of Analytic Generosity in the Treatment of Intergenerational Trauma. Paper presented at the Conference on Intergenerational Trauma, Dublin/London.
Corpt, E. (2013). Peasant in the Analyst's Chair: Reflections, Personal and Otherwise, on Class and the Formation of an Analytic Identity. *International Journal of Psychoanalytic Self Psychology*, 8, 52–69.
Critchley, S. (2007). *Infinitely Demanding: Ethics of Commitment, Politics of Resistance*. London and New York: Verso.
Critchley, S., and Bernasconi, R. (Eds.) (2002). *The Cambridge Companion to Levinas*. Cambridge and New York: Cambridge University Press.

Cushman, P. (2007). A Burning World, an Absent God: Midrash, Hermeneutics, and Relational Psychoanalysis.*Contemporary Psychoanalysis*, 43, 47–88.

Davoine, F., and Gaudillière, J.-M. (2004). *History beyond Trauma: Whereof One Cannot Speak, Thereof One Cannot Stay Silent.* New York: Other Press.

Derrida, J. (1999). *Adieu to Emmanuel Levinas.* Stanford, CA: Stanford University Press.

Ferenczi, S. (1949). Ten Letters to Freud. *International Journal of Psychoanalysis*, 30, 243–250.

Fox, M. (2011). Elisabeth Young-Bruehl, who Probed Roots of Ideology and Bias, Dies at 65. *New York Times*, December 5.

Freud, S., and Strachey, J. (2005). *Civilization and Its Discontents.* New York: Norton.

Fryer, D. (2007). What Levinas and Psychoanalysis Can Teach Each Other, or How to Be a Mensch without Going Meshugah. *Psychoanalytic Review*, 94, 577–594.

Gabbard, G. O. (1994). Sexual Excitement and Countertransference Love in the Analyst. *Journal of the American Psychoanalytic Association*, 42, 1083–1106.

Gabbard, G. O. (1997). Case Histories and Confidentiality. *International Journal of Psychoanalysis*, 78, 820–821.

Gabbard, G. O. (2000). Disguise or Consent. *International Journal of Psychoanalysis*, 81, 1071–1086.

Gabbard, G. O. (2002). Boundary Violations and the Abuse of Power. *Studies in Gender and Sexuality*, 3, 379–388.

Gabbard, G. O., and Williams, P. (2001). Preserving Confidentiality in the Writing of Case Reports. *International Journal of Psychoanalysis*, 82, 1067–1068.

Gadamer, H.-G. (1985). Zwischen Phaenomenologie und Dielektik: Versuch einer Selbstkritik. In *Gesammelte Werke* (Vol. 2, pp. 2–23). Tübingen: JCB Mohr.

Galatzer-Levy, R. M. (2002). The Emergent Ego: Complexity and Coevolution in the Psychoanalytic Process. *Psychoanalytic Quarterly*, 71, 350–356.

Hurwitz, M. R. (1986). The Analyst, His Theory, and the Psychoanalytic Process. *Psychoanalytic Study of the Child*, 41, 439–466.

James, W. (1977). *A Pluralistic Universe.* Cambridge, MA: Harvard University Press.

Kohut, H. (1977). *The Restoration of the Self.* New York: International Universities Press.

Kuriloff, E. A. (2014). *Contemporary Psychoanalysis and the Legacy of the Third Reich: History, Memory, Tradition.* New York: Routledge.

Lear, J. (1998). *Love and Its Place in Nature: A Philosophical Interpretation of Freudian Psychoanalysis.* New Haven, CT: Yale University Press.

Levinas, E. (1969). *Totality and Infinity: An Essay on Exteriority.* Pittsburgh, PA: Duquesne University Press.

Levinas, E. (1981). *Otherwise than Being, or, Beyond Essence.* The Hague and Boston Hingham, MA: M. Nijhoff and Kluwer Boston.

Levinas, E. (1990a). *Difficult Freedom: Essays on Judaism.* Baltimore, MD: Johns Hopkins University Press.

Levinas, E. (1990b). *Nine Talmudic Readings.* Bloomington, IN: Indiana University Press.

Levinas, E. (1999). *Alterity and Transcendence.* New York: Columbia University Press.

Levinas, E., and Nemo, P. (1985). *Ethics and Infinity.* Pittsburgh, PA: Duquesne University Press.

Levinas, E., Peperzak, A. T., Critchley, S., and Bernasconi, R. (1996). *Emmanuel Levinas: Basic Philosophical Writings*. Bloomington, IN: Indiana University Press.

Loewald, H. W. (1960). On the Therapeutic Action of Psycho-Analysis. *International Journal of Psychoanalysis*, 41, 16–33.

Loewald, H. W. (1980). *Papers on Psychoanalysis*. New Haven, CT: Yale University Press.

Loewald, H. W. (1985). Oedipus Complex and Development of Self. *Psychoanalytic Quarterly*, 54, 435–443.

Loewald, H. W. (1988). Termination Analyzable and Unanalyzable. *Psychoanalytic Study of the Child*, 43, 155–166.

Loewald, H. W. (2000). *The Essential Loewald: Collected Papers and Monographs*. Hagerstown, MD: University Publishing Group.

Loewald, H. W. (2007). Internalization, Separation, Mourning, and the Superego. *Psychoanlytic Quarterly*, 76, 1113–1133.

Mitchell, S. A. (2000). *Relationality: From Attachment to Intersubjectivity*. Hillsdale, NJ: The Analytic Press.

Ogden, T. (2010). Why read Fairbairn? *International Journal of Psychoanalysis*, 91, 101–118.

Orange, D. M. (1995). *Emotional Understanding: Studies in Psychoanalytic Epistemology*. New York: Guilford Press.

Orange, D. M. (2006). For Whom the Bell Tolls: Context, Complexity, and Compassion in Psychoanalysis. *International Journal of Psychoanalytic Self Psychology*, 1, 5–21.

Pilecki, W. (2012). *The Auschwitz Volunteer: Beyond Bravery*. Los Angeles, CA: Aquila Polonica.

Poland, W. S. (1975). Tact as a Psychoanalytic Function. *International Journal of Psychoanalysis*, 56, 155–162.

Ricoeur, P. (2006). *On Translation*. London and New York: Routledge.

Shengold, L. (1989). *Soul Murder: The Effects of Childhood Abuse and Deprivation*. New Haven, CT: Yale University Press.

Stern, D. N. (1985). *The Interpersonal World of the Infant: A View from Psychoanalysis and Developmental Psychology*. New York: Basic Books.

Stern, S. (2009). My Experience of Analysis with Loewald. *Psychoanalytic Quarterly*, 78, 1013–1031.

Stolorow, R. D., Atwood, G. E., and Brandchaft, B. (1987). *Psychoanalytic Treatment: An Intersubjective Approach*. Hillsdale, NJ: The Analytic Press.

Suttie, I. D. (1935). *The Origins of Love and Hate*. London: K. Paul, Trench, Trubner.

Taylor, J. (2011). Translating Hospitality: Paul Ricoeur's Ethics of Translation. *The New Arcadia Review*, 4. Retrieved from omc.bc.edu/newarcadiacontent/translating Hospitality_edited.html (accessed September 5, 2015).

Winnicott, D. W. (1960). The Theory of the Parent–Infant Relationship. *International Journal of Psychoanalysis*, 41, 585–595.

Winnicott, D. W. (1965). *The Maturational Processes and the Facilitating Environment: Studies in the Theory of Emotional Development*. New York: International Universities Press.

Winnicott, D. W., and the Institute of Psycho-Analysis (Great Britain) (1975). *Through Paediatrics to Psycho-Analysis*. London: Hogarth Press and the Institute of Psycho-Analysis.

Chapter 3

Is ethics masochism?

Infinite ethical responsibility and finite human capacity[1]

> To respect cannot mean to subject oneself [s'assujettir], and yet the other commands me. I am commanded, that is recognized as capable of a work. To respect is not to bow down before the law, but before a being who commands a work from me. But for this commandment to entail no humiliation—which would deprive me of the very possibility of respecting—the commandment I receive must also be the commandment to command the one who commands me. It consists in commanding a being to command me.
>
> (Levinas, 1998, p. 35)

> [T]he pain and suffering of the masochist (and less obviously the sadist, at least in some instances) may well be the excuse the caretaker self has devised to get the true self to where it has a chance of being found, a signal that something deep inside is rent, a tear in the self, that unbeknown to its bearer, seeks healing, and that the masochistic patterns, especially if a certain satisfaction and pleasure accrues, are really expressions of the patient's efforts at self-cure.
>
> (Ghent, 1990, p. 132)

When I speak of Levinasian ethics to clinical colleagues, without fail the apprehensive questions emerge. Isn't this radical responsibility, this deference to the other, disguised masochism? What about the patient, or the clinician, already exploited as a parentified child, who needs to learn to feel *less* responsible? Isn't ethics, of the type you describe, a form of what Bernard Brandchaft has named "pathological accommodation," or what Winnicott called the "false self"? Have we here narcissism hidden behind a mirage of religion? We need only consult our daily news to see where *that* can lead its hubristic self-deluders.

My colleagues who raise these questions do not wish to evade the ethical call; they want to understand how it works, and to be sure it will destroy neither the humanity they feel called to heal, nor their own. True, these concerns arise less frequently when someone has read my *Suffering Stranger*

(Orange, 2011) all the way through. Still, putting on my philosophical hat, it seems past time to make some distinctions, to help clarify ethics, masochism, accommodation, and subjectivity. I believe we do need to have plenty of worries, but not exactly those listed above.

First, let us look at the ethical demand to live for the other, voiced by various ethical thinkers, by religious traditions, and in literary examples, and radically expressed in the work of the twentieth-century phenomenologist and prophet Emmanuel Levinas. Then let us consider the concept of masochism, primarily as it has been understood in Freudian and relational psychoanalysis, to see where it does and/or does not intersect with forms of ethics inspiring the writers brought together here. Third, let us introduce the work of Brandchaft and recall that of Winnicott, on pathological accommodation and false-self compliance, respectively, to see whether, even if ethics may not be masochistic, living other-wise may still be psychologically dangerous. Along the way, I will introduce careful distinctions, including those made by Emmanuel Ghent, to suggest that it is more than possible to live for-the-other without losing any kind of subjectivity worth having.

Living for-the-other

What threatening message so worries my readers? Emmanuel Levinas returned from five years in Nazi labor camps to find that his entire Lithuanian family was dead, and to learn, as did many others, the scope of the massacre. His philosophy, for his remaining 50 years, challenged us to respond responsibly to the face of the suffering other, not to evade. Solidarity with the other costs me suffering, but so be it. *Me voici, hineni.*[2] That many others require my care, that responsibilities are infinite while I am finite, means that social justice, what he called the third party, must come in. But my passive vulnerability to the other—my useful suffering (Levinas, 1998)—required to respond to the useless suffering of the vulnerable and devastated other, produces experiences of persecution that never end. In the words Levinas never tired of quoting (in various forms) from Dostoevsky's *Brothers Karamazov*, "We are all responsible for everything and guilty in front of everyone, but I am that more than all others." My life is not about me; it is about the other. My always-already responsibility never ends. I never sought this responsibility.

A word of context: as *New York Times* columnist David Brooks (2013) recently noted, egoism and individualism have taken deep root in our everyday talk as well as in our intellectual and political discourse over the past century. He finds the language of community, of the common good, and of solidarity simply disappearing. No wonder, then, that therapeutic work—to appeal to our contemporaries—must be framed in the jargon of self-fulfillment, authenticity, and agency, and that unsurprisingly we may find our thinking upended by someone who proclaims that responding to the other comes first, that human solidarity precedes my own benefit.

Levinasian ethics can be presented in two voices: first, the voice of persecution, substitution, being taken hostage, infinite guilt and responsibility, insistent demandingness. This voice thunders like a biblical prophet: "Thus saith the Lord." (This one truly scares clinicians, I think.) The other voice sounds warm, inviting, hospitable, slow to classify or to judge: "How can I help you?" Let me tell you first about this second Levinas. He was a phenomenologist, a student of both Husserl and Heidegger. But his phenomenology inverts the intentionality of Husserl—that is, the directionality goes not from the knower to the known, but from the other to me. Before any agreements are entered into, the concrete need or suffering of the widow, the orphan, and the stranger requires from me a hospitable response. Responding creates my ethical subjectivity in what Levinas called a "curvature of intersubjective space" (Levinas, 1969, p. 291). The other goes first.

Where did Levinas get these strange ideas? Let us back up a little. He was born in Kovno (Kaunas), Lithuania, in 1906,[3] but in 1914 threats to the Jewish community meant his family moved to Ukraine, where he attended an excellent secondary school. By his own account, he spoke Russian at home all his life, and his first major influences came from Russian literature—Pushkin, Lermontov, and, above all, Dostoevsky—which he credited with leading him into philosophy. (These, I note, were all strongly ethical influences—see Chapter 7.) Back in Lithuania by the age of 14, re-immersed in the very intellectual Judaism he often described, he left for university in Strasbourg in 1923. There he encountered phenomenology, and wrote as his dissertation a book introducing Husserl to such giants as Sartre and Merleau-Ponty. I relate all this to emphasize the three sources of Levinasian thought, which I do not wish to prioritize, as others might do:

1   Russian literature (especially the Dostoevskian notion of responsibility);
2   Torah and Talmud; and
3   Western philosophy, beginning with Plato.

But then, as Primo Levi (1989, 1996) also told us, a radical and massive assault on human dignity occurred.

For our purposes, and for those of Levinas, the crucial point is that phenomenology, and its relationship to psychoanalysis, has been turned upside down. Phenomenology's central idea—intentionality—meant the orientation of mind toward things or states of affairs. To think is to think something, to want is to want something, to feel is to feel something. It all starts from me. Until Levinas. In a drastic reversal, it is no longer about me. It is no longer about *my* death, or *my* losses, or *my* trauma, or *my* anxiety, or *my* finitude. Let us listen a little to this radical discourse, first in its gentler form.

In an interview with the philosopher Francois Poirier, Levinas begins as if this reversal is quite an everyday matter:

> Is not the first word *bonjour?* As simple as *bonjour. Bonjour* as benediction and my being available for the other man. It doesn't mean: what a beautiful day. Rather: I wish you peace, I wish you a good day, expression of one who worries for the other. It underlies all the rest of communication, underlies all discourse.
>
> (Levinas and Robbins, 2001, p. 47)

For-the-other. It's not about me, or about *my* place in the sun. This simple greeting of welcome, and well-wishing in the elevator or on the street, changes phenomenology from a search for essences and definitions and totalities to a response to the other. But let us hear more. Poirier follows up by asking if Levinas has completed his life project. Well, responds Levinas, I never thought of having a well-written biography. (In other words, it wasn't about me.) Instead, he muses,

> the true, the incontestable value, about which it is not ridiculous to think, is holiness. This is not a matter of privations, but it is in the certitude that one must yield to the other the first place in everything, from the *après vous* before an open door right up to the disposition—hardly possible but holiness demands it—to die for the other. In this attitude of holiness, there is reversal of the normal order of things, the natural order of things, the persisting in being of the ontology of things and of the living.
>
> (Levinas and Robbins, 2001, p. 47)

So, phenomenology's famous intentionality—its directedness—always striving, now becomes radically passive and vulnerable to the other. According to a famous rabbinic saying, "the neighbor's material needs are my spiritual needs"—non-indifferent, a complete reversal of the scientific attitude of Husserl's beloved mathematics. Heidegger made the first reversal, and showed that we are born situated and never able to abstract ourselves from the world and our assumptions in the way that Husserl had hoped. But he could not, preoccupied as he was with his "ownmost" (*eigenste*) *Eigentlichkeit*, take the next step. (A great irony, in my view, lies in the very German word that is routinely translated into English as "authenticity." *Eigen* means "own," and both suffixes substantialize it, as if to say, ownness-ness. It is really untranslatable, but it is such a cornerstone of Heidegger's philosophy that it is difficult to capture the Levinasian reversal without feeling the impact of the word *Eigentlichkeit*.)

Though Levinas spoke of holiness, he agreed completely with Nietzsche about "the death of a certain god." Theodicies, arguments that defend a provident god[4] after gulags and holocaust, he found absurd and obscene. But simple holiness, and the unexpected goodness found among ordinary people, these were traces, and he would not stop speaking about them. In his later years he loved the work of the Russian journalist and novelist Vassily Grossman, and he told this story from Grossman's *Life and Fate:*

> [W]hen Stalingrad has already been rescued, the German prisoners, including an officer, are cleaning out a basement and removing the decomposing bodies. The officer suffers particularly from this misery. In the crowd, a woman who hates Germans is delighted to see this man more miserable than the others. Then she gives him the last piece of bread she has. This is extraordinary. Even in hatred there exists a mercy stronger than hatred. I give to this act a religious significance. This is my way of saying that the mercy of God occurs through the particular man—not all because he is organized in a certain way or because he belongs to a society or an institution. There are acts of stupid, senseless goodness.
>
> (Levinas and Robbins, 2001, p. 89)

Levinas considered this to be faithful phenomenological description, and ethics.

In my view, as will become clearer below, this capacity for goodness is the same vulnerability that he calls "ethical subjectivity," which makes us hostage, traumatized by the other's suffering, infinitely responsible. Constituted by its response to the other, this humble subjectivity no longer seeks to grab the microphone or to insist on its own importance. It serves the other unobtrusively. Let us read closely:

> "the one" is for the other of a being who lets go of itself [*se déprend*] without turning into a contemporary of "the other," without taking place next to him in a synthesis exposing itself as a theme; the one-for-the-other. Between the one that I am and the other for whom I answer gapes a bottomless difference, which is also the non-indifference of responsibility, significance of signification, irreducible to any system whatsoever. Non-indifference, which is the proximity of one's fellow, by which is profiled a base of community between one and the other.
>
> (Levinas and Poller, 2003, p. 6)

In other words, you and I are two, in community. We are different, but I can never be indifferent to you. I am my brother's keeper.

Next, let us consider the problem of masochism, usually understood as seeking and enjoying pain.

Masochism: seeking pain

Laplanche and Pontalis (1973) remind us that Richard Krafft-Ebing, an older contemporary of Freud, first described masochism as a sexual perversion in men—an attitude and practice of servility toward dominant women. They provide a more general definition: "Sexual perversion in which satisfaction is tied to the suffering or humiliation undergone by the subject" (1973, p. 245). By 1924, in "The Economic Problem of Masochism", Freud had extended, in his usual style, his understanding of psychological masochism far beyond literal sexuality to encompass what he called "moral masochism." He wrote:

> All other masochistic sufferings carry with them the condition that they shall emanate from the loved person and shall be endured at his command. This restriction has been dropped in moral masochism. The suffering itself is what matters; whether it is decreed by someone who is loved or by someone who is indifferent is of no importance. It may even be caused by impersonal powers or by circumstances; the true masochist always turns his cheek whenever he has a chance of receiving a blow.
>
> (Freud, 1924a, p. 165)

Freud's reference here to religious people ("turns the cheek"), particularly Christians, makes it clear what a wide net he was casting in describing moral masochism and its motivations.[5] The willingness to receive suffering for the sake of the other he now linked to an unconscious desire to suffer:

> It is very tempting, in explaining this attitude, to leave the libido out of account and to confine oneself to assuming that in this case the destructive instinct has been turned inwards again and is now raging against the self; yet there must be some meaning in the fact that linguistic usage has not given up the connection between this norm of behaviour and erotism and calls these self-injurers masochists too.
>
> (Freud, 1924a, p. 164)

In other words, the Freudian moral masochist, referred to by implication in this chapter's title and in the questions so often put to me, unconsciously *enjoys* the suffering taken on from what Freud explained in his essay as guilt resulting from some indefinite crime, never identified and never adequately expiated. The masochist *unconsciously seeks to suffer and owns the suffering as deserved.* Freud continued:

> The fact that moral masochism is unconscious leads us to an obvious clue. We were able to translate the expression "unconscious sense of guilt" as meaning a need for punishment at the hands of a parental

power. We now know that the wish, which so frequently appears in phantasies, to be beaten by the father stands very close to the other wish, to have a passive (feminine) sexual relation to him and is only a regressive distortion of it. If we insert this explanation into the content of moral masochism, its hidden meaning becomes clear to us. Conscience and morality have arisen through the overcoming, the desexualization, of the Oedipus complex; but through moral masochism morality becomes sexualized once more, the Oedipus complex is revived and the way is opened for a regression from morality to the Oedipus complex.

(Freud, 1924a, p. 169)

So, the puzzle is resolved: the conscious goodness of the moral masochist masks a sadistic superego punishing the psychic apparatus for our universal Oedipal crimes. In Freud's view, the Kantian requirement to treat others so that the maxim of our actions would be universalizable—as members of a human community—is heir to the Oedipus complex. It imposes a harsh requirement to seek punishment for crimes of parricide we must all commit (Loewald, 1979) in order to become ourselves and internalize our parents. We—patients and therapists alike—want to suffer and we enjoy it because we know we deserve to suffer.

It is precisely this moral masochism, in patients and therapists alike, that concerns those who question me about Levinasian ethics. Are we simply, in our welcoming response to the other—especially when it stretches us, as working in the service of the other often must—living out unanalyzed moral masochism? Should we be setting better limits, for our own sakes and—as many theorists would argue—for that of the patient as well? Better limits according to whom, though? How do we decide which phone call not to take, which extra session to refuse, which patient to send elsewhere? How do we decide what is service to the other, and what is masochism? These questions remain, no matter how we resolve the masochism question, but I believe them to be questions of practical wisdom. They require clinical experience, the internal chorus, and the community of clinicians.

Meanwhile, some have understood masochism otherwise. Bernhard Berliner (1958, pp. 39, 44; original emphasis), described it in the 1950s most thoroughly and passionately as a relational matter:

the other person does not enter into the picture only after the passive aim is established. The other person is a reality from the very beginning and is instrumental in bringing about the whole masochistic process ... Masochism I do not consider an instinctual phenomenon like sadism or aggression. Masochism is a defensive reaction, motivated by libidinal needs, to the sadism of *another person* ... The experience of hate and ill-treatment is repressed. The child, in its imperative need for love, accepts this hate and ill-treatment as if they were love and is not conscious of the difference. Suffering thus libidinized is introjected.

So, masochism results from internalized mistreatment, much like Ferenczi's (1949) identification with the aggressor. It only superficially resembles the seeking of pain. Instead, it reenacts the childhood situation, where the masochist acts both roles of perpetrator and victim, just as Primo Levi (1989) described among the more privileged "guests," as he ironically called them, of Auschwitz, who inhabited a gray zone. Berliner (1958, p. 53; original emphasis) continued:

> The masochistic patient appears in a double light: he is the *victim* of a traumatic childhood, and he is a *troublemaker* who entangles himself in actual conflicts by which he continuously makes himself the victim again. He is sinned against and sinning, to paraphrase Shakespeare. We [should] give the analysis of the victim priority over the analysis of the troublemaker.

So, we see that already among Freudian psychoanalysts there existed the possibility for genuine empathy with the plight of the patient who seemed forever doomed to a life of suffering; even when, to the observer, life seemed to offer exits from purgatory. They could mention identification with the aggressor—the patient's absorbing of the point of view of the perpetrator— even if they could not dare to mention Ferenczi, just as they could speak of object relations without mentioning Fairbairn or Winnicott.

Not only our patients but also we clinicians who attempt an ethical hospitality—always only an attempt, of course—live this double life. Does this mean we seek pain? If our own history as the "wise babies" Ferenczi (1949) described brings us to clinical work, are we moral masochists? Meanwhile, we have a few more thinkers to help us along.

Next came Harry Stack Sullivan, who called the idea of masochism "foggy thinking" (Sullivan and Perry, 1953, p. 352). But of course, as Ruth Imber (1995) notes, he could not avoid the clinical phenomena that the word so badly connotes. Sullivan described what he called a "malevolent transformation," comprehended at least as empathically as Berliner understood "moral masochism" in the same years. In Imber's paraphrase:

> there were people who had learned, as children, the futility or even danger of seeking love or tenderness from their uncaring and rejecting caretakers. Rather than continue to suffer the hurt and disappointment of trying to get what was not available, such a child would instead learn to change his or her *behavior* from tenderness-seeking to angry rejection or mischievousness. While the need for tenderness went unmet, the malevolent transformation *did* protect against the pain and anxiety of

being rejected or punished for seeking what was not to be had. And if the "malevolence" was met with punishment, that at least was under one's control. The child could thus salvage some sense of security by acting as if to say "If I am the architect of my own misery, I need not fear being at someone else's mercy."

(Imber, 1995, pp. 581–582; original emphasis)

This interpersonalist interpretation points to the effort, in some instances, of seizing one's human dignity, if only by causing one's own pain. Such suffering is sought, not for its own sake, but for its crucial "No!" to the domination by the other.

But soon came Heinrich Racker, unafraid to mention the early subversives Fairbairn and Winnicott, and much concerned about the masochism of the analyst, our particular concern. He believed that "psychoanalytic cure consists in establishing a unity within the psychic structure of the patient. Most of what is ego alien must be relinquished or reintegrated in the ego" (1958, p. 555). He was working here not with ego as substructure (id, ego, superego) but with what Freud called the *Gesamt-Ich* (whole I), or the personality as a whole. Insofar as the analyst was holding parts of the patient, by projection or through various forms of unconscious counter-transference, the cure would be held back. (It would take me too far afield to outline Racker's full and rich account of the countertransferences, perhaps the best we have so far.)

Racker assumed masochism—understood as developmental residue—in every analyst/therapist, but also that each of us has a particular "counter-transference characteropathy," or character pathology, with which we need to be deeply familiar. He warned:

It should be stressed, first of all, that the analyst's masochism aims at making him fail in his task. We should, therefore, never be too sure that we are really seeking success and must be prepared to recognize the existence of an "inner saboteur" (as Fairbairn says) of our professional work. We must likewise reckon with an unseen collaboration between the masochism of the analyst and that of the patient.

(Racker, 1958, p. 558)

Racker used, we see, a concept of masochism that differs from Freud's suffering seeker and also from Berliner's "inner victim." Here we have Fairbairn's "inner saboteur"—the bad internal object making trouble for both therapist and patient, and obstructing our work. In the Fairbairnian world, no longer punished for Oedipal crimes, we remain forever unlovable because we could not get our mothers to love us. We need not seek pain, but we must work for ever to become lovable. The internal saboteur will never let us rest. Racker (1958, p. 559) continued, it predisposes the analyst to feel persecuted by the patient and to see mainly the patient's negative transference and his aggression. Masochism and paranoid anxiety act like smoked glasses, hindering our perception of the patient's love and what is good in him, which in turn increases the negative transference. Our understanding becomes a partial one; while we clearly perceive the present negative transference, we easily become blind to the latent and potential positive transference.

Though I have written much in Racker's spirit of the hermeneutics of trust (Orange, 2011), the precise opposite partial understanding—missing the negative and aggressive transference—can also blind and mislead, with painful results. In either instance, reading our own responses well keeps us from temptations to pre-emptive suspicion and blaming.

Despite reinterpretations, *the word "masochism" itself blames*. Perhaps it would be more accurate to say, given our survey, in classical as well as more relational accounts of masochism, that the word *tends* to blame. Classically, it implied that the masochist, whether patient or analyst, sought and enjoyed suffering. In relational accounts, masochistic relating requires engagement with relational trauma. Perhaps also to be noted, a greater—and generally extremely helpful—attention to shame in recent years (Lansky, 1994; Morrison, 1999; Wurmser, 1991) has shifted our focus away from a pejorative emphasis on masochism. Vulnerability understood as intersubjectively constituted by patterns of humiliation and violent subjugation (Orange, 2008) brings a different focus, in which what seems a desire to suffer may now seem an automatic assumption of a familiar role. Judith Lewis Herman (2011) recently wrote of post-traumatic stress as a shame disorder. Instead of a disparaging, "This patient wants to suffer," we now think, "How does one escape this miserable prison?" No matter the understanding, we do not idealize this suffering. It is, like all suffering in the other, as Levinas (1998) would have clearly said, useless suffering. It becomes useful suffering only when it is accepted for the other's sake.

But what of the person who takes on suffering for the sake of the other, the Levinasian "useful suffering"? This is the trickier question. Now we seem to be in the territory of the ethical, the territory where each of us lives every day in our therapeutic work. Is this moral masochism, the unconscious self-punishment that Freud described? If we take on the suffering of the other too much, we quickly burn out or get into boundary violations. If we avoid and evade the other's suffering, we abandon the other to die alone and reduce our profession to a technology. To complicate matters further, many of our patients come to us as compulsive caregivers (altruists on autopilot) who cannot say no even when they are being grossly, let alone subtly, abused.

Here the "Is ethics masochism?" question becomes practical. Most reasonably wise therapists of all persuasions would respond that they want to help these patients to discover, and to model for them, a life that is reasonably generous but does not consist in being a doormat. How can we conceptualize the difference between Winnicottian false-self compliance—surely an abject and wretched stand-in—and the response to the devastated other (or "holiness") that Levinas described and theorized?

Compliance, accommodation, and ethical subjectivity

Beneath concerns about moral masochism, perhaps, lie related worries, fears that our ethical vulnerability, emotional availability (Orange, 1995), or compassion (Orange, 2006)—our tent flaps as open as we are able to keep them—may involve us in massive false-self compliance. Worse, we may model such a false self for our patients, or fail to help them grow beyond it.

Winnicott described the false self in his early writings—later he wrote more simply of compliance—as the infant's effort to survive impingements. Even in a good-enough early environment, he believed, we develop at least a minimal false self of social compliance. Depending on the extent of impingements—his examples ranged from displacements due to war, family separation, and bombing to all kinds of parental pathologies—the need for development of a protective false self could be more or less extreme, even amounting to experiential eclipse of true selfhood altogether. His compassionate understanding that many symptoms, from lying and stealing to many forms of psychosis, resulted from very early deprivation and impingement allowed forms of therapeutic engagement that sought and welcomed the creativity and spontaneity within the patient into the transitional space of the treatment room. But many worried that it was his overwork, rather than his smoking, that gave him so many heart attacks—more moral masochism. (Personally, I have my doubts about this. All his life he remained playful and involved in cultural pursuits and friendships.) It is no accident, however, that psychoanalytic readers of Levinas often think of Winnicott (Alford, 2007) and Ferenczi, both for their open-hearted practice and for their foreshortened lives.

Similarly and even more clearly, Bernard Brandchaft (Brandchaft et al., 2010) has written of a form of what Leonard Shengold (1989) calls "soul murder." He described patients, unfortunately very common among us clinicians too, for whom a radical choice was early and long required. They had to decide between surrender to dominating caregivers and development of one's own soul, self, or path. The victim accommodates by passivity, rebellion, or some mad combination of the two to form almost all the pathologies we find in the manuals.

"Pathological accommodation" sounds less extreme than soul murder, but instead forms a desperate attempt to survive such destruction. It sounds as if the patient is the perpetrator of the crime, but this is not Brandchaft's meaning. While he intended to describe an intersubjective wrong that the patient continues endlessly to memorialize, only a child born to (often unconsciously) exploitative parents suffers from this torture. The patient feels that the price of any significant attachment must be the sacrifice of her own soul, of her own path, of her own desire. Unconscious until it meets the analyst/therapist who can feel its terrible grip, this conviction keeps the patient in a depressive pit, a furious defiance, an obsessive terror, or a chaotic combination of all of three. Dante could not have imagined a hell worse than pathological accommodation.

In the face of such hell, I began to think and write some years ago—even before reading much of Levinas—about the absence of compassion discourse in psychoanalytic literature, musing:

> psychoanalytic compassion is not reducible to moral masochism on the part of the analyst, nor is it to be contrasted with properly psychoanalytic work, usually seen as explicitly interpretive. It is, instead, an implicitly interpretive process of giving lived meaning and dignity to a shattered person's life by enabling integration of the pain and loss as opposed to dissociation or fragmentation. A compassionate attitude says to every patient: your suffering is human suffering, and when the bell tolls for you, it also tolls for me.
>
> (Orange, 2006, p. 16)

Over time, I believe, each clinician finds a way of working that ranks service to the other (Poland, 2000) first, but allows ongoing life, including health, family, and those pursuits that make living precious. But each of us can lose our balance. If therapeutic work in the spirit of service to the patient becomes felt as submission, not as response engendering my subjectivity—and it has sometimes felt so to me—it is time for consultation. Perhaps the therapist has idealized the patient, mistaking traumatic suffering for uncomplicated goodness. This patient may explode at the mere suggestion that she or he is less than perfectly benevolent. Something—perhaps an absolutely needed rage in the transference–countertransference system—is occurring in the space between to evoke the therapist's (possibly traumatic) history of annihilation. When the therapist has regained calmness, and the capacity for hospitality in the Levinasian sense, survival in Winnicott's words, or surrender in Ghent's terms, words like "masochism" no longer seem fitting. Human dignity may be sought, modeled, and brought into conversation. Or at least, if relevant to the therapist's and patient's experience, masochism will not be confused with ethical surrender and response, to which we now turn.

Ethical subjectivity and clinical humility

To conclude, let us revisit a now classic distinction by Emmanuel Ghent— between masochism and surrender—as well as the contrast drawn by Levinas between useless and useful suffering.

Levinas wrote:

> Without introducing any deliberate seeking of suffering or humiliation (turning the other cheek) it [the prophetic text] suggests, in the primary suffering, in suffering as suffering, a hard unbearable consent that animates passivity, strangely animates it in spite of itself, whereas passivity as such has neither force nor intention, neither like it or not. The impotence or humility of "to suffer" is beneath the passivity of submission. Here the word *sincerity* takes all its sense: to discover oneself totally defenseless, to be surrendered. Intellectual sincerity, veracity, already refers to vulnerability, is founded in it.
>
> (Levinas and Poller, 2003, pp. 63–64)

This text contains two of the three words compared by Ghent, and it refers to all three: masochism, submission, and surrender (Ghent, 1990). Over the years I have often simply replied to colleagues worried about whether Levinasian ethics concealed masochism: "Please read Manny Ghent." He described masochism as a kind of false-self organization that longs for surrender to release the creative true self that Winnicott described. Such masochism, "which may be rooted in a deep quest for understanding, for undoing . . . isolation" (Ghent, 1990, p. 127), should never be confused with real surrender, nor with the submissive compliance that is the behavioral expression of common masochism. Levinas, in the text quoted above, says the same thing. Suffering without ego, without intention, with sincerity, does not seek pain; it simply suffers it for the sake of the other. To surrender is not to seek pain or punishment.

Ghent (1990, p. 133) warned that analysts too may seek surrender but fall into masochism:

> Let us not overlook the role of masochism and surrender in being a member of our profession. What other occupation requires of its practitioners that they be the objects of people's excoriations, threats and rejections, or be subjected to tantalizing offerings that plead "touch me," yet may not be touched? What other occupation has built into it the frustration of feeling helpless, stupid and lost as a necessary part of the work? And what other occupation puts its practitioners in the position of being an onlooker or midwife to the fulfillment of others' destinies? It is difficult to find a type of existence, other than that of the psychoanalyst, who fits this job description. In a sense it is the portrait of a masochist. Yet I suspect that a deep underlying motive, in some analysts at least, is again that of surrender, and their own personal growth. It may be acceptably couched in masochistic garb or denied by narcissistic and/or sadistic exploitation. When the yearning for surrender is, or begins to be, realized by the

analyst, the work is immensely fulfilling and the analyst grows with his patients.

It seems to me that rereading this article carefully can help us to sort out the residues of our history, which haunt our clinical lives, from the ethical spirit in which we attempt to respond to the other.

Mostly, I try to live my clinical life between two values, for my patients and for myself: basic human kindness, and restoration of dignity. (Neither of these words, by the way, appears much in the psychoanalytic literature, nor in the work of philosophers.) Though kindness and hospitality are never simple, often they require immediate response, with reflection and theorizing later. Restoration of dignity, I think, begins precisely in this response to the naked and devastated face of the other, even though, as Jean Améry (1986, p. 40) reminded us:

> Whoever has succumbed to torture can no longer feel at home in the world. The shame of destruction cannot be erased. Trust in the world, which already collapsed in part at the first blow, but in the end, under torture, fully, will not be regained. That one's fellow man was experienced as the antiman remains in the tortured person as accumulated horror.

When these values fail me, and I find myself faced by more trouble than my personal limitations can bear, I need the help of a third value, clinical humility (to which the final chapter of this volume is devoted). Ghent alluded to this situation: "'touch me,' yet may not be touched." Just as I have always tried to hold theory lightly, every so often comes a time to surrender to the vulnerability and passivity of my clinical limitations, and to admit that this is beyond me.

Unfortunately, young clinicians often develop the impression that they should be able to work with every patient who comes to them. Goodness of fit and the sense that each of us has strengths and weaknesses to be welcomed rarely feature in their training. Rarely do they learn how to estimate whether this patient fits the therapist's range of capacities, or how to understand when this therapy has reached its limits. Instead, young therapists are assessed for their ability to keep patients in treatment. Combining this training bias with an ethical desire to serve the other can create a trap for otherwise superb therapists. Remembering, however, that we work in service to the other in the context of a larger community can keep us more modest, and help us to surrender our hubris. Though my immediate *hineni* of ethical response and emotional availability may be crucial, I am not the only person who can help, and I must humbly realize that I work within a beloved community (Martin Luther King's term). Humility means, among other things, giving up the solipsistic ego.

What has all this to do with the question of ethics and masochism with which we began? Without humility, compulsive service to the other will indeed resemble superficially the classical story of the desire to suffer, or false-self compliance with patients whose needs come to rule our lives. With clinical humility, working within community (the third party, Levinas would have said), we will have a better—though never perfect—sense of whether we are still responding to the other, or whether it is time to turn to the resources of community.

A word of transition for readers

The next four chapters will consider some communitarian resources that I have internalized. I do not intend or imagine that the voices in my internal chorus will be yours, but rather hope to give some sense of how a clinician or other humanitarian worker may nourish and be nourished by whomever most inspires them. I will begin by providing some "life and work" background on each of my choristers (aside from in Chapter 6, for reasons explained there), followed by an explanation of why this person is so important as support for an ethical life of one kind or another. Ethics, as you may have surmised already, forms the thread woven throughout this book, but not everyone means exactly the same thing when using this word. My own chorus sings polyphony. Still, ethics requires courage, and courage needs support.

Notes

1 Earlier versions of this chapter formed a keynote address at the 2013 Psychology and the Other conference in Cambridge, MA, and a further version appears as a chapter in *The Ethical Turn: Otherness and Subjectivity in Contemporary Psychoanalysis* (Goodman and Severson, forthcoming).
2 Levinas used "*hineni*" repeatedly to express his sense of ethical subjectivity without ego or agency. My thanks to Karen Starr for explaining that this Hebrew word contains nothing of "I" or "me." It simply expresses full willingness to respond to the call. It appears several times in Genesis.
3 Interested readers can find more easily accessible "life and work" information on Levinas in my two most recent books (Orange, 2010, 2011). For more depth, consult Critchley and Bernasconi (2002) as well as the primary sources (Levinas, 1969, 1981).
4 Western religions, in their theologies and piety, tend to employ upper case when referring to their (masculine) deity. In this book I use religious discourse for ethical purposes, but I am not writing from within any specific religion, so I generally refrain from this honorific, and I apply scare quotes to the masculine pronoun where necessary (see Chapter 8, note 4).
5 The German expression for "to turn the other cheek" is "*die andere Wange hinhalten*," and it seems always to be used in this way. Freud (1924b, p. 378) says, "*der richtige Masochist hält immer seine Wange hin, wo er Aussicht hat, einen Schlag zu bekommen*" (literally, "the real masochist holds his cheek always ready

to receive a blow"). So we cannot be sure he was referring to the Christian idea, but it seems likely.

References

Alford, C. (2007). Levinas, Winnicott, and Therapy. *Psychoanalytic Review*, 94, 529–551.

Améry, J. (1986). *At the Mind's Limits: Contemplations by a Survivor on Auschwitz and Its Realities*. New York: Schocken.

Berliner, B. (1958). The Role of Object Relations in Moral Masochism. *Psychoanalytic Quarterly*, 27, 38–56.

Brandchaft, B., Doctors, S., and Sorter, D. (2010). *Toward an Emancipatory Psychoanalysis: Brandchaft's Intersubjective Vision*. New York: Routledge.

Brooks, D. (2013). What Our Words Tell Us. *New York Times*, May 13.

Critchley, S., and Bernasconi, R. (Eds.) (2002). *The Cambridge Companion to Levinas*. Cambridge and New York: Cambridge University Press.

Ferenczi, S. (1949). Confusion of the Tongues between the Adults and the Child (the Language of Tenderness and of Passion). *International Journal of Psychoanalysis*, 30, 225–230.

Freud, S. (1924a). The Economic Problem of Masochism. In *The Standard Edition of the Complete Psychological Works of Sigmund Freud* (Vol. 19 (1923–1925), pp. 155–170). London: Hogarth.

Freud, S. (1924b). Das ökonomische Problem des Masochismus. In *Gesammelte Werke* (Vol. 13, pp. 371–383). Frankfurt am Main: Fischer.

Ghent, E. (1990). Masochism, Submission, Surrender: Masochism as a Perversion of Surrender. *Contemporary Psychoanalysis*, 26, 108–136.

Goodman, D., and Severson, E. (Eds.) (Forthcoming). *The Ethical Turn: Otherness and Subjectivity in Contemporary Psychoanalysis*. New York: Routledge.

Herman, J. (2011). Posttraumatic Stress Disorder as a Shame Disorder. In R. Dearing and J. Tangney (Eds.), *Shame in the Therapy Hour* (pp. 261–276). Washington, DC: American Psychological Association.

Imber, R. (1995). The Role of the Supervisor and the Pregnant Analyst. *Psychoanalytic Psychology*, 12, 281–296.

Lansky, M. (1994). Shame. *Journal of the American Academy of Psychoanalysis*, 22, 433–441.

Laplanche, J., and Pontalis, J. (1973). *The Language of Psycho-Analysis*. New York: Norton.

Levi, P. (1989). *The Drowned and the Saved*. New York: Vintage International.

Levi, P. (1996). *If This Is a Man: The Truce*. London: Vintage.

Levinas, E. (1969). *Totality and Infinity: An Essay on Exteriority*. Pittsburgh, PA: Duquesne University Press.

Levinas, E. (1981). *Otherwise than Being, or, Beyond Essence*. The Hague and Boston Hingham, MA: M. Nijhoff and Kluwer Boston.

Levinas, E. (1998). *Entre Nous: On Thinking-of-the-Other*. New York: Columbia University Press.

Levinas, E., and Poller, N. (2003). *Humanism of the Other*. Urbana and Chicago, IL: University of Illinois Press.

Levinas, E., and Robbins, J. (2001). *Is It Righteous to Be? Interviews with Emmanuel Levinas.* Stanford, CA: Stanford University Press.

Loewald, H. (1979). The Waning of the Oedipus Complex. *Journal of the American Psychoanalytic Association, 27,* 751–775.

Morrison, A. (1999). Shame in Context. *International Journal of Psychoanalysis, 80,* 616–619.

Orange, D. (1995). *Emotional Understanding: Studies in Psychoanalytic Epistemology.* New York: Guilford Press.

Orange, D. (2006). For Whom the Bell Tolls: Context, Complexity, and Compassion in Psychoanalysis. *International Journal of Psychoanalytic Self Psychology, 1,* 5–21.

Orange, D. (2008). Whose Shame Is It Anyway? Lifeworlds of Humiliation and Systems of Restoration. *Contemporary Psychoanalysis, 44,* 83–100.

Orange, D. (2010). *Thinking for Clinicians: Philosophical Resources for Contemporary Psychoanalysis and the Humanistic Psychotherapies.* New York: Routledge.

Orange, D. (2011). *The Suffering Stranger: Hermeneutics for Everyday Clinical Practice.* New York: Routledge.

Poland, W. (2000). The Analyst's Witnessing and Otherness. *Journal of the American Psychoanalytic Association, 48,* 17–34.

Racker, H. (1958). Psychoanalytic Technique and the Analyst's Unconscious Masochism. *Psychoanalysis Quarterly, 27,* 555–562.

Shengold, L. (1989). *Soul Murder: The Effects of Childhood Abuse and Deprivation.* New Haven, CT: Yale University Press.

Sullivan, H., and Perry, H. (1953). *The Interpersonal Theory of Psychiatry.* New York: Norton.

Wurmser, L. (1991). Shame: The Underside of Narcissism. *Psychoanalysis Quarterly, 60,* 667–672.

Chapter 4

Philosophy as a way of life[1]

Pierre Hadot

In modern university philosophy, philosophy is obviously no longer a way of life or form of life—unless it be the life of a professor of philosophy.

(Hadot and Davidson, 1995, p. 271)

I sincerely believe that our most urgent and difficult task today is, as Goethe said, to "learn to believe in simplicity." Might it not be the case that the greatest lesson which the philosophers of Antiquity ... have to teach us is that philosophy is not the complicated, pretentious, and artificial construction of a learned system of discourse, but the transformation of perception and of life, which lends inexhaustible meaning to the formula—seemingly so banal—of the love of the Good?

(Hadot, 1993, p. xi)

There is no such thing as good or bad fortune for the individual; we live in common.

(Seneca, 1932, 48.3)

Why treasure Pierre Hadot? Least known of my choristers, he lived not for himself, but to make the work of ancient Greek and Roman philosophers accessible and useful to us. More than anything, Hadot wanted us to know that philosophy back then was no abstruse academic discipline full of "recondite jargon" (Chase, 2007) as Western philosophy became after medieval Christianity relegated it to its status as "handmaiden of theology." Much less was it a technical study or the working of conceptual puzzles as Anglo-American philosophy had become in the years of my graduate studies in the 1970s.[2] The Dutch philosopher Jeanne Peijnenburg (2000) characterizes the philosophical world I remember from those years:

concentration on language and meaning and analysis as the decomposition or the breaking down of wholes; a clear style and the precise definition of terms; the prevalent use of logical symbols and formulae;

the avoidance of metaphysical, social, and religious questions; the lack of interest in the history of philosophy, and a proximity to and respect for the natural sciences.

(Quoted in Chase, 2007)

Instead, ancient philosophy meant transforming one's life, under the guidance of teachers who worked endlessly at transforming their own. It sought self-knowledge and self-discipline for the sake of life in the human community.

Life and work

Pierre Hadot (1922–2010) transformed his own life from that of the Roman Catholic priesthood for which he studied during the Second World War, under the influence of his mother's desires, into the scholar and philosopher he became on his own. Though he retained from his early life in the Church his love for textual study and interpretation (hermeneutics) in historical context, in adolescence he had personal experience of what many have called "oceanic sentiment": "the impression of being a wave in a limitless ocean, of being part of a mysterious and infinite reality" (Hadot et al., 2009, p. 8). He found this experience expressed in various literatures from Lucretius onwards (including, by the way, Dostoevsky in *The Brothers Karamazov*), but found no place for it in Roman Catholicism. Worst of all, he was forced, like every seminarian, to take the infamous "Oath against Modernism". In his words:

I had not been warned of this formality and I was made to read a text almost every line of which repelled me. I believe that this oath is no longer in use. It had been introduced in a directive by Pius X dated September 1, 1910. I was to declare, among other things, that I believed that the doctrine of faith transmitted by the apostles and Fathers had remained absolutely immutable since its origins and that the idea of the evolution of dogma was heretical. I had also to declare that a purely scientific exegesis of the Holy Scriptures and of the writings of the Fathers was inadmissible and the freedom of judgment in this situation forbidden. I remember that I was terribly perplexed in this unexpected situation, but I finally told myself, "let us see how things turn out"—an attitude that I can now, with the perspective of age, say is, like pity, disastrous and engenders many tragedies . . . I only discovered the realities of life little by little.

(Hadot et al., 2009, p. 16)

Already grateful to Hadot for his writings on ancient philosophy, so confirming my long-felt intuitions, as well as for his conviction that philosophy concerns a way of life more than an expertise, this story of his youth endeared him to me. True, life in religion provided us both with the educational means to make our later contributions and to make our very escape from its dogmatic and institutional forms. Unfortunately, it also involved us in compromises we later regretted and repented. As he puts it so well, "let us see how things turn out" can evade seeing what faces us— from disastrous marriages, to ethical violations, to bystandership during dictatorships. Pointing ahead to the chapter on humility at the conclusion of this book, who among us cannot remember having accommodated to trouble, small and serious, saying to ourselves, "let us see how things turn out"?

Similarly, Hadot's short phrase "like pity" already gives me pause. Disastrous pity, so different from true compassion, suffering-with, places me above, in a position to condescend to the one who suffers. Already we sense the depth of Hadot's moral understanding, again from the perspective of age.

His "conversion"—his word—further involved both his desire to marry and his encounter with the philosophy of Ludwig Wittgenstein.[3] Hadot's fluent German, learned from his father's Lorraine family, allowed him to introduce Wittgenstein to the French in the early 1950s. From Wittgenstein, he learned the concepts of language games, meaning as use,[4] and philosophy as ethics. Wittgenstein taught him to understand the ancient philosophers he was studying as a philologist—that is, as a historian—to see what use their texts had for their "forms of life." Instead of looking for a coherent system in the work of an ancient thinker, he began to search for the function of the text: to instruct, to remind, to challenge, and so on. Gradually he became convinced that he had been presented with a false choice: to be a historian of philosophy or a philosopher. He refused this choice, and for the next 50 years lived out this refusal. In the process he made his central discovery: "Philosophy was a method of spiritual progress which demanded a radical conversion and transformation of the individual's way of being" (Hadot and Davidson, 1995, p. 265).

Only recently has his profound message begun to reach beyond the French-speaking world, where Foucault's interest in him had made him known. From 1964 to 1982 he taught at the École des Hautes Études; then at the Collège de France from 1982 through 1991, when he retired to work on his books. Though we have only three of his books in English, as well as a wonderful collection of interviews, Hadot has been unusually well served by his translators (Hadot, 1998, 2002; Hadot and Davidson, 1995; Hadot et al., 2009). Still, ancient philosophy may seem far from the worries of clinicians and other humanitarian workers, especially those worried about injustices outside our doors.

In the face of hunger, poverty, and wrongs, why a life devoted to ancient philosophy? Hadot loved to quote in response:

To take flight every day! At least for a moment, which may be brief, as long as it is intense. A "spiritual exercise" every day—either alone, or in the company of someone who also wishes to better himself. Spiritual exercises. Step out of duration ... Try to get rid of your passions, vanities, and the itch for talk about your own name, which sometimes burns you like a chronic disease. Avoid backbiting. Get rid of pity and hatred. Love all free human beings. Become eternal by transcending yourself.

This work on yourself is necessary; this ambition justified. Lots of people let themselves be wholly absorbed by militant politics and the preparation for social revolution. Rare, much more rare, are they who, in order to prepare for the revolution, are willing to make themselves worthy of it.

(Georges Friedmann, *La puissance de la sagesse*, quoted in Hadot and Davidson, 1995, p. 35)

Hadot began with the discipline of studying ancient texts in the contexts in which they had taken form. He gradually realized that not only Plato's dialogues but all the ancient texts seemed so chaotic and difficult because they had never been written as organized treatises. Instead, most of them reflected students' memories of conversations with revered teachers like Socrates, Aristotle, Epicurus, Musonius Rufus, Epictetus, and others. Some were letters from the old (Seneca) instructing the young; others notes or reminders to oneself (the *Meditations* of Marcus Aurelius). In every instance, Hadot learned and later taught us, the original form and context of the ancient text provided clues to its purpose. Above all, these studies led him radically to revise his understanding of the nature and purpose of philosophy itself.

In other words, Hadot's life's work itself exemplified the process this book attempts to explain: the creation and support of an interior life—from interiorized mentors—that supports an ethical life. His own internal chorus, as readers will discover, included Socrates, Marcus Aurelius, Seneca, and Goethe, among others. Though he lived the quiet life of a scholar and professor, he understood the philosophical life as any reflective, unselfish life devoted to the service of the community. Stories about him report that he was always ready to interrupt his own path to help another.

Living as a philosopher

Philosophy, as lived and taught in the ancient world—and, Hadot believed, more recently by Montaigne, Spinoza, Goethe, Nietzsche (at least in some moods), Henri Bergson, and certainly Wittgenstein[5]—bore little resemblance to philosophy as taught in universities in the Western world today. Hadot (Hadot and Davidson, 1995, pp. 270–271) wrote:

One of the characteristics of the university is that it is made up of professors who train professors, or professionals who train professionals. Education was thus no longer directed toward people who were to become educated with a view to becoming fully developed human beings, but to specialists, in order that they might train other specialists . . . In modern university philosophy, philosophy is obviously no longer a way of life or form of life—unless it be the form of life of a professor of philosophy.

No wonder students fear to study or read philosophy.

In the ancient world, people avoided and ridiculed philosophy, but not because the technical discourse intimidated them. Instead, philosophers walked about in simple clothes, unconcerned about the latest fashions, or about accumulating wealth or fame. This made them seem really weird and impractical. The famously ugly Socrates, inspiration for all ancient philosophical schools, constituted an ongoing reminder that superficial appearance had nothing whatever to do with goodness, or even with beauty in its more important senses. The Emperor Marcus Aurelius, a Stoic philosopher, made sure to remove his imperial purple as soon as he returned home, to remind himself that he wore it only in the service of the community.

Philosophers also spoke differently from those around them. The Sophists showed this contrast most clearly. The political spin-doctors of the ancient world, they provided Socrates with his perfect foil. Like young people of today who study marketing, finance, and communication, ancient youth flocked to the Sophists to learn how to get ahead in the world. Socrates engaged these young people in conversations that challenged all their heroes' assumptions, and for this he was condemned to death. Marcus Aurelius, probably Hadot's favorite among the ancients, adopted an unadorned style and recommended it to himself: "the work of philosophy is simple and discreet. Let us not get carried away by the swollen puffiness of solemn affectation" (Marcus Aurelius, 2011, 9.29).[6] Hadot, long before his greatest works on philosophy as a way of life, commented:

> I sincerely believe that our most urgent and difficult task today is, as Goethe said, to "learn to believe in simplicity." Might it not be the case that the greatest lesson which the philosophers of Antiquity . . . have to teach us is that philosophy is not the complicated, pretentious, and artificial construction of a learned system of discourse, but the transformation of perception and of life, which lends inexhaustible meaning to the formula—seemingly so banal—of the love of the Good?
>
> (Hadot, 1993, p. xi)

Simplicity, of course, conjures the ever-enigmatic figure of Socrates.

Hadot's Socrates (and mine) remains not only the central figure for ancient Greek philosophy, but for all Western thought indebted to it. Tempted to give him extended treatment, I provide only this concise summary:

- Socrates acted the ethical gadfly—in religious traditions, the prophetic function—calling the community back from injustice. Better to suffer than to commit injustice.
- Socrates initiated, so far as we know, the tradition of teaching through dialogue. Though he knew where he wanted the conversation to go—through the student's confusion to eventual recognition of the injustice of the starting assumption—Socrates traveled the road with the student. In Hadot's words, "Socrates splits himself in two, so that there are two Socrates: the Socrates who knows in advance how the discussion is going to end, and the Socrates who travels the entire dialectical path along with his interlocutor" (Hadot and Davidson, 1995, p. 153).
- Socrates lived the simple philosophical life he espoused—no double standard here, in contrast to what we often find in professional philosophy.
- Socrates understood more than he communicated directly. Hadot wrote: "here we come upon one of the most profound reasons for Socratic irony: direct language is not adequate for communicating the experience of existing, the authentic consciousness of being, the seriousness of life as we live it, or the solitude of decision making" (Hadot and Davidson, 1995, p. 156).
- Socrates remained strange, a teacher without a system to teach: "Throughout, his philosophy was a spiritual exercise, an invitation to a new way of life, active reflection, and living consciousness" (Hadot and Davidson, 1995, p. 157).

Spiritual exercises every day

Indispensable for most of my internal chorus, some regular time for refueling the spirit sustains us who respond to the widow, the orphan, and the stranger, who hear the demand of infinite responsibility. Whether nurses or therapists, doctors without borders, or caregivers for aging parents, we would-be philosophers must have a few minutes each day to gather ourselves. Pierre Hadot believed this practice crucial to the philosophical life, and entitled his most important book *Exercices spirituelles*. Marcus Aurelius began each day by calling to mind his moral teachers; Dietrich Bonhoeffer in prison by reading a biblical passage. Nelson Mandela concluded each day in prison by spending 15 minutes considering how he had treated the people he had encountered that day, and what he wished he had done differently (not what he wished *they* had done differently, even though it would be easy enough to focus on that in prison).

This version of spiritual exercise, like the tradition of spiritual reading to which this book is much indebted (Malone, 2003), involves interior dialogue, quite different from more Asian-inspired meditative forms during which one seeks to drop or ignore difference or distinction.[7] Hadot commented:

> Only he who is capable of genuine encounter with the other is capable of an authentic encounter with himself, and the converse is equally true . . . From this perspective, every spiritual exercise is a dialogue, insofar as it is an exercise of authentic presence, to oneself and to others.
>
> (Hadot and Davidson, 1995, p. 91)

People who take time for these exercises live each day in peace and serenity, claimed Philo of Alexandria. They learn to regard the whole world as their city, and train themselves to be indifferent to indifferent things: "they do not give in under the blows of fate because they have calculated its attacks in advance" (see Hadot and Davidson, 1995, pp. 264–265). Imagining death meant to the ancients knowing without fear that it would come, and thus embracing the present. *Carpe diem*, they taught. Seize the present moment. While our conversations with Primo Levi, Emmanuel Levinas, and others in later chapters may lead us to question whether such spiritual exercises suffice in extreme situations, they surely keep us steady and prepared to respond to the other, day by day. They also help us to refind our footing when confronted with violence, with what exceeds our capacities, and even with the demonic.

Philosophical exercises, though quiet, do not separate us from the world of practical concerns; they prepare us to act in the world. The Stoic[8] philosopher Epictetus, a former slave, explained:

> A carpenter does not come up to you and say, "listen to me discourse about the art of carpentry," but he makes a contract of a house and builds it . . . Do the same thing yourself. Eat like a man, drink like a man . . . get married, have children, take part in civic life, learn how to put up with insults, and tolerate other people.
>
> (Quoted in Hadot and Davidson, 1995, p. 267)

Hadot shows us how to read other-wise, as a form of spiritual exercise (Laugier, 2011). Instead of expecting the ancient author—or even one closer to our time, such as Thoreau, Kierkegaard, or Wittgenstein—to conform to our expectations, Hadot teaches us to pause meditatively and listen, to let the text sink in. He instructs us in reading as a spiritual exercise. It brings us into contact with the ordinary, and pitches us into our citizenship in the world. This reading has no intent to inform, but rather to form. Carefully chosen reading, slowly absorbed, nourishes my life every day, reminding me of great and beloved ones who have thought and served before me, providing me with internal reminders, warnings, and support. My work emerges from theirs.

Marcus Aurelius (Roman Emperor 161–180 CE), Hadot's favorite and one of mine too, practiced a form of philosophical exercise called *hypomnemata*, or written reminders. His famous *Meditations* were written to keep himself focused on the philosophical life. He recalled the people who had taught him Stoicism, he rehearsed its most important principles, and he kept himself a philosopher in the ancient sense. Let us listen in:

> Concentrate every minute . . . on doing what's in front of you with precise and genuine seriousness, tenderly, willingly, with justice. And on freeing yourself from all other distractions. Yes you can—if you do everything as if it were the last thing you were doing in your life, stop being aimless, stop letting your emotions override what your mind tells you, stop being hypocritical, self-centered, irritable. You see how few things you have to do to live a satisfying and reverent life?
>
> (Marcus Aurelius, 2002, 2.5)

> Don't be put off by other people's comments and criticisms. If it's right to say or do it, then it's the right thing for you to do or say . . . Don't be distracted. Keep walking.
>
> (Marcus Aurelius, 2002, 5.3)

> No matter what anyone says or does, my task is to be good.
>
> (Marcus Aurelius, 2002, 7.15)

Marcus's reminder-writing, read by Hadot, becomes my reminder-reading. The discourses of Epictetus, and the letters of Seneca, serve as similar buttresses for the always-threatened ethical life.

Gratitude and the present moment as our happiness

The daily meditation—whatever its form—leads easily to the embrace of the present moment. The Greco-Roman schools Hadot studied, especially his favorite Epicureans and Stoics—challenged us to embrace and enjoy the present. The past, with its alleged glories and remembered sorrows, may teach us something, but we cannot live there. The future we can neither know nor possess. *Carpe diem*, the ancients taught, not in a reckless sense, but with reverence and gratitude.

Marcus Aurelius devoted the first long section of his *Meditations*, "Debts and Lessons," to a detailed list of the people to whom he was grateful for very particular aspects of his upbringing and moral education. He assumed that whatever he became was a gift from others, not his own doing.

For clinicians and for many humanitarian workers, this aspect of ancient philosophy can form a strong foundation. We work every day with unbearable and unspeakable wrongs and sorrows, toward uncertain futures. Our own strong sense that each day is precious can communicate itself to those whom we serve, often without being said, and can sustain us through many storms.

"It is precisely because the Epicureans considered existence to be the result of pure chance that they greeted each moment with immense gratitude, like a kind of divine miracle" (Hadot and Davidson, 1995, p. 252). All the ancient philosophers, as Hadot constantly reminded us, considered philosophy as a practice in dying.[9] Not a morbid exercise, this focus attempted to remind us of the seriousness of now. Paraphrasing Marcus Aurelius, he wrote:

> one must spend every day as though it were one's last. It is a matter of becoming aware that the moment one is still living has infinite value. Because death may interrupt it, it is a matter of living in an extremely intense manner as long as death has not arrived.
>
> (Hadot et al., 2009, p. 105)

The meditation on death ranked high among the "spiritual exercises" Hadot found among the ancient philosophers he studied so closely.

Philosophy as therapy[10]

Like Martha Nussbaum (1994), Hadot emphasized the therapeutic function of philosophy itself as understood in the ancient world. To live as the Stoics and Epicureans recommended was to develop and care for what I have called a pre-Cartesian self, and they called variously soul, *daimon*, psyche, or *hegemonikon*. Listen to Socrates, who proclaimed, before all, an ethical self. To the suggestion that they might acquit him if he agreed to live quietly, he responded:

> Men of Athens, I am grateful and I am your friend, but I will obey the god rather than you, and as long as I draw breath and am able, I shall not cease to practice philosophy, to exhort you and in my usual way to point out to any of you whom I happen to meet . . . are you not ashamed of your eagerness to possess as much wealth, reputation and honors as possible, while you do not care for nor give thought to wisdom or truth, or the best possible state of your soul?
>
> (Plato, 1997, *Apology*, 27d–e)

What might be this "soul" that is so worthy of protection at all costs? Earlier Socrates had explained that we are mistaken if we think that questions of life and death matter at all when compared with whether we are acting as good or bad people. Surely this soul, for Socrates, as for Plato and Aristotle, was an ethical self, perhaps the only kind worth being. Before and after the modern era, we may no longer need to worry about having or not having something called a self, and just concern ourselves more, as Socrates and the Stoics did, with the care for the inherent dignity, the core humanity, in those despised by others. Socrates warned us that the moment when we consider ourselves more important than the convict or peasant next to us, we have lost our soul.

We find also in Plato—our primary access to Socrates, of course—a concept of, and arguments for, a soul that survives embodied life. Just noting that these views interweave with religious traditions to give us the medieval soul supplanted by the infamous modern self of Descartes and beyond, I would point out that this pre-Cartesian soul was never a substantialized thing, but rather remained much closer to the center of personal and ethical continuity (Kohut, 1985).

Back to Socrates, we must pause over the *daimon*, which great scholars and popular culture have considered and we can only glimpse. The *locus classicus* appears in the *Apology*: "it is a voice, and whenever it speaks it turns me away from something I am about to do, but it never encourages me to do anything" (Plato, 1997, *Apology*, 31d). Primarily it kept Socrates out of public life, where people say what pleases the crowd. (Unlike the voice heard by the Hebrew prophets, this *daimon* warned *against* speaking and doing.) Of course, with our psycho-analytic sophistication, we would characterize his *daimon* as some aspect of himself, of perhaps his wisdom or self-knowledge. In Plato's dialogue *Theaetetus*, speaking of decisions about which students might or might not be teachable, Socrates explained, "the divine sign [*daimon*] that visits me forbids me to associate with them [some prospective interlocutors]; in others it permits me, and then they begin again to make progress" (Plato, 1997, *Theaetetus*, 151a). Which of us has not needed to listen to ourselves to understand whether to take a new patient into our care or how to respond to the next humanitarian crisis? The *daimon*, perhaps, forms an aspect of the soul, something like wisdom or discretion, later articulated within Aristotelian ethics as *phronesis*. The *phronimus/a* is a contextually good and wise person, one good at what Hubert Dreyfus (1992) describes as "skilled coping" (James and James, 1955). But Socrates was always more extreme, like Levinas, proclaiming like a prophet (see Chapter 8) that we should prefer death to murder, even in its more subtle forms. The *daimon* warns me against evasion, against murder I might not recognize.

Hadot acknowledged Socrates as the only true philosophical sage. For everyone who aspires to philosophy understood as ethical life, he quoted Nietzsche to illustrate the standing of Socrates:

The genius of the heart, as that great concealed one possesses it, the tempter god and born pied piper of consciences whose voice knows how to descend into the netherworld of every soul; who does not say a word or cast a glance in which there is no secret goal of seduction . . . the genius of the heart who silences all that is loud and self-satisfied, teaching it to listen; who smooths rough souls and lets them taste a new desire— to lie still as a mirror, that the deep sky may mirror itself in them . . . the genius of the heart from whose touch everyone walks away richer, not having received grace and surprised, not as blessed and oppressed by alien goods, but richer in himself, newer to himself than before, broken open, blown at and sounded out by a thawing wind, perhaps more uncertain, perhaps, tenderer, more fragile, more broken, but full of hopes that as yet have no name.

> (Nietzsche, *Beyond Good and Evil*, § 295, quoted in Hadot and Davidson, 1995, p. 170)

The Greek and Roman Stoics followed Socrates, and idealized him, even as they lived more apparently conventional lives. The more famous among them included both the slave Epictetus and the Roman Emperor Marcus Aurelius, whom you will still find sitting astride his horse in the center of the Museo Capitolini in Rome, as well as Seneca and Cicero. What they all held in common, with each other and with Socrates, were the convictions that everyone could be a philosopher, that philosophy was a way of life, not a body of knowledge or a profession, and that only the philosophical life was worth living for a human being.

For the Stoics—those who inhabited the structure along the side of the *agora* or marketplace called the *stoa*—to live as a philosopher meant to disregard fame, fortune, wealth, reputation, all that could come and go, and to live according to one's *hegemonikon*.[11] A more familiar word is probably "hegemony"—rule or dominance, a related idea. What the Stoics meant by *hegemonikon* was that philosophers live according to their own ruling principle, that which makes them who they are. "Know thyself," said the Delphic oracle—not an epistemological project but an ethical and existential one that involves turning down the noise and listening differently, a project of drastic self-transformation (Honneth and Joas, 1988). "Live according to *who* you are, in accordance with your nature," said the Stoics. Your nature as a member of the human community meant that the very care of your soul signified living in the service of the human community (Erdmann et al., 1990). Living as a philosopher meant a lifelong effort to understand this, and to live in this way. Historian of ancient philosophy Julia Annas (1992, p. 64) comments:

> the *hegemonikon* can be thought of, not too misleadingly, as the mind, and the Stoic theory of the soul as a theory of our mental life. As such a

theory, it is strikingly un-Cartesian; the Stoics show no interest in the kinds of concern that led Descartes to his conclusions about the mind. The contents of the *hegemonikon* are not taken to be accessible to introspection by privileged inner view [thus not vulnerable to Wittgenstein's and Heidegger's devastating critiques]; nor are they epistemologically basic, nor in any interesting sense private. But the *hegemonikon* is very like a non-Cartesian mind: it centralizes, unifies, and interprets what goes on in the rest of the soul.

This kind of selfhood, neither subjective nor objective, may correspond in part to what the eminent scholar of Hellenistic philosophy A. A. Long, referring to Homer, calls

> normative identity, that manifests itself when one hero rebukes himself or another hero for falling short of what the situation requires . . . the idea of a universal norm, a true self, a standard of general human excellence to which this particular person is currently not living up.
> (Long, 2006, p. 366)

The ancient psyche functioned as ethical voice.

"*Vindica te tibi* [claim yourself for yourself]," wrote the Roman Stoic Seneca (quoted in Honneth, 2000, p. 371). The verb *vindicare* suggests the lifelong project of liberation involved in becoming a philosopher, or in our work of service, therapeutic or humanitarian, to the devastated other. "To know oneself means, among other things, to know one *qua* non-sage: that is, not as a *sophos*, but as a *philo-sophos*, someone *on the way toward* wisdom" (Hadot and Davidson, 1995, p. 90; original emphasis). The way toward wisdom and the way toward humility converge.

In the service of the community

Modesty and balance have earned Hadot his front-row seat in my internal chorus in recent years. To my knowledge, he unpretentiously promoted his understanding of the philosophical life, but not himself. Often mentioned in the same breath with Michel Foucault, who used Hadot's work to support his aesthetics of self-creation, Hadot never became a personage. He remained a quiet scholar.

Moreover, Hadot quite specifically understood the philosophical life as an ethical life:

> This concern for living in the service of the human community, and for acting in accordance with justice, is an essential element of every philo- sophical life. In other words, the philosophical life normally entails a communitary engagement. This last is probably the hardest part to

carry out. The trick is to maintain oneself on the level of reason, and not allow oneself to be blinded by political passions, anger, resentments or prejudices. To be sure, there is an equilibrium—almost impossible to achieve—between the inner peace brought about by wisdom, and the passion to which the sight of the injustices, suffering and misery of mankind cannot help but give rise. Wisdom, however, consists in precisely such equilibrium, and inner peace is indispensable for efficacious action.

(Hadot and Davidson, 1995, p. 274)

Inner peace: does this come first, or apart from one's service to others? No, answered Hadot in a late interview: "I would say that there is no real concern for others if there is no self-forgetting" (Hadot et al., 2009, p. 108). But service to others, self-forgetting, depends on continual, daily nourishing of one's internal life. Hadot went on to quote Socrates: "Ask yourself if it is humanly possible to neglect, as I have, all one's personal interests . . . for so many years and thus to be able to take care only of you" (Plato, 1997, *Apology*, 32b, 31b). Here Socrates resonates with the self-diremption (self-emptying) emphasis in Buddhism, in Christianity, and surely in Levinas's understanding of ethical responsibility. We can understand him to speak of a radical self-decentering for the sake of the other. Again and again Hadot emphasized that the care of the soul is not egotistical or egocentric, but the condition for the possibility of work in the service of the community. Speaking of meditation—"the practice of dialogue with oneself"—he wrote: "Only he who is capable of a genuine encounter with the other is capable of an authentic encounter with himself, and the converse is equally true" (Hadot and Davidson, 1995, p. 91). Socrates enjoins us to "know thyself" and Hadot would have us converse with a radically non-self-centered self.

Hadot felt that the Stoics' central contribution was their emphasis on the common good and on service to the human community:

The notes in Marcus Aurelius' book are precious. There is an extraordinary lucidity in the advice the emperor gives himself to make out all the dangers that threaten the person of action. One must take care to respect others, to remain perfectly impartial, to be totally disinterested [read, with Levinas, dis-interested], to do good without being aware of it, to avoid egotistically attaching oneself to one's action, to accept the advice of others. All these remarks are valuable today.

(Hadot et al., 2009, p. 172)

Hadot associates these attitudes in the twentieth century with, for example, Albert Einstein and Vaclav Havel. He quotes the latter (who often noted his indebtedness to Levinas): "The only politics, the only one worthy of this name, and moreover the only one I consent to practice, is politics in the service of the neighbor, in the service of the community." This, continues Hadot, is philosophical action "in the strongest and most noble sense of the word" (Hadot et al., 2009, p. 173).

Balance remains the ongoing challenge of the philosophical life in the service of the human community. Once again, according to Hadot:

> To be sure there is an equilibrium—almost impossible to achieve—between the inner peace brought about by wisdom, and the passions to which the sight of the injustices, sufferings and misery of mankind cannot help but give rise. Wisdom, however, consists in precisely such an equilibrium, and inner peace is indispensable for efficacious action.
>
> (Hadot and Davidson, 1995, p. 274)

Further reading

Hadot's book on Marcus Aurelius, *The Inner Citadel* (Hadot, 1998) has found its way into my all-time shortlist of indispensables, and I recommend it to anyone who wants to go deeper into the philosophical life as personal conversion. Next, pick up *Philosophy as a Way of Life* (Hadot and Davidson, 1995), and the book of interviews with Hadot, *The Present Alone Is Our Happiness* (Hadot et al., 2009).

The work of A. A. Long, in particular his *Epictetus: A Stoic and Socratic Guide to Life* (Long, 2002), has also been extremely important to me. I cannot recommend this book too highly for meditative reading.

Notes

1 The title is borrowed from Hadot's best-known book in English translation (Hadot and Davidson, 1995).
2 Michael Chase, Hadot's principal translator, provides a vivid portrait of these years when philosophers wanted to be scientists: "Analytic philosophers often seemed slightly embarrassed about being 'philosophers' at all, to the point that their goal, sometimes implicitly and sometimes avowedly, was the elimination of philosophy itself" (Chase, 2007, p. 9).
3 Also one of my important influences, about whom I have written earlier (Coburn, 2009; Orange, 2010).
4 These two concepts refer to understanding words and concepts by their use and function in their practical contexts (see Wittgenstein, 1953).
5 Hadot introduced the French to Wittgenstein (Hadot et al., 2004). A fascinating figure, hero both for analytic philosophers, who reduce philosophy to puzzle-working, and for Hadot, who saw philosophy as the pursuit of simple life in the service of the community, Wittgenstein tests the limits of both. In his last years, Hadot took ever more interest in the ways Chinese Taoist and Buddhist philosophers similarly pursued philosophy as a way of life.
6 This form of quoting from Marcus Aurelius allows readers to find quotations in any translation they may have.

7 I am grateful to Donald A. Braue, a specialist in the history of religions, for pointing out this contrast.
8 Stoicism has an unfortunate bad name among psychotherapists who know only its teaching against overreacting to misfortune. Its therapeutic potential for self-regulation, and its constant reminders that we are small in the universe, and members of a human community, make reading in the texts of Seneca, Epictetus, and especially Marcus Aurelius a source of spiritual stability.
9 Simon Critchley (2009) has further reminded us.
10 This section borrows from an earlier work (Orange, 2013).
11 I have also discussed this idea in Orange (2013).

References

Annas, J. (1992). *Hellenistic Philosophy of Mind*. Berkeley, CA: University of California Press.
Chase, M. (2007). Observations on Pierre Hadot's Conception of *Philosophy as a Way of Life*. Retrieved from www.society-for-philosophy-in-practice.org/journal/pdf/8-2%2005%20chase%20-%20Hadot.pdf (accessed September 5, 2015).
Coburn, W. (2009). Attitudes in Psychoanalytic Complexity. In R. Frie and D. Orange (Eds.), *Beyond Postmodernism: New Dimensions in Clinical Theory and Practice* (pp. 183–200). New York: Routledge.
Critchley, S. (2009). *The Book of Dead Philosophers*. New York: Vintage Books.
Dreyfus, H. L. (1992). *What Computers Still Can't Do: A Critique of Artificial Reason*. Cambridge, MA: MIT Press.
Erdmann, E., Forst, R., and Honneth, A. (1990). *Ethos der Moderne: Foucaults Kritik der Aufklärung*. Frankfurt and New York: Campus.
Hadot, P. (1993). *Plotinus, or The Simplicity of Vision*. Chicago, IL: University of Chicago Press.
Hadot, P. (1998). *The Inner Citadel: The Meditations of Marcus Aurelius*. Cambridge, MA: Harvard University Press.
Hadot, P. (2002). *What is Ancient Philosophy?* Cambridge, MA: Belknap Press of Harvard University Press.
Hadot, P., and Davidson, A. I. (1995). *Philosophy as a Way of Life: Spiritual Exercises from Socrates to Foucault*. Oxford and New York: Blackwell.
Hadot, P., Anscombe, G. E. M., and Gabriel, G. (2004). *Wittgenstein et les limites du langage*. Paris: Librairie Philosophique J. Vrin.
Hadot, P., Djaballah, M., Carlier, J., and Davidson, A. I. (2009). *The Present Alone Is Our Happiness: Conversations with Jeannie Carlier and Arnold I. Davidson*. Stanford, CA: Stanford University Press.
Honneth, A. (2000). *Das Andere der Gerechtigkeit: Aufsätze zur praktischen Philosophie*. Frankfurt am Main: Suhrkamp.
Honneth, A., and Joas, H. (1988). *Social Action and Human Nature*. Cambridge and New York: Cambridge University Press.
James, W., and James, W. (1955). *Pragmatism, and Four Essays from* The Meaning of Truth. New York: Meridian Books.
Kohut, H. (1985). On Courage. In C. Strozier and E. Kohut (Eds.), *Self Psychology and the Humanities* (pp. 5–50). New York: Norton.
Laugier, S. (2011). Pierre Hadot as a Reader of Wittgenstein. *Paragraph*, 34, 322–337.

Long, A. A. (2002). *Epictetus: A Stoic and Socratic Guide to Life*. Oxford and New York: Clarendon Press and Oxford University Press.

Long, A. A. (2006). *From Epicurus to Epictetus: Studies in Hellenistic and Roman Philosophy*. Oxford and New York: Clarendon Press and Oxford University Press.

Malone, N. M. (2003). *Walking a Literary Labyrinth: A Spirituality of Reading*. New York: Riverhead Books.

Marcus Aurelius (2002). *Meditations*. Translated by G. Hays. New York: Modern Library.

Marcus Aurelius (2011). *Meditations: With Selected Correspondence*. Translated by R. Hard. Oxford and New York: Oxford University Press.

Nussbaum, M. C. (1994). *The Therapy of Desire: Theory and Practice in Hellenistic Ethics*. Princeton, NJ: Princeton University Press.

Orange, D. (2010). *Thinking for Clinicians: Philosophical Resources for Contemporary Psychoanalysis and the Humanistic Psychotherapies*. New York: Routledge.

Orange, D. (2013). A Pre-Cartesian Self. *International Journal of Psychoanalytic Self Psychology*, 8, 488–494.

Peijnenburg, J. (2000). Identity and Difference: A Hundred Years of Analytic Philosophy. *Metaphilosophy*, 4, 365–381.

Plato (1997). *Complete Works*. Edited by J. M. Cooper; associate editor D. S. Hutchinson. Indianapolis, IN: Hackett.

Seneca, L. A. (1932). *Seneca's Letters to Lucilius*. Translated by E. P. Barker. Oxford: The Clarendon Press

Wittgenstein, L. (1953). *Philosophical Investigations*. New York: Macmillan.

Chapter 5

Witness to indignity
Primo Levi

Determined to tell and despairing of being truly heard, the poet Paul Celan, the philosopher Jean Améry, and the chemist and writer Primo Levi emerged from hell in 1945. Yet all three succumbed in the end to suicide. Levi, my primary interest here, apparently thought of suicide before his captivity in Buna/Monowitz at Auschwitz, but the suicides of the other two had an impact on him. Each of their voices reminds us that the destruction of human dignity—by enslavement and torture, by calculated or indifferent degradation, by genocide—may be the ultimate crime, one that time, the balm of human kindness, and even poetry can never adequately heal. Their stories, like the stories of former slaves (Yetman and Federal Writers' Project, 2002), help to keep me unpretentious in my work and grateful to them for their witness, while their suicides challenge any certainties that I may be tempted to claim. Another of my favorite fallibilists, reminding me of the American philosopher Charles Sanders Peirce and of the psychoanalytic pioneer Sandor Ferenczi, Primo Levi himself warned, "There is trouble in store for anyone who surrenders to the temptation of mistaking an elegant hypothesis for a certainty" (Levi, 1996, p. 157).[1] Precise scientist that he always attempted to be, determined reporter of the truth as he saw it and lived it, poet that he could not escape being, he left us his demise as an enigma.

Life and work

Born in 1919 into an educated and non-observant Jewish family from Torino (Turin), Primo Levi received a classical Italian education and decided to study chemistry, at which he excelled. Small for his age, shy, often ill, younger than his peers in school because precocious, he was often bullied. He understood the torment to relate to his Jewishness. Later, at university, he gained respect for his talents, developed hardiness, and compensated for his size by making friends among mountaineers.

In the late 1930s Levi, like his Italian friends and colleagues, believed Italy would protect its Jews. As Italian Fascism succumbed to the alliance with Hitler during the war, however, he joined the partisans. In February 1944 he and his best friends, including Luciana Nissim,[2] were betrayed and deported to Auschwitz, where, of the 650 who made the train journey, only 18 survived. Of those not gassed immediately, the average survival time was three months. Levi "lived" in the camp for 11 months, in part because his lifelong friend Alberto Dalla Volta immediately announced that Levi was an expert in chemistry (Angier, 2002), in part because the civilian worker Lorenzo Perrone, after whom Levi later named his son, smuggled him an extra ration of soup each day. Too ill to go on the infamous "death march" at the end of the war, he and a few others were left behind and found by the Russians. After his liberation it took him nearly ten months to reach home, where few even recognized him.

Levi said later that he felt compelled to survive Auschwitz and to return, so that he could tell exactly what had occurred there. He often quoted Coleridge's Ancient Mariner, duty-bound to repeat his "ghastly tale" incessantly. Of this time in his life, Levi later wrote:

> The things I had seen and suffered were burning inside of me; I felt closer to the dead than the living, and felt guilty as being a man, because men had built Auschwitz, and Auschwitz had gulped down millions of human beings, and many of my friends, and a woman who was dear to my heart. It seemed to me that I would be purified if I told its story, and I felt like Coleridge's Ancient Mariner, who waylays on the street the wedding guests going to the feast, inflicting on them the story of his misfortune.
>
> (Levi, 1984a, p. 151)

But, as he often said, he returned as a witness, reporting in scientific detail the methods used to destroy human dignity. "*I giudici siete voi*" (Levi and Belpoliti, 1997, Vol. 1, p. 175). "You are the judges."

Levi's own "Shemà," the poem naming his first book and written in Milano, where he had gone to find work after his return, thunders with prophetic fury:[3]

> Consider that this has been:
> I commend [*comando*] these words to you.
> Engrave them on your hearts . . .
> Repeat them to your children.
> Or may your house crumble,
> Disease render you powerless,
> Your offspring avert their faces from you.
> (Levi et al., 1992, p. 9)

Soon, however, he turned to prose, writing in 1946 the chapters that would become within a year *Se questo e un uomo* (*If This Is a Man*) (1984b).[4] The title, drawn from the poem, refers to the dehumanization of both victims and victimizers.[5] It took years to find the book a small publisher, but gradually acclaim and many translations came. Though working full time as an industrial chemist, writing short fiction, and fighting bouts of serious depression, Levi obsessively checked the translations when he could, especially into German, wanting to be sure that people understood his message precisely.

His message was that human beings, considered as members of groups, can become inhuman. (We will return in a later chapter to Levi's robust and prophetic humanism, impatient with postmodernist waffling, as he saw it, in the face of injustice.) Levi depicted Dante's hell constructed by twentieth-century "humans": the selections, the slave labor, the seemingly small indignity of a capo wiping grease off his hand on Levi's shoulder without apparent contempt. His scientist's eye for detail recorded an account more damning than generalizations about "the holocaust." Desperately thirsty, he reached for an icicle, then asked why it was roughly snatched away from him. *"Hier ist kein Warum!* [Here there is no why]," the SS guard snapped at him.[6] Reporting such details reminded him, like Coleridge's Ancient Mariner and Odysseus on return, that human beings were involved. Human beings decided, immediately and methodically, to strip away the human status of other human beings. (Attempting to report methods of destroying humanity, Levi tended to understate the violence perpetrated against him personally. Writing of the arrest that led to his deportation to Auschwitz, he wrote, "*Ci picchiarono un po*" ("They hit us a bit"). A companion arrested with him reports that "Primo Levi was beaten violently, so that hours later he still had the imprint of a hand on his face" (Sessi, 2013, p. 58; my translation).)

When discussing one of the hopeless drowned, Levi observed, "it is as if everyone was aware that only a man was worthy of a name, and Null Achtzehn is no longer a man." *Null Achtzehn* (Zero Eighteen) had formerly been a person;[7] now "he carries out all the orders that he is given, and it is foreseeable that when they send him to his death he will go with the same total indifference" (Levi, 1986b, pp. 42, 43). The drowned, the *Muselmänner* (Muslims; *muselmani* in Italian), so called in Auschwitz though named differently in other camps, had lost all sense of dignity and hope, as well as all memory of the people they had formerly been. They had been reduced to one of Levi's favorite words: "*nulla*" (nothing, in the mathematical sense). The entire methodology of the *Lager*[8]—as Levi almost always referred to the camps—oriented itself toward the production of such former humans, according to Levi. He described with scientific precision the methods used to accomplish this depersonalization: stripping naked, starving, shaving, beating, tattooing, night latrine duty, senseless brutality that he called "useless violence," threat of selections, and above all substitution of numbers for names. The vast majority came to look like *Null Achtzehn*, and the world of the *Lager* resembled Thomas Hobbes's war of all against all, where life is famously "solitary, poor, nasty, brutish, and short" (Hobbes and

Curley, 1994, p. 76). Levinas's ethics, as well as Dostoevsky's literary vision, are directly aimed against the Hobbesian egoism and social contract theory, which, in both Levi's and Levinas's views, made Auschwitz possible. Only a few managed a quiet resistance: keeping minimally clean, maintaining friendships, sustaining the shards of an interior life, closely related to the theme of this book; but even so, very few returned home.

Levi's post-Auschwitz life was long and complex: he worked as an industrial chemist for thirty years, living in Torino with his wife and depressed mother (Thomson, 2003) until his suicide in 1987. He both sought fame and was overwhelmed by it. Periods of serious depression had plagued him prior to his deportation; he did not blame them on the *Lager*. Still, he always had many and close friends, including such Italian literary stars as Italo Calvino and Leonardo Sciascia. They valued him as an extraordinary writer, as a moral and political voice (against neo-Fascism and for calling on Israeli Prime Minister Menachem Begin to resign[9]), and just as a friend.

We will return to Levi's life story in the meditation on suicide.

The gray zone

What I find remarkable, and what earns Primo Levi an ever-larger place in my thinking about ethics, is his personal integrity and fidelity to his values of human dignity and care for the other, regained immediately on liberation. His version of Levinasian substitution consisted in recalling and retelling his story no matter what it cost him. As a prisoner, though careful not to mistreat others, he could worry only for his own survival. Afterwards he struggled beyond his original descriptive task, leaving behind what he regarded as simplistic judgments. His "gray zone" did not provide him with peace of mind;[10] it forced him to see human beings in impossible situations in all their moral complication.

His final and darkest book, *I sommersi e i salvati* (*The Drowned and the Saved*) (1989), attempting to articulate this complexity, portrayed the grayness of Auschwitz as a moral gray zone where anyone who was "saved" deserved to be damned. Auschwitz turned Dante's *Inferno* upside down. To be a survivor meant you were doubly ashamed: for what you had done to survive; and to live in a world where such slaughter can be planned and executed. By the end, he had quietly but clearly indicted not only the planners of the genocide but all those complicit in it, even afterwards. Once this final book came out, he seemed to cross over from the saved to the drowned. He had nothing more to say, and the despair of being unheard finally overwhelmed this ever-sensitive soul.

But who are the drowned and who are the saved? The drowned, the vast majority, Levi tells us, were those destined for the gas chambers, those without any hope, those whose sense of humanity and personal dignity had been completely destroyed (*Null Achtzehn* had been the clearest exemplar in his earlier book). Nothing in them remained to object to dehumanizing treatment. Like many other witnesses, Levi called them *"muselmani"* (Muslims: "This word 'Muselmann', I do not know why, was used by the old ones of the camp to describe the weak, the inept, those doomed to selection" (Levi 1986c, p. 94)).[11] Those with empty hopes, who always thought liberators were coming next week, also tended to die.

The 18 who returned home to Italy presented moral problems for the ever-truth-seeking Levi.[12] *The Drowned and the Saved* asks questions that he could not, from the immediate perspective of 1946, have asked before. His early testimony was full of detail that would have faded or fogged with time and been faced with the perpetrators' *"Non mi ricordo"* ("I don't remember"). But it lacked the scope of what he later, especially in interviews, emphasized as the *"strage"* ("massacre").[13] He had subsisted in one section of Auschwitz, Buna/Monowitz, a synthetic rubber factory, and had never seen Auschwitz–Birkenau, the gas chambers, or the crematoria up close. He knew of their existence, but it was not until later that he realized the extent and complexity of the whole "final solution." Forty years later he attempted to surpass the experiential world of victim–perpetrator, and to address the moral complexities of what he called "the gray zone" (*"la zona grigia"*).

First and last, he reminded us, there endures a difference between good and evil. Examining the gray zone means a humble recognition that, as witnesses, our judgments of others remain fallible. If we were not there, we cannot be sure how we would have acted. Nonetheless, good and evil remain different. He wrote:

> it is necessary to declare the imprudence of issuing hasty moral judgment on such human cases. Certainly the greatest responsibility lies with the system, the very structure of totalitarian state; the concurrent guilt on the part of the individual big and small collaborators (never likable, never transparent!) is always difficult to evaluate. It is a judgment that we would like to entrust only to those who found themselves in similar circumstances and acted in a state of coercion.
>
> (Levi, 1989, pp. 43–44)

No one who survived, he believed, was a saint. Instead, as he explained in his first book, one had to learn immediately how to steal and to bargain, how to manage one's relationships with the privileged prisoners, and how to watch one's back and possessions (e.g., a precious spoon) at all times, to figure out whom to trust.[14] Then there were those who bargained for oppressing others in small ways just to get a bit more soup or bread—the lowest level of the gray zone, who were easy to forgive, Levi thought. Considering those Jews whom the Nazi system used to oppress their own people, *i priveligiati* (prisoner-functionaries), or even the *Sonderkommandos*, used to carry out the most grisly tasks in the extermination camps and elsewhere, here Levi places the blame squarely on the Nazi system. But he believed we must look closely at the gray zone:

> the time has come [in the 1980s] to explore the space which separates the victims from the persecutors . . . Only a schematic rhetoric can claim that that space is empty: it never is, it is studded with obscene or pathetic figures (sometimes they possess both qualities simultaneously) whom it is indispensable to know if we want to know the human species, if we want to know how to defend our souls when a similar test should once more loom before us.
>
> (Levi, 1989, p. 40)

He noted that the privileged prisoners returned far more often than the others: they had more food, and more protection. These prisoner-functionaries had been willing to do what was needed, to oppress their fellows, to survive themselves. When it came to the capos, though usually not Nazis themselves, sometimes even Jews, but left without any supervision to perpetrate useless cruelty, Levi's grays became very dark. He wondered about the many motivations that predisposed people to this role. The camp commandants who chose them for it clearly needed such enthusiastically and dependably sadistic collaborators.

The SS delegated the operation of the gas chambers and crematoria, the deception of the victims, the extraction of gold teeth, the transportation of the corpses, and so on to the *Sonderkommandos*, composed at Auschwitz of prisoners, largely fellow Jews, from 1943 to 1945, when 90–95 percent of those arriving were Jewish. They accepted their assigned tasks, hoping for a few extra months of life, but were invariably murdered so that no one would be left to tell the story of what happened there. Levi (1989, p. 53) writes:

> Conceiving and organizing the squads was National Socialism's most demonic crime. Behind the pragmatic aspect . . . this institution represented an attempt to shift onto others—specifically, the victims—the burden of guilt, so that we were deprived of even the solace of innocence.[15]

But Levi's most extended meditation on the gray zone focuses on the members of these squads: why did they not refuse? Some did, he reports, and died immediately. So there was a choice, and thus some responsibility.

Finally, he wanted us to understand, the gray zone does not erase the possibility of moral distinctions:

> I am not an expert on the unconscious and on the mind's depths [this he knew because his oldest friend, Luciana Nissim, another of the 18 who

returned home to Italy from Auschwitz, was a famous psycho-analyst], but I do know that few people are experts in this sphere and that these few are most cautious. I do not know, and it does not much interest me to know, whether in my depth there lurks a murderer, but I do know I was a guiltless victim and I was not a murderer. I know that the murderers existed, not only German, and still exist, retired or on active duty, and that to confuse them with their victims is a moral disease or an aesthetic affectation or a sinister sign of complicity; above all it is a precious service rendered (intentionally or not) to the negators of truth.

(Levi, 1989, pp. 48–49)

Shame and guilt

Levi belongs to my inner chorus in part for the depth and complexity of his reflections on guilt (*colpa*) and shame (*vergogna*), words he used differently but not consistently so.[16] Where guilt, primarily Oedipal, preoccupied classical Freudian psychoanalysis, shame has taken center stage among relational clinicians more confronted with the humiliated and traumatized (Herman, 2011). Thus Levi's reflections, thankfully, can prevent our own from oversimplification.

Levi is sometimes misunderstood as viewing survivor guilt as merely living on when the best did not survive. In his view, the clearest guilt, as we have seen, belonged to the Nazis, and to those who organized the genocide, as well as to those who stood by and did nothing about it. To the darker shades of the gray zone belonged some guilt as well, but here he was less willing to assign blame. Levi insisted on explaining that one could feel wrong in living on, even without having mistreated anyone. "Return to your shadows," he wrote to the ghosts: "I have not eaten anyone's bread."[17]

But much more importantly for Levi, the disappearance of shame in the *Lager* marked the death of human dignity in everyone involved:

> The personages in these pages are not men. Their humanity is buried, or they have buried it, under an offence received or inflicted on someone else. The evil and insane SS men, the Kapos, the politicals, the criminals, the prominents, great and small, down to the indifferent slave *Häftlinge* [inmates], all the grades of the mad hierarchy created by the Germans paradoxically fraternize in a uniform internal desolation.
>
> (Levi, 1986, pp. 121–122)

In the perpetrators, shamelessness precisely manifested itself in their transfor-mation into mindless robots or sadistic, ruthless torturers. In the victims, the loss of shame meant that, from the first days, in order to survive one would lie, steal, smuggle, work as little as possible—behavior that was unthinkable in life before Auschwitz. Memories of having so lived form one source of shame afterwards—"what I did to survive." Only after the Germans had fled and before the Russians arrived, he reported, could he begin to care for his fellow prisoners.

Much later (Levi, 1989), he distinguished—and Amy Simon (2011) has discussed in his work—at least four kinds of shame in survivors:

1   the extreme dehumanization beginning from arrival but only fully realizable retrospectively;[18]
2   the shame felt over not having actively resisted, notwithstanding the impossibility of doing so;
3   the memories of "having failed in terms of human solidarity"; and
4   what preoccupied Levi most, the "shame of the world," which he felt from the moment of liberation, and saw in others.

In the Russians who arrived after the Germans had abandoned the camp with the death march, Levi (1965, p. 16) observed

> a confused restraint, which sealed their lips and bound their eyes to the funereal scene. It was that shame we knew so well, the shame that drowned us after the selections, and every time we had to watch, or submit to, some outrage; the shame the Germans did not know, that the just man experiences at another man's crime; the feeling of guilt that such a crime should exist, that it should have been introduced irrevocably into the world of things that exist.

We sense this type of shame at being the same species as those who commit such crimes against the humanity of our brothers and sisters. Levi could feel it in their eyes, and he reported it many years later.[19] He wrote of *"una vergogna più vasta, la vergogna del mondo"* ("a vaster shame, the shame of the world"):

> The just among us . . . experienced remorse, shame, suffering, for the misdeeds that others and not they had committed, and in which nevertheless, they felt themselves involved, because they could see that what had happened around them and in their presence was irrevocable . . . that man, the species man, we in short, are capable of constructing an infinite enormity of pain.
> (Levi, 1986a, pp. 66–67, translated in Kleinberg-Levin, 2005, p. 221)

And yet, he believed this kind of shame was important, even indispensable: "I command to you (plural) [these words:] . . . Carve/engrave them into your heart, repeat them to your children . . . or may your house be destroyed, illness disable you, and your children turn their faces from you" (Levi, 1984b,

p. 5; my informal translation). In other words, without this kind of shame, we should be cursed. Not only is there no cure for shame over crimes against humanity; awareness that we belong to a species capable of dehumanizing its fellows to this extent is a shame from which we turn away at the peril of our own further dehumanization. This kind of shame forms the exact counterpart to the universal guilt and responsibility we will consider in Chapter 7 in the reading of Dostoevsky.

It may, however, be ultimately unbearable for some of its most prophetic witnesses, ethically sensitive, who had to live *"abbrutitto"* (brutish).

Suicide and human dignity

Levi considered suicide an act of human dignity, unavailable to the sub-humans *Lager* existence created, and wrote that, despite the constant availability of the highly electrified barbed wire, there were few suicides in the camps. Only when some minimal sense of dignity had been restored, he thought, could survivors consider whether a bearable life remained, and avail themselves of this "right we all have" (Thomson, 2003, p. 423). For Levi, this question did not occur in a vacuum. His grandfather had committed suicide in 1888 by precisely the method Levi himself employed a century later (Thomson, 2003). Little noticed, a reference to the earlier event occurs in Levi's *Il sistema periodico (The Periodic Table)* (1984a).

In my view—and that of both of his English-language biographers (Angier, 2002; Thomson, 2003)—Levi may have considered suicide, on and off, ever since his bullied childhood. On his return from the *Lager*, he felt, like the Ancient Mariner, a duty to tell the world, and especially the Germans, his ghastly tale. As he grew older, and more revisionists and minimizers dominated public discourse, he realized that he needed to write one more time. In interviews he suggested that to forget (*dimenticare*) meant to deny (*negare*), which would eventually mean to remake or redo (*rifare*) what he called the *strage* (massacre). He had told his story in memoir and fiction; now he needed to write reflections.

According to Cynthia Ozick (1988), *The Drowned and the Saved* forms Levi's long suicide note. She believes that his apparent clarity and detachment covered a rage that he finally expressed, that he could not maintain his distance from Jean Améry's fury.[20] Ultimately she subscribes to the Kleinian view that suicide is an act of rage, and uses this view to interpret Levi's last book. Much, though perhaps not all, in Levi's biography justifies her view. From childhood he had learned not to fight the bully but to walk away to the gym and the mountains and make himself stronger for the next trial. He learned to use his extraordinary intellect to out-wit the oppressor, and credited all these lessons with helping him to survive the *Lager*, and teaching him not to confront those who would simply have shot him. He often explained that having learned German quickly allowed him to obey the barked commands that others simply did not understand, and were shot for "disobeying"—"*morti per non capire*" ("dead for not understanding"). His first book, full of dispassionate and scientific description, damns more surely than any more passionate or eloquent tirade. A sleeper for many years, *If This Is a Man* exploded as he intended:

> Yes, I had written the book in Italian for Italians, for my children, for those who did not know, those who did not want to know, those who were not yet born, those who willing or not had assented to the offense; but its true recipients, those against whom the book was aimed like a gun, were they, the Germans. Now the gun was loaded . . . I would corner them, tie them before a mirror . . . Not that handful of high-ranking culprits, but them, the people, those I had seen from close up, those from among whom the SS militia were recruited, and also those others, those who had believed, who not believing had kept silent, who did not have the frail courage to look into our eyes, throw us a piece of bread, whisper a human word.
>
> (Levi, 1989, pp. 168–169)

These would not have been Levi's words, but, like Dostovesky and Levinas, he precisely understood ethics as the capacity to see the misery of others without turning away. Millions "did not have the frail courage to look into our eyes." To see would have been to be obligated, to be responsible. Toward the end of his long odyssey home in October 1945, he observed Germans in their own country:

> We felt we had something to say, enormous things to say, to every single German, and we felt that every German should have something to say to us; we felt an urgent need to settle our accounts, to ask, explain and comment, like chess players at the end of a game. Did "they" know about Auschwitz, about the silent daily massacre, a step away from their doors? If they did, how could they walk about, return home and look at their children, cross the threshold of a church? If they did not, they ought, as a sacred duty, to listen, to learn everything, immediately from us, from me; I felt the tattooed number on my arm, burning like a sore . . .
>
> [E]verybody should interrogate us, read in our faces who we were, and listen to our tale in humility. But no one looked us in the eyes, no one accepted the challenge; they were deaf, blind and dumb, imprisoned in their ruins, as in a fortress of willful ignorance, still strong, still capable of hatred and contempt, still prisoners of their old tangle of pride and guilt.
>
> (Levi, 1965, pp. 204–205)

"No one looked us in the eyes." For many years after the war, Levi visited Germany on business for his chemical company, perhaps twice a year. Often, he told interviewers, Germans would ask how an Italian came to speak German—this was unusual. "Oh," he replied simply, "I learned in Auschwitz." No one knew what to say next. Or he might be a guest in one of their homes where a child might ask about his tattoo. "Shall I tell her?" he would ask the parents. Clearly, they had not. He found both individual Germans and Germans generally without shame, and in his understated style observed that the industrialists of mass murder (Siemens, Bayer, Krupp) in West Germany continued to prosper: "The crematoria ovens themselves were designed, built, assembled, and tested by a German company Topf of Wiesbaden (it was still in operation in 1975, building crematoria for civilian use, and had not considered the advisability of changing its name)" (Levi, 1989, p. 16).

All over the world in the postwar years, he noted in interviews, the firms that had profited from the Nazi period flourished as millions bought "Hitler cars" (Volkswagens)[21] and Bayer aspirin. The Germans would never need to think about what they had done. But he did not give up easily. In the preface to the German edition of *If This Is a Man* he explicitly invited Germans to write to him to help him understand more. In his last book, having received their letters, he considered their justifications and evasions with his usual allergy to hypocrisy and to the slippage of memory.

Whether Levi viewed his last book as a lengthy suicide note, as Ozick (1988) believes, it functions as a transition from testimony to testament. The *Lager* had become his origin, deeply internalized. Asked by a Polish man where he came from, he responded, "I come from Auschwitz. *Sono hebraio italiano* [I am an Italian Jew]" (Levi, 1983). He explained to Alexander Stille (1987) that "he could remember literally everything that happened during his year as a prisoner. Forty years later he could recall entire sentences he had heard in languages he did not even know: Polish, Yiddish, Hungarian and Greek." Levi himself wrote that

> a host of details continued to surface in my memory and the idea of letting them fade distressed me. A great number of human figures especially stood out against that tragic background: friends, people I'd traveled with, even adversaries—begging me one after another to help them survive and enjoy the ambiguous perennial existence of literary characters.
>
> (Levi, 1986b, p. vii)

Ultimately, this burden of remembering—so similar to the one clinicians carry for their many seriously devastated patients—may have overwhelmed him. He had already fought off serious depressions before he was ever deported, and he seemed to be saying he had done all he could—for his wife and mother, for the world. *Non ce lo faccio piu* (I can't do it any more). I read his suicide less as rage than as the exhaustion of a sensitive soul. He joined the ranks of the drowned, finally, but with dignity, of his own choice, with his work done.

My partial guess—given the biographical hints we have, surely nothing Levi's scientific mind would accept as cast-iron evidence—would be that his early life with a mother who never freed him to his dying day left him forever incarcerated. Jean-Jacques Blévis, a French Lacanian, warns us to think contextually about trauma even in Levi's extreme instance (Blévis, 2004). My colleague Anna Ornstein, who also bears the Auschwitz tattoo, believes that those who had solid family resources in early life recovered better afterwards. She also notes without explaining, however, that

> Suicide was also the fate of several writers who survived the Holocaust: Jean Améry, Primo Levi, Paul Celan, and Tadeusz Borowski. Considering the relatively small number of survivors who were accomplished writers, this is a very high number, especially since suicide among Holocaust survivors was not more frequent than in the general population.
>
> (Ornstein, 2006, p. 301)

More recently, Rachel Rosenblum (2009) has speculated that the very telling and retelling of the "ghastly tale" of a major historical trauma (I think also of the Chilean and Argentinian dictatorships, of apartheid in South Africa, of slavery in the United States, and many others), the very work of witnessing in the face of so much indifference, may finally have cast them into despair. Rosenblum (2009, p. 1319) writes:

> When survivors remain silent, they are often condemned to desiccated existence, a dried-out life, a death in life. But when they speak out, and in particular when they do so in public, they are running an even greater risk. Telling the "ghastly tale" may, in some cases, trigger not only serious somatic trouble, psychotic episodes, but suicide.

She notes that Levi himself told of a recurrent dream in the camp of returning home, trying to tell his story, and meeting complete indifference. Everyone walks away. The dreamer feels despair and futility—in some views the primary explanation for Levi's suicide (e.g., Titelman, 2006). Both Rosenblum (2009) and Chasseguet-Smirgel (2000), on the other hand, believe that Levi could not believe his own testimony at some level; that he was of "split mind"; that some realities simply destroy our capacity to integrate. Telling again and again what he himself could not believe, when his initial psychological conditions had not been good enough, may ultimately have created a strain he could not bear.

Rosenblum questions the extent to which the clinician should upset the fragile balance produced by extreme dehumanization and the impossibility of normal feeling and mourning in these situations. Doing our ordinary job with survivors of torture and death camps may be playing with fire. Just as Leonard Shengold—explicitly relating his work to Primo Levi's story—writes that working with the soul-murdered is never for the faint of heart or for those who do not have many years to give (and which of us really knows about this?), therapy with victims of massacres requires special conditions.

Didier Anzieu writes of this contrast: "To analyse, in its original sense, means to unbind, to cut, to undo the links. However there are extreme situations where, on the contrary, binding is absolutely necessary" (Anzieu, 1990, quoted in Rosenblum, 2009, p. 1335). Dori Laub (Felman and Laub, 1992), who has given so much of his life to recording the testimonies of survivors (Levi would simply have said "those who returned"), has also spoken of what they need if testifying of what they have seen and suffered is not to destroy them.

According to Rosenblum (2009, p. 1335), the analyst or therapist functions in three ways: "authenticating witness, the sanctuary provider, the experience-sharing companion." The listener–witness confirms, first, that the victim is not the perpetrator. We must note that, as in child abuse and rape, victims of genocide and torture have usually been convinced by their torturers that something about them causes them to be so mistreated. This greatly complicates working with the guilt and shame discussed briefly above. Doing evil and suffering mistreatment remain fundamentally different, even if the victims had to cooperate, steal, lie, and smuggle to survive. The listener–witness also continually confirms, against the fogginess of memory, against the revisionists, and contrary to those who say, "You must be exaggerating," that these historical events actually occurred, and were actually greater in horror and scale than any one victim could realize.[22]

Second, the "sanctuary provider" provides a binding-up function that the survivor can stabilize to some degree, placing some limit on the power of the past to overwhelm the present. The patient gradually becomes witness to his or her own completely unbearable history, holding it away from everyday life, but not denied.

Third, sharing the experience "into the eye of the hurricane" means that the victim no longer remains completely alone. The therapist becomes the listener who does not walk away from the "ghastly tale" as in Primo Levi's dream, so that he does not have to keep walking away from it himself.

Back to Primo Levi, chemist that he was, he turned to chemistry first for his recurrent bouts of extreme depression. Antidepressants were, of course, relatively primitive in those years. His lifelong friend and fellow Auschwitz survivor Luciana Nissim Momigliano, one of Italy's most prominent psychoanalysts, must have urged him toward therapy. Reserved and self-reliant Torinese that he was, he seems not to have tried it until the very end, and too late. But I believe that he needed witnesses, sanctuary, as well as someone who could understand his original emotional situation. We can never know, however: he often said that he chose not to forget anything, to live with his memories, for the sake of the rest of us who need to remember better. On a return visit to Auschwitz, he answered his interlocutor: "*Mi ricordo benissimo!* [I remember very well!]."

Levi's belief that suicide could be an act of human dignity in the face of unbearable humiliation stands as a challenge to any of us who rush to interpret his suicide too quickly, or any suicide as an unalloyed failure. His years of relentless testimony, likewise, stand as ringing testament to the centrality of human dignity in all humanitarian work, including the clinical. Now we turn to his inner resources.[23]

Levi's internal chorus: a song of humanity

Even after Levi's death, the central chapter from *If This Is a Man* haunts. Famously entitled "The Canto of Ulysses," it follows story upon story of dehumanizing degradation, and precedes the story of the October selection with the coming of the dreaded second winter. It seems a moment of light in the darkness (or, as Levi put it, the bottom).

A young Frenchman, Jean, known to the commando as the Pikolo, was designated to walk for an hour each day to fetch the soup at noon for the prisoners. For a few days Levi, appointed to help him, took advantage of the chance for conversation and lighter work. Jean wanted to learn Italian, so Levi—having been required as a child to memorize much of Dante's *Commedia*—began to recite Canto XXVI from the *Inferno*—the story of Odysseus' return home—explaining it in French and Italian to his young companion as they walked along:

> *Considerate la vostra semenza:*
> *Fatti non foste a viver come bruti,*
> *Ma per seguir virtute e conoscenza.*
> [Think of your breed:
> You were not made to live like brutes,
> But to pursue excellence and knowledge.] . . .

> As if I was hearing it for the first time: like the blast of a trumpet, like the voice of God. For the moment I forget who I am and where I am.
> (Levi, 1996, p. 113)

What is Levi telling us here? Surely not only that there were isolated moments in which his cultural heritage helped him to survive. He proclaims with Dante that human dignity is more than the absence of dehumanizing degradation, that we are meant to pursue what Aristotle called "*arête*", excellence, and wisdom. Still, a moment later he feels himself nothing but a hungry stomach and a shirt on which a capo can mindlessly wipe his greasy hand. Reminders of human dignity, in Levi's ironic idiom, may be little more than teases and temptations. But well he knew about words carved on the heart.

Much as he loved Dante—and Dante echoes in much of his work—he had no patience for any religious worldview that appealed to divine providence. Perhaps his angriest words came out after the selection:

> From my bunk on the top row, I see and hear old Kuhn praying aloud, with his beret on his head, swaying backwards and forwards violently. Kuhn is thanking God because he has not been chosen . . . Kuhn is out of his senses. Does he see Beppo the Greek in the bunk next to him, Beppo who is twenty years old and is going to the gas-chamber the day after tomorrow and knows it and lies there looking fixedly at the light without saying anything and without even thinking any more? Can Kuhn fail to realize that next time it will be his turn? Does Kuhn not understand that what has happened today is an abomination, which no propitiatory prayer, no pardon, no expiation by the guilty, which nothing at all in the power of man can ever clean again.
>
> If I was God, I would spit at Kuhn's prayer.
>
> (Levi, 1996, p. 91)

We will take up the question of forgiveness in a later chapter, but for the moment note that Levi joins my other skeptical choristers, Dostoevsky and Levinas, on petitionary prayer to a providential god who prefers some over others, a god who selects just as the Nazis did. His task, at which he ultimately judged himself to have failed, was to make others—in particular, collaborators who had pretended not to know what was happening in the camps—see themselves. Of his first book in German translation, he wrote (and I quote again here), "Its true recipients, those against whom the book was aimed like a gun . . . Before they were oppressors or indifferent spectators, now they would be readers: I would corner them, tie them before a mirror" (Levi, 1989, p. 168).

But no matter the reasons for Levi's ultimate choice of suicide, Samuel Gerson's (2009) understanding makes sense to me. He reads Levi's late poem "Unfinished Business" as "a vision of living one's life with a sense of integrity" (2009, p. 1351), even if it cannot be all that one hoped. Creativity, comments Gerson, does not erase destruction. It may have enabled Levi, as it enables many of us, to live useful and generative lives for many years, to witness to crimes against humanity, to protest injustice and to work to restore dignity where we can. But in the face of massacres, the "fundamental work" may be beyond us.

Even the secondary work, to which Levi gave his remaining life—the work of telling the "ghastly tale" and exploring its dire meanings—was thwarted.

In the *Lager* he learned "*Hier ist kein Warum!*" For a scientist, such a statement was not only an insult, but an ultimate absurdity. He then spent 40 years asking why, and trying to explain, and concluded "too bad." It was too much, and besides, people were not interested. Tzvetan Todorov (1996, p. 271) writes of him: "Just as Levi overestimated his ability to understand the enemy without suffering the consequences of that understanding, so did he underestimate the weight of the world." Humanitarian workers, including clinicians, may be familiar with this.

During and after his year in Auschwitz, Levi suffered a recurrent nightmare in which he left the *Lager* to return home and tell in detail what the camp had been like. No one listened; they continued talking as if he were not there; finally they got up and walked away without saying a word. Unfortunately, the dream, not unique to Levi, came true. He failed to persuade us to hear.

In Chapter 7 we will consider, via Dostoevsky and Levinas, ethical seeing. It seems that we need both our eyes and our ears open to be vulnerable enough to the suffering of others to respond. Otherwise we deserve Levi's prophetic curse. Like those of Dostoevsky and Levinas, Levi's voice in the chorus warns against complacency and indifference to the plight of others, against ethical blindness, against ignoring the lessons of history. It perhaps speaks to displaced Palestinians and Syrians, to the homeless and humiliated everywhere, and, above all, to those of us who may not see our brothers and sisters. Levi's poetry, near his death, no longer distinguished so clearly between the drowned and himself. By then they had become his companions, his brothers and sisters, those whose fate he barely escaped and could no longer carry.

Notes

1 I am grateful to Nancy Smith's (2004) brief but elegant piece on Levi for bringing this sentence to my attention.
2 For me, it has been touching to discover that one of his closest companions, deported with him and later refound, was the same Luciana Nissim Momigliano whose book with Andreina Robutti I reviewed about twenty years ago. Though I knew nothing of her history, I felt she possessed a clear and honest psychoanalytic voice. She provided Levi's biographer Ian Thomson with a great deal of personal and valuable information about their lives before, during, and after Auschwitz. Levi himself was more reserved.
3 This despite his repeated disavowal of the prophet's vocation.
4 Describing these first months, he wrote:

> I, too, began to tell my story even before my physical hunger was satiated, and I have not finished even now. I had become similar to the ancient mariner in Coleridge's ballad, who goes into the street and buttonholes guests on their way to a party in order to inflict on them his sinister story of evil doings and ghosts. I repeated my stories dozens of times in just a few days, to friends, enemies and strangers. Then I realized that my tale was crystallizing into a

definitive and unchanging form. All I needed in order to write all down was paper, pen and time. Time, which now is so scarce, grew up around me as if by enchantment: I wrote at night, in the train, in the factory canteen, in the factory itself, in the middle of the din of machinery. I wrote quickly, with no hesitation and no order . . . everything seemed to write itself. In just a few months the work was finished. Prompted by the urgency of my memories, I had written the seventeen chapters almost exactly in reverse order, starting, that is, with last one. Then I wrote the preface, and finally I added an epigraph, a poem which had been dancing around my head even while I was in Auschwitz, and which I had written down a few days after my return.

(Levi et al., 2005, pp. 24–25)

5 His book was published in the United States as *Survival in Auschwitz* (1986c). Levi hated this change of title. For him, the book was not about his survival; it concerned the methods of dehumanization of both perpetrators and victims. His second book, *La Tregua* (*The Truce*), the story of his long journey home from Auschwitz, appeared in English as *The Reawakening* (1965).

6 James Hatley comments:

it can be argued that the guard physically dismisses him not simply because Levi has spoken out of turn but because he has spoken at all. The guard desires, in his rage against Levi [I would say against a nameless nobody], to intimidate Levi to the point that he would not even dare to speak. The guard does not simply wish that Levi would obey him, he would have Levi behave *as if* he were faceless.

(Hatley, 2005, p. 43; original emphasis)

7 Langer (2011) points out that 18 is the Hebrew character for life, so Levi's decision to describe this particular prisoner as *Null Achtzehn* (No Life) was probably intentional. "018" would have been the last three of the six numbers tattooed on this man's arm. He had lost his previous name.

8 Short version of "*Konzentrationslager*" (KZ), the term still used today on directional signs pointing to the former camps.

9 Levi resolutely opposed Israeli settlements in the occupied territories, and signed a letter to *La Repubblica* in 1982 calling on Menachem Begin to resign (Thomson, 2003). He lost old friends, including a close one from the *Lager*, over this stance.

10 In a great irony, the great preacher of "peace of mind" Rabbi Joshua Liebman (1946) prevented Levi's work from being published in the United States for almost 20 years (see Thomson, 2003). Levi disturbed the peace too much for Liebman's liking.

11 Some scholars speculate that the name came from the hunched-over posture of these hopeless ones, reminding others of Muslims at prayer.

12 He usually spoke of "*i rediti*" ("the returned") rather than "survivors."

13 Watching Levi in interviews, one gains a sense of him as a compact, understated Italian whose hand gestures are small, eyes expressive, language extremely clear and carefully chosen (as in his writing). Nothing is exaggerated, so his words strike hard. Like Dostoevsky, he had returned from the house of the dead, but he knew this house had been precisely planned to eliminate his people, and others, from the earth.

14 A clinical reflection here on the patterns we survivors of early trauma develop and carry along into our later lives would be easy, but it would disrupt the story about Levi.

15 Clinicians may recognize the phenomenon that Leonard Shengold, borrowing from Schreber, has called "soul murder." For Shengold's meditation on Levi's

discussion of the *Sonderkommandos*, and their relation to the difficulty of clinical work with the soul-murdered, see Shengold (1992).

16 Recent psychoanalytic studies of shame generally distinguish clearly between guilt for transgressions creating debt and/or feelings of guiltiness, as in Freud's Oedipal guilt for the desired parricide, and shame over one's very being in the eyes of others or one's own eyes (Kilborne, 1999; Lansky, 1994; Morrison, 1984; Orange, 2008; Wurmser, 1991).

17 This is an extract from my own translation of Levi's "The Survivor." The full poem (with a different translation) is available in Levi et al. (1992).

18 Perhaps the shame described by Jean Améry belongs here: "Whoever has succumbed to torture [I think he means whomever has been tortured] can no longer feel at home in the world. The shame of destruction cannot be erased" (Améry, 1980, p. 40).

19 Unlike Giorgio Agamben (1999), Levi firmly refused to conflate the guilt and shame of perpetrators, victims, and bystanders.

20 Améry had called Levi a "forgiver." Levi (1989, p. 137) commented:

> I consider this neither insult nor praise but imprecision. I am not inclined to forgive. I never forgave our enemies of that time, nor do I feel I can forgive their imitators in Algeria, Vietnam, the Soviet Union, Chile, Argentina, Cambodia, or South Africa, because I know no human act that can erase a crime, but I am not able, personally, to trade punches, or return blows.

21 With shame I now realize that the only car I wanted in my youth was a VW Beetle. I gave no thought to its origins; nor did I ask who might be profiting from my purchase.

22 I am deeply grateful to Dori Laub and Rachel Rosenblum for these understandings, and apologize to them if my elaborations are unfaithful to their insights in any way.

23 Late in life, he edited an anthology of 30 of his favorite pieces of literature. He said that this exposed him more than anything he had ever done previously (Levi, 2001).

References

Agamben, G. (1999). *Remnants of Auschwitz: The Witness and the Archive*. New York: Zone Books.

Améry, J. (1980). *At the Mind's Limits: Contemplations by a Survivor on Auschwitz and Its Realities*. Bloomington, IN: Indiana University Press.

Angier, C. (2002). *The Double Bond: Primo Levi, a Biography*. London and New York: Viking.

Anzieu, D. (1990). *Psychic Envelopes*. London: Karnac Books.

Blévis, J. (2004). Remains to be Transmitted: Primo Levi's Traumatic Dream. *Psychoanalytic Quarterly*, 73, 751–770.

Chasseguet-Smirgel, J. (2000). Trauma et croyance. *Revue Francaise Psychanalyse*, 64, 39–46.

Felman, S., and Laub, D. (1992). *Testimony: Crises of Witnessing in Literature, Psychoanalysis, and History*. New York: Routledge.

Gerson, S. (2009). When the Third is Dead: Memory, Mourning, and Witnessing in the Aftermath of the Holocaust. *International Journal of Psychoanalysis*, 90, 1341–1357.

Hatley, J. (2005). Beyond Outrage: The Delirium or Responsibiity in Levinas's Scene of Persecution. In E. Nelson, A. Kapust, and K. Still (Eds.), *Addressing Levinas* (pp. 34–51). Evanston, IL: Northwestern University Press.

Herman, J. (2011). Posttraumatic Stress Disorder as a Shame Disorder. In R. Dearing and J. Tangney (Eds.), *Shame in the Therapy Hour* (pp. 261–276). Washington, DC: American Psychological Association.

Hobbes, T., and Curley, E. M. (1994). *Leviathan: With Selected Variants from the Latin Edition of 1668.* Indianapolis, IN: Hackett.

Kilborne, B. (1999). Shame in Context. *Journal of the American Psychoanalytic Association*, 47, 949–952.

Kleinberg-Levin, D. (2005). Persecution: The Self at the Heart of Metaphysics. In E. Nelson, A. Kapust, and K. Still (Eds.), *Addressing Levinas* (pp. 199–235). Evanston, IL: Northwestern University Press.

Langer, L. (2011). The Survivor as Author: Primo Levi's Literary Vision of Auschwitz. In R. Sodi and M. Marcus (Eds.), *New Reflections on Primo Levi* (pp. 133–147). New York: Macmillan.

Lansky, M. R. (1994). Shame. *Journal of the American Academy of Psychoanalysis*, 22, 433–441.

Levi, P. (1965). *The Reawakening (La tregua): A Liberated Prisoner's Long March Home through East Europe* (1st US edn.). Boston: Little.

Levi, P. (1983). *Primo Levi, Back to Auschwitz* [video interview]. Retrieved from https://www.youtube.com/watch?v=lA7Xa2ANx2c (accessed August 24, 2015).

Levi, P. (1984a). *The Periodic Table* (1st US edn.). New York: Schocken Books.

Levi, P. (1984b). *Se questo e un uomo* (14th edn.). Torino: G. Einaudi.

Levi, P. (1986a). *I sommersi e i salvati.* Torino: G. Einaudi.

Levi, P. (1986b). *Moments of Reprieve.* New York: Summit Books.

Levi, P. (1986c). *Survival in Auschwitz and The Reawakening: Two Memoirs.* New York: Summit Books.

Levi, P. (1989). *The Drowned and the Saved.* New York: Vintage International.

Levi, P. (1996). *Survival in Auschwitz: The Nazi Assault on Humanity.* New York: Simon & Schuster.

Levi, P. (2001). *The Search for Roots: A Personal Anthology.* London: Allen Lane and Penguin Press.

Levi, P., and Belpoliti, M. (1997). *Opere.* Torino: G. Einaudi.

Levi, P., Belpoliti, M., and Wood, S. (2005). *The Black Hole of Auschwitz.* Cambridge and Malden, MA: Polity.

Levi, P., Feldman, R., and Swann, B. (1992). *Collected Poems* (new edn.). London and Boston, MA: Faber & Faber.

Liebman, J. (1946). *Peace of Mind.* New York: Simon & Schuster.

Morrison, A. (1984). Working with Shame in Psychoanalytic Treatment. *Journal of the American Psychoanalytic Association*, 32, 479–505.

Orange, D. (2008). Whose Shame Is It Anyway? Lifeworlds of Humiliation and Systems of Restoration. *Contemporary Psychoanalysis*, 44, 83–100.

Ornstein, A. (2006). Artistic Creativity and the Healing Process. *Psychoanalytic Inquiry*, 26, 386–406.

Ozick, C. (1988). The Suicide Note. *The New Republic*, March 21, pp. 32–35.

Rosenblum, R. (2009). Postponing Trauma: The Dangers of Telling. *International Journal of Psychoanalysis*, 90, 1319–1340.

Sessi, F. (2013). *Il lungo viaggio di Primo Levi: la scelta della resistenza, il tradimento, l'arresto: una storia taciuta.* Venezia: Marsilio.

Shengold, L. (1992). Commentary on "Dissociative Processes and Transference–Countertransference Paradigms ..." by Jody Messler Davies and Mary Gail Frawley. *Psychoanalytic Dialogues,* 2, 49–59.

Simon, A. (2011). Guilt or Shame? In S. Pugliese (Ed.), *Answering Auschwitz: Primo Levi's Science and Humanism after the Fall* (pp. 31–40). New York: Fordham University Press.

Smith, N. (2004). "To Return, to Eat, to Tell the Story": Primo Levi's Lessons on Living and Dying in the Aftermath of Trauma. *International Forum of Psychoanalysis,* 13, 66–70.

Stille, A. (1987). Primo Levi: Reconciling the Man and the Writer. *New York Times,* July 5.

Thomson, I. (2003). *Primo Levi: A Life* (1st US edn.). New York: Metropolitan Books.

Titelman, D. (2006). Primo Levi's Loneliness: Psychoanalytic Perspectives on Suicide-Nearness. *Psychoanalytic Quarterly,* 75, 835–858.

Todorov, T. (1996). *Facing the Extreme: Moral Life in the Concentration Camps* (1st US edn.). New York: Metropolitan Books.

Wurmser, L. (1991). Shame: The Underside of Narcissism. *Psychoanalytic Quarterly,* 60, 667–672.

Yetman, N. R., and Federal Writers' Project (2002). *When I Was a Slave: Memoirs from the Slave Narrative Collection.* Mineola, NY: Dover Publications.

Chapter 6

Substitution

Nelson Mandela and Dietrich Bonhoeffer

As I walked out the door toward the gate that would lead to my freedom, I knew if I didn't leave my bitterness and hatred behind, I'd still be in prison.

(Mandela)

I pray for the defeat of my country, for I think that is the only possibility of paying for all the suffering that my country has caused in the world.
(Bonhoeffer quoted in Schlingensiepen, 2010, p. 269)

Ethical responsibility, in extreme situations, calls for radical sacrifice. Two members of my internal chorus came to understand this clearly, and prepared themselves to undertake it from their early years. Both built up their own interior lives, and relied on others to support their radical decisions. Both, in a strong sense, chose their awful fate, and reflected on it, fortunately for us. Their stories therefore illustrate what clinicians need for survival, even if we may never be called to live in prison, to fear torture, or to be murdered. Each wrote of his prison experiences from prison (Bonhoeffer and Bethge, 1971; Mandela, 1995), so we have some primary sources.

First, however, having already considered forms of responsibility beyond personal and professional integrity, fidelity to contractual obligations, and even the ordinary norms of goodness, having imagined the turn to the other's face, let us listen again. Suppose the habit of response to the other, of being at the other's disposal, of seeing the other as infinitely valuable, begins to create a crisis of conscience. It is as if we begin to see and hear differently, as if traces and resonances from that irrecuperable, unrepresentable past come over us, and there seems "no limit or measure for this responsibility" (Levinas, 1981, p. 47). In extreme situations human limits may face a clear requirement for an ultimate sacrifice for the sake of human others, a substitution, whose nature becomes increasingly clear. I tell the stories of these two examples of ethical substitution to inspire clinicians—even if these extreme sacrifices may not be demanded of each of us—and to illustrate the process of using our internal resources.

Because this chapter considers two figures of great importance to me, its structure will differ from that of these other central chapters. Life and work will embed themselves in the ethical story; indeed they *are* the ethical story.

Nelson Mandela: dignity for all

Nelson Mandela learned Afrikaans. Neither by chance nor by brilliance, nor in the end by force, did he mitigate the fears of the ruling white minority in apartheid South Africa. He studied their language, their history, their culture and habits, even their sports. Just as clinicians and other humanitarians learn the languages of those they serve and seek to understand, Mandela practiced his language skills on his prison warders for many years. When he needed to negotiate in secret the freedom and full equality for his comrades and indeed all his people, he already spoke Afrikaans fluently.[1] Former *New York Times* Johannesburg bureau chief John F. Burns reported an act of "particular kindness" from his press conference at Desmond Tutu's residence the day after Mandela left prison in 1990:

> a white reporter stepped forward and identified himself as Clarence Keyter, the chief political correspondent of the Afrikaans-language service of the state-run broadcasting monopoly, SABC. Sensing Mr. Keyter's unease, Mr. Mandela shook the reporter's hand and thanked him, saying that in his last years in prison, when he had been given a radio, he had relied on Mr. Keyter's reports to learn "what was going on in my country." Mr. Keyter, stunned, had tears welling in his eyes.
>
> (Burns, 2014)

Such an act of kindness became possible, of course, not only because Mandela had devoted years to learning Afrikaans, but also because he then possessed the sensitivity to respond in the moment. Few have noticed, in celebrating the life of "the great reconciliator," his disciplined attention to the specific proficiencies needed for such peacemaking. To make war skill-fully, as he had learned as a young man from Walter Sisulu and Oliver Tambo, demanded planning, preparation, and a cool head. To stop war, to overcome hatred and fear, to build a functioning nation demanded different skills, but no less unrelenting effort.

To introduce a man whose quiet dignity inspires me and others through-out the world, I begin with this concrete example, chosen not at random but because language itself both murders and welcomes. This moment of Mandela's recent "transition" gives those he has taught the chance to listen again to what he would be telling us now. I am told that in the world of his origins, dying means he has transitioned into a state from which he can now speak to us more directly than before. I hear several messages coming through his life and words.

My own voice speaks, of necessity, from a hesitant place in these matters. The path of return requires hard reconciliation—none of what Dietrich Bonhoeffer called "cheap grace" (Bonhoeffer and Fuller, 1949, p. 43)—after extensive human rights abuses and explosive conflicts, as well as answers to the insistent demands of transitional justice. Not only has my indirect contact with this giant of history—whom South Africans affectionately call "Madiba," his clan name, or "Tata" (Dad)[2]—been limited to a three-day visit to Cape Town, including excursions to his tiny cell on Robben Island and to the museum of the Sixth District. Much more, I write from the United States, where the work of confronting our legacy of human rights violations, destruction of indigenous peoples, and hundreds of years of slavery (Davis, 2006) has scarcely begun. We white Americans, barely realizing that we are white because we assume we are simply "normal," almost never speak directly of our own crimes.

Mandela delegated the problems of human rights abuses to the Truth and Reconciliation Commission (TRC). He understood his own responsibility as the first president of all South Africans in a specific way, and believed it must fall to others to detail the injustices he had spent his life working to abolish. But South Africa after apartheid has inherited overwhelming economic injustice and continuing mental apartheid, so that the silent rage of so many years has begun to explode. Without faulting Mandela's trade-off—his clarity placed political equality before everything else—South Africans now find themselves faced with his unfinished work even as we and they mourn his departure.

In another instance of official forgetting, British and American victors colluded to silence those who would have faced ordinary Germans with their responsibility for the deliberate massacre called holocaust or shoah.[3] In April 1945, British filmmakers accompanied the British and US soldiers who liberated Bergen-Belsen and eight other concentration camps. They compiled 55 minutes of indescribably gruesome footage in which well-fed SS guards were made to bury thousands of horribly emaciated bodies, while similarly well-fed townspeople from no more than two or three kilometers away were made to watch. From other camps, also right next to towns, the footage showed gas chambers and crematoria. In some camps there were survivors to be nursed back to life, survivors too ill to eat or drink; in other camps there was evidence that inmates had been shot on the approach of the Allies. Alfred Hitchcock assembled all this extremely harrowing footage and prepared its narration by Trevor Howard; but then it was buried, deemed too difficult for the German people to see. Someone made the decision that Germany's postwar reconstruction was more important. Only in January 2014 did the film become available for anyone who wanted to Google "Memory of the Camps." As in South Africa, we buried stories of atrocity in the service of important political objectives, but this decision has borne costs.

A third instance: American slavery. Perhaps if we do not say these words, we can all get along as if we all just fell out of the sky onto the North American continent, intended by a provident god to have the social and economic privileges that we have. Puzzling, then, why some people seem resentful about their lower-class status. If they would just work harder, stay out of prison, remain in school, they could do as well as my children do. All these bemused reactions make sense when history remains invisible: the atrocities of apartheid; memories of the camps; the daily indignities and violence of slavery.

Madiba—here I use his South African name deliberately—accomplished something extraordinary that few have noticed: he articulated in English and acted out in Afrikaans the African communitarian philosophy of *ubuntu* (we are what we are together)—in the context of the United Nations Declaration of Human Rights. Misunderstood, even by philosophers as prominent as Derrida (Mandela et al., 1987), to be writing a new version of Rousseau's social contract theory (a radical Western individualism), Mandela instead assumed a fundamental human solidarity; egoistic behavior is a deviation. When, in all his early writings, he contrasted law with conscience, he meant that laws like apartheid were unjust because conscience called everyone to struggle for basic human solidarity and equality. Born into the African assumptions, he could learn and love Western culture and law without ever accepting its foundational ethics. Like his friend Desmond Tutu—the poet Antjie Krog (1998, 2013) speaks of the politician and his prophet—Mandela could talk of Western justice ethics while working from their own native communitarian *ubuntu*.

Born in 1918 to a Xhosa family of African royalty but completely without rights in a South Africa ever more dominated by apartheid, Nelson (a name assigned to him in school) Rolihlahla Mandela said that he inherited from his father, who died in his childhood, both his rebelliousness and his intense sense of fairness. Taken into the care of the local chieftain, he was sent to the local Methodist school, where he was impressed by European culture. Later, he finished high school at an African boarding school, then began his studies at the University of Fort Hare, an elite institution for black students. Involved in a student boycott over the quality of the institution's food, he was suspended and did not receive his degree. But he met friends like Oliver Tambo who would be important in later anti-apartheid struggles.

On his return home in 1941, he learned that a marriage had been arranged for him, so he fled to Johannesburg, where he attended law school and began to work in the legal profession. He also made his first contacts with the African National Congress (ANC). The rest of the 1940s saw him developing relationships with all those who would be central in his later struggles and trials, while refusing to join with the communists—that is, to turn the struggle against racism into a class struggle—and insisting that the struggle must be kept non-violent. (He later explained that non-violence failed to achieve justice in South Africa, so it had to be abandoned.) He also married for the first time and started a treasured family in these years, but this ultimately fell victim to the political struggles that lay ahead.

In 1948, the government codified apartheid so that it controlled every aspect of life for blacks, whites, and "coloreds." Every black resident of South Africa had to carry a pass, and was banned from white areas except at specified times and for specified purposes. Immediately the ANC began to organize serious resistance, and Mandela, devoting most of his time to political struggle, failed his university exams three times. Gradually he became convinced that, much as he admired Gandhi, non-violent means would not suffice for South Africa, so he lobbied the ANC to allow him to organize the section of the organization that was devoted to armed struggle— the Umkhonto we Sizwe (Spear of the Nation).

Because of his education and legal training, Mandela became the voice of the movement in two famous trials, though others did much of the organizational work. During the 1950s, and later in prison, he worked closely with these colleagues, several of whom were imprisoned with him. Gradually, he became the international face of South African oppression, as many of us remember. "Free Nelson Mandela" became the rallying cry. He, however, would not allow himself to be freed until all South Africans obtained full equality. He would frequently declare: "This isn't right."[4]

Injustice bothered Mandela all his life. As a young man faced with the blatant injustice of increasingly rigid apartheid laws, he channeled his rage into physical training and legal education, eventually becoming South Africa's first black attorney and preparing himself to represent his people in the great trials and the country's first truly representative government. For a time he willingly lived in hiding because the state regarded him as a terrorist. In prison he calmly confronted the small injustices: the differences in food, clothing, privileges. Why should black political prisoners have to wear short pants while Indian and colored prisoners were granted the dignity of long pants? "This isn't right."

He endured nearly 20 years on Robben Island,[5] where his eyesight suffered from working in the limestone quarry without sunglasses. From 1982 to 1988 he lived in Pollsmoor Prison near Cape Town, until he contracted tuberculosis in the dank conditions and was transferred to Victor Verster to serve out the final two years of his imprisonment. Only once in all these years did he erupt in rage, over an insult to his second wife Winnie. "I have mellowed," he told Richard Stengel, who helped him write his autobiography. "I was very radical as a young man, fighting everybody, using high-flown language" (Stengel, 2010, p. 51). By the time he emerged from prison after 27 years of incarceration, he had become the quietly dignified leader of his people.

How did this transformation happen? In prison Mandela learned to value self-control over self-expression. The "man without bitterness" whose measured style reassured white leaders and whose response prevented civil war when Chris Hani was assassinated in 1993 also hid his pain and anger. Just as he considered courage a choice to act in the face of real fear, he chose his calm and measured public style at a personal cost he rarely acknowledged. In addition to "Robben Island University"—which he organized with his comrades Walter Sisulu and Ahmed Kathrada to study history and political science during their incarceration—he developed his spiritual resources while in prison.

Who belonged to Mandela's internal chorus? An intense sense of justice and human equality seems to have undergirded all the voices; for him, other elements (non-violence, socialism, and so on) served only as "tactics." He had attended a Methodist school as a child, and he went to church with his family, but he kept any religious beliefs very much to himself. African tribal leaders remained important inspirations, but he refused to consider thinkers like Marx and Gandhi, who have proved so crucial for others, authoritative. Two voices clearly ring out as key influences: William Shakespeare and Abraham Lincoln.

When someone brought the complete works of Shakespeare to Robben Island in 1980 and asked the prisoners to choose a favorite passage, Mandela did not hesitate (Stengel, 2010). He turned straight to *Julius Caesar* (Act 2, Scene 2):

> Cowards die many times before their deaths;
> The valiant never taste of death but once.
> Of all the wonders that I yet have heard
> It seems to me most strange that men should fear,
> Seeing that death, a necessary end,
> Will come when it will come.

In addition to drawing inspiration from Shakespeare, Mandela engaged in the ancient philosophers' meditation on death, the spiritual practice intended to help us to live in the present moment. He often used this exercise to reduce his fear, as we can hear in his closing words at the "Rivonia Trial" of 1963–1964, when he faced the probability of a death sentence:

> During my lifetime I have dedicated myself to this struggle of the African people. I have fought against white domination, and I have fought against black domination. I have cherished the ideal of a democratic and free society in which all persons live together in harmony with equal opportunities. It is an ideal which I hope to live for and to achieve. But if needs be, it is an ideal for which I am prepared to die.
>
> (Mandela, 2010, pp. 121–122)

So the meditation on death (see Chapter 4) had begun even before the Robben Island years.

Abraham Lincoln appears in Mandela's image-conscious style of leadership, in his keeping rivals close (Stengel, 2010) and learning their language, and even in his speeches. In his crucial address to the nation on the death of Chris Hani in 1993, prior to the first free elections that carried him to the presidency, we can hear Lincoln:

> This is a watershed moment for all of us. Our decisions and actions will determine whether we use our pain, our grief, and our outrage to move forward to what is the only lasting solution for our country—an elected government of the people, by the people, and for the people.
>
> (Mandela, 2010, p. 338)

We might wish to know more of Mandela's inner life and its inhabitants, but what we do glimpse provides continuity with his public life. His example of deliberate personal growth based on reflection on the example of others offers a way to reflect on his extraordinary work toward justice.

Unexpectedly, Mandela developed his character through the examination of conscience. One might not expect a South African political prisoner to practice this spiritual exercise, which is taught to every monastic novice. Nevertheless, he described it in detail in a letter from prison to his wife Winnie, who was imprisoned herself in 1975. First he set out the values to be sought:

> In judging our progress as individuals we tend to concentrate on external factors such as one's social position, influence and popularity, wealth and standard of education. These are, of course, important in measuring one's success in material matters and it is perfectly understandable if many people exert themselves mainly to achieve all these. But internal factors may be even more crucial in assessing one's development as a human being. Honesty, sincerity, simplicity, humility, pure generosity, absence of vanity, readiness to serve others are the foundation of one's spiritual life.
>
> (Mandela, 2010, p. 271)

To refocus on these matters, however, would require discipline. Mandela had found a method that worked for him:

> [Y]ou may find that the cell is an ideal place to learn to know yourself, to search realistically and regularly the process of your own mind and feelings ... Development in matters of this nature is inconceivable without serious introspection, without knowing yourself, your weaknesses and mistakes. At least, if for nothing else, the cell gives you the opportunity to look daily into your entire conduct, to overcome the bad and develop whatever is good in you. Regular meditation, say about

15 minutes a day before you turn in, can be very fruitful in this regard. You may find it difficult at first to pinpoint the negative features in your life, but the 10th attempt may yield rich rewards. Never forget that a saint is a sinner who keeps on trying.

(Mandela, 2010, pp. 271–272)

His method reminds me that injustice thrives on prejudice and, as Gillian Straker (2006, p. 750) writes, on "stereotyped interchanges, which, at the level of their subtly choreographed prosody, interpellate us again and again as the homophobic and racist subjects we would wish not to be." She recommends relentless mindfulness as a corrective, much as Mandela did.

He developed a personal style that alternated between understatement and irony. In the face of injustice, he often quietly uttered only those familiar three words: "That's not right." Describing his early years on Robben Island, he wrote:

In general, Coloureds and Indians received a slightly better diet than Africans, but it was not much of a distinction. The authorities liked to say that we received a balanced diet; it was indeed balanced—between the unpalatable and the inedible. Food was the source of many of our protests, but in those early days, the warders would say, "Ag, you kaffirs are eating better in prison than you ever ate at home!"

. . . For supper, Coloured and Indian prisoners received a quarter loaf of bread (known as a *katkop*, that is, a cat's head, after the shape of the bread) and a slab of margarine. Africans, it was presumed, did not care for bread as it was a "European" type of food.

(Mandela, 1995, pp. 392–393)

Mandela was regarded as a leader both by warders and fellow prisoners. A younger comrade from Robben Island, Neville Alexander, described him:

The point about Nelson, of course, is that he has a tremendous presence, apart from his bearing, his deportment and so on. He's a person who's got real control over his behavior. He is also quite conscious of the kind of seriousness he radiates. And because he's got a legal training and so on, he sizes up other people, particularly those that he has to engage with, often in a hostile sort of way. He sizes them up very carefully and then addresses them in the way that he thinks will make the most impact.

(Alexander, 1999)

Mandela emerged from prison a peacemaker, focused on only one goal—full equality for all South Africans—without retribution toward either the white oppressors or his African rivals. At his death, John Dramani Mahama, the president of Ghana, wrote of him:

His utilization of peace as a vehicle of liberation showed Africa that if we were to move beyond the divisiveness caused by colonization, and the pain of our self-inflicted wounds, compassion and forgiveness must play a role in governance. Countries, like people, must acknowledge the trauma they have experienced, and find a way to reconcile, to make what was broken whole again.

(Mahama, 2013)

Mahama remembered his childhood, imagining that Mandela would never come out of prison. When he did, "we waited for an indescribable rage." Had Mandela wanted retribution, who would not have understood?

Twenty-seven years of his life, gone. Day after day of hard labor in a limestone quarry, chipping away at white rock under a merciless sun—without benefit of protective eyewear—had virtually destroyed his tear ducts, and for years, robbed Mandela even of his ability to cry.

(Mahama, 2013)

In contrast with Mandela's letter to Winnie quoted above, here is another, dated February 4, 1985, reflecting the cost of his sacrifices for justice:

Yet there have been moments when that love and happiness, that trust and hope, have turned into pure agony, when conscience and a sense of guilt have ravaged every part of my being, when I have wondered whether any kind of commitment can ever be sufficient excuse for abandoning a young and inexperienced woman [Winnie] in a pitiless desert, literally throwing her into the hands of highwaymen.

(Quoted in Mandela et al., 1985, pp. 148–149)

But because his suffering, and enormous personal losses, had been for justice, Mandela saw no need for resentment: "To go to prison because of your convictions and be prepared to suffer for what you believe in is something worthwhile. It is an achievement for a man to do his duty on earth irrespective of the consequences" (Mahama, 2013).

In the face of blatant dishonesty, he tended to say, well, people act in their own self-interest. In his last years, he sadly noted that "we have now learned that even those that fought beside us in the struggle for freedom can be corrupted" (quoted in Abuya, 2013). Whatever his private suffering, he refused to demonize those who had subjugated his people,[6] and, as many have noted, even invited some of his prison guards to his inauguration as the first president of all South Africans. His oppressors had never succeeded in crushing his spirit. His critics may argue that government exists to protect people from those who disregard the common good, and that he ought to have done more to structure such protection from gross inequality.

His private notes from 1993 show that he knew exactly where the crucial agenda lay:

> Priority is commitment to oppressed.
> Will fall or rise depending on our success or failure to address their needs, to accommodate their aspirations. Specifically we must get them houses and put an end to informal settlements; end unemployment, school crisis, lack of medical facilities.
>
> (Mandela, 2010, p. 339)

For the clinicians and humanitarian workers for whom this book is written, your vulnerability, your creativity, your courage, your questions, your humility, your audacity make you Nelson Mandela's legitimate heirs in the spirit and work of *ubuntu*. Just as you do every day, he substituted, in the Levinasian sense, the needs of others for his own self-interest. In the face of complacent injustice, in the face of the sufferings for his people, in the face of systemic and daily indignities, he saw other-wise and heard the cries of the other, and could not remain indifferent or comfortable. He practiced non-indifference.

Dietrich Bonhoeffer: theologian of costly grace

In a sense, Dietrich Bonhoeffer arrived in South Africa at the time when Nelson Mandela was working in Robben Island's lime quarry in the 1970s. Eberhard Bethge—Bonhoeffer's best friend, literary executor, and biographer—introduced him to the country via a series of lectures to the Anglican churches (de Gruchy, 2007). Carefully avoiding comparisons between apartheid and Nazi genocide, he simply told Bonhoeffer's story again and again, and explained its connection with his theological development. But some heard the overtones.

Born into a cultured but not particularly church-going Berlin family in 1906, Dietrich Bonhoeffer knew from early adolescence that he wanted to study theology. His father Karl was Germany's most prominent psychiatrist of the era; his eldest brother Karl-Friedrich was a physicist working at the Max Planck Institute alongside Fritz Haber and Albert Einstein;[7] and his brother Klaus was an attorney. The family thought Dietrich's choice odd, but supported it. His mother came from a Pietist family, and had read Bible stories to the children. All the family played musical instruments, and Dietrich played the piano so well that music was his other vocational option. German religious music lived in their bones. When Klaus was shot by the Nazis, the score of Bach's *St. Matthew Passion* was found open in his cell. This family opposed Hitler before almost anyone had heard of the National Socialists, lost two sons and two sons-in-law as a result of the 1944 assassination plot, and found the spiritual resources deep in their heritage when most of Germany, including the Church, fell in line. Maybe young Dietrich's chorus lived at home.[8]

But how does a theologian come to be hanged in a concentration camp by Hitler's personal order at the age of 39? A brilliant student, by the age of 21 he had written a dissertation, "*Sanctorum Communio*: A Dogmatic Investigation of the Sociology of the Church," recognized by Karl Barth as a "theological miracle." But pastoral work, especially with the poor and disadvantaged, attracted him more than academic work, so he found himself in Berlin, Barcelona, and Harlem, connecting with people very different from his upper-middle-class family. Again and again, he found himself interpreting and reinterpreting the Sermon on the Mount: "Blessed are the poor . . ."

The poor, however, turned out to have, for Bonhoeffer, a different face from what he had expected. Naively, he and his older brother Karl-Friedrich (Rasmussen, 2009) initially thought only America had a serious race problem. However, though educated into some older Christian ideas about Jews and the Hebrew scriptures, Dietrich quickly saw the injustice and danger of the Nazi program, and spoke out without fear. From the moment Hitler came to power, and the German Christians went along, he understood that someone had to try to persuade as many pastors as possible to state clearly what the Gospels required, and wrote to his friend Erwin Sutz that "here the most intelligent people have totally lost both their heads and their Bible" (quoted in Schlingensiepen, 2010, p. 121).[9] As early as 1933, with Karl Barth, Martin Niemoeller, and a few others, he formed the Pastors' Emergency League and then joined the Confessing Church (*Die Bekennende Kirche*) to develop the Barmen Declaration of Faith. From 1935 to 1939 he led a seminary to train pastors of the Confessing Church at Zingst and Finkenwalde, where young men, including Eberhard Bethge, learned communal life, scriptural meditation, theology, and reflection on the meaning of their faith in dangerous times.

Meanwhile, at an ecumenical conference in Fano, Sweden, the 28-year-old Bonhoeffer spoke for peace. He had learned from one of his Union Theological Seminary friends, the young French pastor Jean Lassere, to regard the Christian message as pacifist. At the same time, he saw Germany rearming, operating under totalitarian lawlessness, and threatening its neighbors more than ever. All young men of his age group were being conscripted. He told the conference:

> There is no way to peace along the way of safety. For peace must be dared, it is itself the great venture, and can never be safe. Peace is the opposite of security. To demand guarantees is to mistrust, and this mistrust in turn brings forth war. To look for guarantees is to want to protect oneself. Peace means giving oneself completely to God's commandment, wanting no security, but in faith and obedience laying

down the destiny of the nations in the hand of Almighty God, not trying
to direct it for selfish purposes. Battles are won, not with weapons, but
with God. They are won when the way leads to the cross.

(Bonhoeffer et al., 1970, p. 286)

One of the participants reported that when they were sitting around
afterwards, someone asked Bonhoeffer what he would do if he were drafted.
He thought for a long time, twisting his pencil around, then answered slowly,
"I hope God will give me the strength not to take up arms" (Bethge, 1970,
p. 389). Everyone in the room knew that conscientious objection was not an
option in Nazi Germany.

Next let us consider 1938. Until then Bonhoeffer had been involved in the
church struggle and in education. Late in the year, though, two things happened: first, he learned from his brother-in-law Hans von Dohnanyi—who
had been recording all the crimes of the Nazis since 1933—of a conspiracy;
and, second, on November 9, synagogues were burned all over Germany in
the infamous *Kristallnacht* (Night of Broken Glass). In his Bible, Bonhoeffer
underlined the line "they burned all the meeting-places of God in the land"
from Psalm 74 and wrote the date: "9 Nov 1938" (Schlingensiepen, 2010,
p. 216). Most of his fellow pastors had already been called up for military
service, and he knew it would soon be his turn. His biographer Ferdinand
Schlingensiepen (2010, p. 222) recounts the immense personal struggle that
followed:

> [W]as it worthwhile, this struggle which was consuming the crucial
> years of his life? Was it right to object conscientiously to military service,
> at the sacrifice of his own life, when no one in the Confessing Church
> could even understand such a sacrifice, much less approve of it? And
> what of his being party to the conspiracy? Wasn't that a mission in
> which people belonging to the military would be useful, but not a
> theologian?

While he agonized, Reinhold Niebuhr and others—hoping to keep him
safe—urged him to accept an invitation to return to the United States, to
work and lecture at the Union Theological Seminary. He arrived in New
York in June 1939 but immediately felt he had abandoned something
imperative. After three dark and confusing weeks, he returned to Germany,
"a sojourner on this earth," to work as a double agent. He wrote to Niebuhr:

> I have made a mistake in coming to America. I must live through this
> difficult period of our national history with the Christian people of
> Germany. I will have no right to participate in the reconstruction of
> Christian life in Germany if I do not share the trials of this time with my
> people . . . Christians in Germany will face the terrible alternative of

either willing the defeat of their nation in order that Christian civilization may survive, or willing the victory of their nation and thereby destroying our civilization. I know which of these alternatives I must choose; but I cannot make that choice in security.

(Quoted in Bethge and Barnett, 2000, p. 665)

The choice, for a scholar of Christian ethics (similar to that faced by the young Nelson Mandela in turning toward violence in the fight against apartheid), had been a terrible one. Sabine Dramm formulated it in this way:

The dilemma Bonhoeffer faced was that he would incur guilt not only if he stood idly by as a spectator of violence *but also* if he participated even indirectly in putsch plans, violence, and concrete actions designed to take human life while in the guise of an agent of military intelligence.

(Dramm, 2007, p. 181, quoted in Ballor, 2008, p. 469; Dramm's emphasis)

Either way, he could not evade guilt and responsibility. He chose to assume it. For the next three years he seemed to conform (even giving the Nazi salute)—working for military intelligence (and thus escaping the draft), working as a spy, and writing theology. His ethical writings in particular became focused at this time on the understanding of "thou shalt not kill." He also fell in love for the first time, and became engaged to Maria von Wedemeyer. Well informed about several early coup attempts, he communicated through his theological contacts outside Germany on behalf of the conspirators. He wrote in his well-known meditation on Psalm 119:

With God we do not take up a stance—we walk along a path. It goes forward, otherwise we are not with God. God knows where the path goes, throughout its length, we know only the next step and the ultimate destination . . . To know the way, to be going the right way, never spares us any of the responsibility and guilt, but only makes them harder to bear.

(Bonhoeffer et al., 1996, Vol. 15, p. 508)

On April 5, 1943, five days after the latest conspiracy's assassination attempt on Hitler's life had failed, Bonhoeffer was arrested alongside Hans and Christine (Dietrich's sister) von Dohnanyi. A few weeks before their arrest, Bonhoeffer had written of what he called "the view from below:"

There remains an experience of incomparable value. We have for once learnt to see the great events of world history from below, from the perspective of the outcast, the suspects, the maltreated, the powerless, the oppressed, the reviled—in short, from the perspective of those who suffer. The important thing is that neither bitterness nor envy should have gnawed at the heart during this time, that we should have come to look with new eyes at matters great and small, sorrow and joy, strength and weakness, that our perception of generosity, humanity, justice and mercy should have become clearer, freer, less corruptible. *We have to learn that personal suffering is a more effective key, a more rewarding principle for exploring the world in thought and action than personal good fortune.*

(Bonhoeffer and Bethge, 1971, p. 17; emphasis added)

Bonhoeffer, like Dostoevsky and Levinas, believed in "useful suffering": personal suffering, embraced, could transform us in the direction of generosity and justice.

In prison, the conspirators concentrated on keeping their captors from knowing more. Though, to his biographers' knowledge, Dietrich escaped torture (his brother Klaus did not), he was interrogated daily. His *Letters and Papers from Prison* (Bonhoeffer and Bethge, 1971), many written to his family, probably understate his suffering. Clearly, his family's support—they made enormous efforts to see him, bring him books and food, and encode messages from the conspirators in his books—sustained his courage. Of course, all letters to his family passed the censors first, so both he and the family deliberately communicated calmness to the interrogators. In smuggled letters to his best friend, Eberhard Bethge, however, he painted a more complex picture, which was nevertheless courageous for its searching honesty:

[T]hings here are revolting . . . my grim experiences often pursue me into the night, and . . . I can shake them off only by reciting one hymn after another, and . . . I'm apt to wake up with a sigh rather than with a hymn of praise to God. It's possible to get used to physical hardships, and to live for months out of the body, so to speak . . . but one doesn't get used to the psychological strain; on the contrary, I have the feeling that everything that I see and hear is putting years on me, and I'm often finding the world nauseating and burdensome.

(Bonhoeffer and Bethge, 1971, p. 162)

Bethge's previous letter had commented on Bonhoeffer's appearance at their recent visit after eight months in prison: "Cheerful, fresh, not at all pale, and in everything, as usual, in command of the situation, a little concerned to communicate comfort and confidence about your situation to us, no matter what" (Bonhoeffer and Bethge, 1971, pp. 153–154). Bonhoeffer continued:

I often wonder who I really am—the man who goes on squirming under these ghastly experiences in wretchedness that cries to heaven, or the man who scourges himself and pretends to others (and even to himself) that he is placid, cheerful, composed, and in control of himself, and allows people to admire him for it (i.e., for playing the part—or is it not playing a part?). What does one's attitude mean, anyway? In short, I know less than ever about myself, and I am no longer attaching any importance to it. I have had more than enough psychology, and I am less and less inclined to analyze the state of my soul . . . There is something more at stake than self-knowledge.

(Bonhoeffer and Bethge, 1971, p. 162)

What more is at stake? He could not avoid his own complexity, and had suffered from depressive episodes, but remained convinced that, as he put it in musical terms, the basic melody—in his language, "the love of God"—or *cantus firmus* had to hold steady: "Where the *cantus firmus* is clear and plain, the counterpoint can be developed to its limits" (Bonhoeffer and Bethge, 1971, p. 303). Many other lives were at stake should he weaken and disclose any secrets in the face of possible torture or other kinds of intimidation, or from sheer exhaustion. Photos make it clear that he lost significant weight in his first year in Tegel Prison.

But like Mandela, and as if he had read Hadot, as well as from his own exposure to the Roman Catholic monastic tradition, he did his best to convert the noisy, smelly, bombing-threatened prison cell into a monastic cell. He invented routines for prayer, meditation, scripture reading, physical exercise, disciplined reading, and study, and followed them closely. Of homesickness, he wrote:

An outward and purely physical régime . . . itself provides some support for one's inner discipline. Further, there is nothing worse in such times than to try to find a substitute for the irreplaceable. It just does not work, and it leads to still greater indiscipline, for the strength to over-come tension (such strength can come only from looking the longing straight in the face) is impaired, and endurance becomes even more unbearable.

(Bonhoeffer and Bethge, 1971, p. 168)

He interacted with others when he felt he could listen in a pastoral way— "it seems to me much more important actually to share someone's distress than to use smooth words about it" (Bonhoeffer and Bethge, 1971, p. 203)—but otherwise kept to himself. Thus, like the others we have studied, he strengthened himself for the trials of each day's interrogations, and for the worse that he knew could lie ahead, while trying to sustain hope for a future of freedom and marriage. Gradually, however, he came ever more clearly to hope for Germany's defeat, understanding this feeling as true patriotism.

Had Primo Levi met a surviving Bonhoeffer in Germany after the war, what could we imagine? Bonhoeffer and Bethge (1971, p. 203) agreed that people tend to feel "shamelessly at home," and Bonhoeffer remarked, "The man who feels neither responsibility towards the past, nor desire to shape the future is one who 'forgets,' and I don't know how one can really get at such a person and bring him to his senses." To both Levi and Bonhoeffer, this kind of forgetting threatens a repeat of the massacre. Feeling "shamelessly at home" may be inconsistent with the kind of ethical seeing and responsibility that both Dostoevsky (Slavic Christianity) and Levinas (Talmudic Judaism) deemed central to humanity. Here we find the objection voiced by Western Christians, lonely voices abandoned by most Western European Catholics and Protestants of the *Nazizeit.* "Shamelessly at home":

> You who live secure
> In your warm houses
> Who return at evening to find
> Hot food and friendly faces:
>
> Consider whether this is a man,
> Who labours in the mud
> Who knows no peace
> Who fights for a crust of bread
> Who dies at a yes or a no
>   (Levi et al., 1992, p. 9)

May you be cursed if you forget. Bonhoeffer and his family did not forget, and he did not live to meet Levi. He prayed for Germany's defeat so that fewer would be murdered, and so that Germans might feel the needed shame, and actually suffer for their crimes. Levi found them unable or unwilling to see, even afterwards.[10]

After 14 months in Tegel, Bonhoeffer began to include in his letters to Bethge (with the Wehrmacht in Italy) reflections and questions of a radical theology that he called "religionless Christianity":

> What is bothering me incessantly is the question what Christianity really is, or who Christ really is, for us today. The time when people could be told everything by means of words, whether theological or pious, is over, and so is the time of inwardness and conscience—and that means the time of religion in general. We are moving towards a completely religionless time; people as they are now simply cannot be religious any more. Even those who honestly describe themselves as "religious" do not in the least act up to it, and so they presumably mean something quite different by "religious."
>
> (Bonhoeffer and Bethge, 1971, p. 279)

This Bonhoeffer, steeped in the Jewish and Christian scriptures, in the theology of Karl Barth, in the monastic and communitarian traditions of Roman Catholicism, had now lived an unusual 14-month sabbatical, and had become convinced that any Christianity worth having needed to be worldly, secular. No "god of the gaps" would do for him, nor, I suspect, one constructed from theodicies, but a church of the guilty and responsible for the world that does not treat god as a bailout resource (Rasmussen, 2009). He continued:

> What do a church, a community, a sermon, a liturgy, a Christian life mean in a religionless world? How do we speak of God—without religion, i.e. without the temporally conditioned presuppositions of metaphysics, inwardness, and so on? How do we speak (or perhaps we cannot now even "speak" as we used to) in a "secular" way about "God"? In what way are we "religionless-secular" Christians, in what way are we the *ecclesia* [church], those who are called forth, not regarding ourselves from a religious point of view as specially favored, but rather as belonging wholly to the world? In that case Christ is no longer an object of religion, but something quite different, really the Lord of the world. But what does that mean? What is the place of worship and prayer in a religionless situation?
>
> (Bonhoeffer and Bethge, 1971, pp. 280–281)

No theologian, I claim no familiarity with the vast literature to which these words have given rise; still, I can only wonder what might have followed from Bonhoeffer's no longer "specially favored" Christianity. Religious pluralism, perhaps?[11] Famous for saying that "only those who cry out for the Jews may sing Gregorian chants" (Bethge and Barnett, 2000, p. 512), and well known resolutely to oppose every Nazi anti-Semitic measure, he was also understood, based on his 1933 essay "The Church and the Jewish Question" (Bethge, 1970), as thinking that Jews should convert to Christianity.[12] Bonhoeffer was therefore unanimously denied a listing among the "righteous Gentiles" at Yad Vashem.[13] His serious reading of the Old Testament, meant to take the Jewish contribution seriously, instead reduced it to pre-Christology in the eyes of some Jewish scholars, such as W. Harrelson (Marty, 1962). Perhaps in prison his views became more pluralistic, but even his death—in his eyes and in those of the other conspirators clearly intended to cry out for the Jews—had not saved any. I feel sure that he would have wanted others to be honored instead.

Bonhoeffer remains important to me not for his faultlessness, but for his sincerity. Like Mandela, he knew himself to be no saint, no hero, not even a righteous Gentile. He entered the resistance both because conscientious objection to military service was not an option in the Nazi system, and because he could not stand by and pretend not to see what his country was doing, or not attempt to put "a spoke in the wheel," as he put it. "Things do exist," he once wrote to his brother Karl-Friedrich, "that are worth standing up for without compromise" (quoted in Rasmussen, 2009, p. 103). A saint, Mandela often repeated, is simply a sinner who keeps on trying. After the failed assassination attempt on Hitler's life in July 1944, "trying" became sustaining the inevitable. As his brother-in-law and closest collaborator Hans von Dohnanyi said to his wife in the spring of 1945, "Dietrich and I didn't do the thing as politicians. It was simply the way a decent person had to go" (quoted in Dramm, 2009, p. 239).

After a trove of their papers surfaced, every member of the conspiracy was arrested and imprisoned. Bonhoeffer was moved to a Gestapo prison in Berlin, then to Buchenwald, and finally to Flossenbürg concentration camp, where he was hanged on April 9, 1945, four weeks before Germany surrendered. (Hitler personally ordered the murder of all the conspirators, even though he knew the war was lost.) His parents heard months later, when the BBC broadcast a memorial service for the lost theologian.

Ethics

Both Mandela and Bonhoeffer lived the hyperbolic ethics of responsibility verbalized in Dostoevsky's *The Brothers Karamazov* (the topic of the next chapter), and in the philosophy of Emmanuel Levinas, inspired by Dostoevsky from childhood. So we turn the clock back, and *nachträglich*, having listened to Levi, Mandela, and Bonhoeffer speak from their perspectives on extreme crimes against humanity, we will read Dostoevsky. But first, a few words in parting from Bonhoeffer's vision of a future church, written in Tegel after July 20, 1944 but before his involvement in the plot was discovered:

> The church is the church only when it exists for others. To make a start, it should give away all its property to those in need . . . The church must share in the ordinary problems of human life, not dominating, but helping and serving. It . . . will have to take the field against the vices of *hubris*, power-worship, envy, and humbug, as the roots of all evil. It will have to speak of moderation, purity, trust, loyalty, constancy, patience, discipline, humility, contentment, and modesty.
>
> (Bonhoeffer and Bethge, 1971, pp. 382–383)

Just as the pragmatic Mandela saw politics as the servant of justice for all, the more mature Bonhoeffer saw the church as the servant of all, and we can hope that his youthful supercessionism (all roads lead to Christianity) gave way, or would have given way, to genuine pluralism. I do believe he risked his life to support the conspiracy because he knew what was happening to the Jews, and wanted to help end the massacre sooner; an example of Levinasian substitution, or what Bonhoeffer, in his *Ethics*, named "deputyship": "Deputyship [*Stellvertretung*], and therefore also responsibility, lies only in the complete surrender of one's own life to the other man. Only the selfless man lives responsibly, and this means that only the selfless man lives" (Bonhoeffer and Bethge, 1995, p. 222).

Notes

1   Mac Maharaj (one of Mandela's closest early friends and colleagues) recalled:

> When we went to prison most of us were not speaking Afrikaans. I argued with Mandela about whether we should study the language. He'd say: "Let's do it together." I'd say I'm not interested in this language, first of all it's not even an international language, and second it's the language of the oppressor. He'd reply: "Look, man, we're in for a long struggle, a protracted struggle. It's going to be a war of attrition." He'd say: "How are we going to lead the enemy forces into an ambush? To do that we look at the enemy's commander and try to understand him. To do that, we've got to read his literature, read his poetry. So shall we study Afrikaans?"
>
> (Maharaj, 2013)

2   For me, a point of contact comes in his original name, Rolihlahla (Tree-shaker or Troublemaker), so appropriate in his early life, and an epithet that my psychoanalytic teachers also applied disparagingly to me. One could only wish to have transformed one's troublemaking as Mandela did.

3   I hesitate in naming this disaster, knowing that some object to either choice: holocaust (sacrifice by fire) or shoah (catastrophe). The choice of lower case indicates its belonging with other historical massacres discussed in this book; upper case would have recognized the uniqueness of this deliberate extermination.

4   According to Richard Stengel (2010), who assisted Mandela in the preparation of his autobiography *Long Walk to Freedom,* Mandela would often listen quietly to a long conversation, and then utter these words.

5   On my 2009 visit to Cape Town, my day free from teaching took me to Mandela's Robben Island cell, seven feet by eight, barely large enough for the six-foot-four Mandela to lie down. Our guide, a former prisoner, clearly explained the differences in diet among the groups of prisoners, and described the daily routine and living conditions. The Africans who took me there asked about our elections and were amazed to meet a white person who had voted for a black man. Some remembered with pride Obama's visit to Robben Island.

6   His "people" came to include, for him, all who fought injustice. He wrote in 1976 from prison:

> The first condition for victory is black unity. Every effort to divide the blacks, to woo and pit one black group against another, must be vigorously repulsed. Our people—African, Colored, Indian and democratic whites—must be united into a single massive and solid wall of resistance, of united mass action.
>
> (Mandela, 1986, p. 191)

7   He switched to chemistry during the Nazi period because he did not want to work on nuclear weapons for the Nazi regime (Rasmussen, 2009).

8   When the plot of July 20, 1944 failed, Klaus Bonhoeffer's wife asked him what she should do when he was arrested. He replied that she would be unable to do anything for him, but urged her to protect the children. At least they would

know that their father was not one of those who knew about the crimes against humanity yet chose to do nothing. The documentary evidence that Hans von Dohnyani—brother-in-law of Dietrich and father of the conductor Christoph— gathered to convince all the conspirators that they had to do something to decapitate the regime was later used in the Nuremberg trials.

9   But this seriously problematic attempt, analyzed by Stephen Haynes (2002) in the context of his study of the anti-Semitism of the minority Confessing Church—which I formerly idealized for its opposition to the Nazis—not only accepts without question the formulation "*Judenfrage*" ("Jewish question") but also blames Jews for Christ's death, and assumes that they should "return to God" by way of Christianity. It is easy to see why some have judged him "the best of a bad lot." Haynes (2002, p. 367) concludes that his actions were better than his theology.

10 Some, perhaps many, younger Germans have wanted to learn about and confront the crimes. Austrians, perhaps because many of their schools were never fully denazified, have been slower. But that is another story.

11 Both philosophers (Bernasconi, 2009) and historians of religion (Smith, 1991) have since warned against the imperialistic use of the term "religion," and argued for pluralism.

12 He never, to my knowledge, repeated this opinion when he was older, and I want to make it completely clear that I do not share this view. Ruth Zerner (1999, p. 191), who has studied Bonhoeffer's relation to the "Jewish question" extensively, believes that, had he lived, he would have been a leader among postwar Germans in transcending these inherited views.

13 From Rubinstein (2011):

> On July 28, 2000, Dr. Mordecai Paldiel, Director of the Department for the Righteous of Yad Vashem, Israel's Holocaust Martyrs' and Heroes' Remembrance Authority wrote to a very distinguished group of Jewish and Christian scholars and religious leaders giving a detailed explanation of the reasons why on July 2, 2000, Yad Vashem's Commission for the Designation of the Righteous deferred action on their petition to have Dietrich Bonhoeffer named a "righteous gentile." Judging from Dr. Paldiel's letter, it is highly unlikely that Bonhoeffer will be so named. According to Dr. Paldiel, the title of "Righteous Gentile" is awarded to "persons who risked their life in the attempt to save one or more Jews from the Nazis, where the rescuer was personally and directly involved in the rescue operation, and where no distinction was made between Jews faithful to their religion and community and baptized Jews." In addition, a person in "high office or influential position" who unambiguously denounced the persecution of Jews faithful to their inherited tradition rather than baptized Jews alone may be awarded the title. Paldiel cites the examples of Jules-Gérard Cardinal Saliège, Archbishop of Toulouse, and Bishop Pierre-Marie Théas, Bishop of Montauban, who spoke out explicitly against the persecution and who may be eligible . . . On the contrary, Paldiel concludes:

>> on the Jewish issue, the record of Bonhoeffer is to publicly condone certain measures by the Nazi state against the Jews (save only baptized Jews), and to uphold the traditional Christian delegitimization of Judaism, coupled with a religious justification of the persecution of Jews. His words against the extreme form of the Nazi anti-Jewish measures were uttered in private and among trusted colleagues; his denunciation of Judaism and justification of the initial anti-Jewish measures were voiced in writing.

References

Abuya, K. (2013). Special Tribute: Nelson Rolihlahla Mandela. Retrieved from www.saybrook.edu/rethinkingcomplexity/posts/12-22-13/special-tribute-nelson-rolihlahla-mandela-great-leader-and-elder-took-stand-humanity (accessed August 25, 2015).

Alexander, N. (1999). Interview. *Frontline*. Retrieved from www.pbs.org/wgbh/pages/frontline/shows/mandela/interviews/alexander.html (accessed August 24, 2015).

Ballor, J. (2008). Bonhoeffer in America: A Review Essay. *Christian Scholar's Review*, 37, 465–482.

Bernasconi, R. (2009). Must We Avoid Speaking of Religion? The Truths of Religions. *Research in Phenomenology*, 39, 204–223.

Bethge, E. (1970). *Dietrich Bonhoeffer: Man of Vision, Man of Courage*. New York: Harper & Row.

Bethge, E., and Barnett, V. (2000). *Dietrich Bonhoeffer: A Biography* (rev. edn.). Minneapolis, MN: Fortress Press.

Bonhoeffer, D., and Bethge, E. (1971). *Letters and Papers from Prison* (enlarged edn.). London: SCM Press.

Bonhoeffer, D., and Bethge, E. (1995). *Ethics*. New York: Simon & Schuster.

Bonhoeffer, D., and Fuller, R. (1949). *The Cost of Discipleship*. New York: Macmillan.

Bonhoeffer, D., Müller, G., Schönherr, A., Reuter, H.-R., Green, C. J., and Kelly, G. B. (1996). *Dietrich Bonhoeffer Works* (1st English edn.). Minneapolis, MN: Fortress Press.

Bonhoeffer, D., Robertson, E., and Bowden, J. (1970). *No Rusty Swords: Letters, Lectures and Notes, 1928–1936*. In *The Collected Works of Dietrich Bonhoeffer* (Vol. 1). London: Collins, the Fontana Library.

Burns, J. (2014). Memories of Mandela. Retrieved from www.abreakingnews.com/africa/memories-of-mandela-h96833.html (accessed August 24, 2015).

Davis, D. B. (2006). *Inhuman Bondage: The Rise and Fall of Slavery in the New World*. New York: Oxford University Press.

de Gruchy, J. (2007). Eberhard Bethge: Interpreter Extraordinaire of Dietrich Bonhoeffer. *Modern Theology*, 23, 349–368.

Dramm, S. (2007). *Dietrich Bonhoeffer: An Introduction to His Thought*. Peabody, MA: Hendrickson.

Dramm, S. (2009). *Dietrich Bonhoeffer and the Resistance*. Minneapolis, MN: Fortress Press.

Haynes, S. (2002). Who Needs Enemies? Jews and Judaism in Anti-Nazi Religious Discourse. *American Society of Church History*, 71, 341–366.

Krog, A. (1998). *Country of My Skull*. Johannesburg: Random House.

Krog, A. (2013). The South African Statesman and His Prophet: A Relook at Aspects of Vocabulary and Tolerance after a Period of Transitional Justice. Retrieved from http://otjr.crim.ox.ac.uk/index.php/events/Seminar/161-the-south-african-statesman-and-his-prophet-a-relook-at-aspects-of-vocabulary-and-tolerance-after-a-period-of-transitional-justice.html (accessed September 5, 2015).

Levi, P., Feldman, R., and Swann, B. (1992). *Collected Poems* (new edn.). London and Boston, MA: Faber & Faber.

Levinas, E. (1981). *Otherwise than Being, or, Beyond Essence*. The Hague and Boston Hingham, MA: M. Nijhoff and Kluwer Boston.

Mahama, J. (2013). He Taught a Continent to Forgive. *New York Times*, December 6.

Maharaj, M. (2013). The Nelson Mandela I Knew. *Guardian*, December 6.

Mandela, N. (1986). *The Struggle Is My Life: His Speeches and Writings Brought Together with Historical Documents and Accounts of Mandela in Prison by Fellow-Prisoners*. London: International Defence and Aid Fund for Southern Africa.

Mandela, N. (1995). *Long Walk to Freedom: The Autobiography of Nelson Mandela* (1st paperback edn.). Boston, MA: Back Bay Books.

Mandela, N. (2010). *Conversations with Myself*. New York: Farrar, Straus & Giroux.

Mandela, N., Derrida, J., and Tlili, M. (1987). *For Nelson Mandela*. New York: Seaver Books.

Mandela, W., Benjamin, A., and Benson, M. (1985). *Part of My Soul Went with Him* (1st US edn.). New York: Norton.

Marty, M. E. (1962). *The Place of Bonhoeffer: Problems and Possibilities in His Thought*. New York: Association Press.

Rasmussen, L. (2009). Dietrich and Karl-Friedrich Bonhoeffer: The Brothers Bonhoeffer on Science, Morality and Theology. *Zygon*, 44, 97–113.

Rubenstein, R. (2011). Was Dietrich Bonhoeffer a Righteous Gentile? Retrieved from www.newenglishreview.org/custpage.cfm/frm/86357/sec_id/86357 (accessed August 25, 2015).

Schlingensiepen, F. (2010). *Dietrich Bonhoeffer, 1906–1945: Martyr, Thinker, Man of Resistance*. London and New York: T. & T. Clark.

Smith, W. C. (1991). *The Meaning and End of Religion*. Minneapolis, MN: Fortress Press.

Stengel, R. (2010). *Mandela's Way: Fifteen Lessons on Life, Love, and Courage*. New York: Crown.

Straker, G. (2006). The Anti-Analytic Third. *Psychoalytic Review*, 93, 729–753.

Zerner, R. (1999). Church, State and the "Jewish Question." In J. de Gruchy (Ed.), *The Cambridge Companion to Dietrich Bonhoeffer* (pp. 190–205). Cambridge: Cambridge University Press.

Chapter 7

Ethics as optics

Fyodor Dostoevsky

Written in collaboration with Maxim Livshetz[1]

> The full horror of what happened you cannot know for you did not see it.
>
> (Sophocles, *Oedipus Rex*, 9.1)

From his early childhood in his father's Kovno bookstore (Malka, 2006), Emmanuel Levinas absorbed the intensity of Russian literature, including Pushkin, Lermontov, and Tolstoy, but above all, as he often noted, Dostoevsky.[2] The Russian type of Christianity Levinas thus knew, so visual and engaged with suffering, preceded his study of Western philosophy and perhaps even of Jewish texts. Reportedly, he learned to read Russian at home before learning to read Hebrew, and spoke Russian at home throughout his life. The quotation most recurrent in his writing and interviews comes neither from the scriptures nor from philosophical sources, but from *The Brothers Karamazov.*

But, first, who is this Dostoevsky who has haunted me since my twenties and haunted Levinas from his childhood? Like many English-speaking readers, I knew him only from his novels, from *Notes from Underground* and *Crime and Punishment*, through the complex and intense world of *The Brothers Karamazov*, including the elder Zosima's discourses and the Grand Inquisitor. Psychological struggles and philosophical arguments fill these masterpieces, forming an undercurrent to everything I would learn later. But it would require meeting Emmanuel Levinas to send me back to these books and others, to test the claim that responsible love for one's neighbor underpinned all Dostoevsky's complex literary productions.

As literary critics often say, especially of Dostoevsky, we must not attribute to the author his fictional characters' passionately expressed opinions on religion, on politics, on immortality, on ethics, or on anything else. Dostoevsky provided us, thankfully, with other points of access to his own views. Fortunately for those of us who do not read Russian, we have secondary sources with full access to his correspondence, his notebooks, and his nonfiction, including his *Writer's Diary* (Dostoyevsky, 1993b). Of these, I have found particularly useful *Dostoevsky the Thinker* (Scanlan, 2002),

Dialogues with Dostoevsky (Jackson, 1993), *A Karamazov Companion* (Terras, 1981), and, of course, *Problems of Dostoevsky's Poetics* (Bakhtin, 1973). Fortunately, my collaborator on this chapter speaks Russian as his first language, and reads Dostoevsky through an ethical lens.

This chapter, like the preceding three, will first present the life and work of a person who has been or become important to me (DMO) in nourishing and sustaining the search for an ethical professional/personal life. Next will come sections explaining and illustrating major themes we have found worth internalizing. With Dostoevsky, these include: seeing poverty and suffering; the repudiation of egoism, rational or otherwise; two distinct forms of guilt and responsibility; and, albeit briefly, the memory of goodness. In his last years Dostoevsky consciously assumed a prophetic role (Frank, 2002), leading into my next chapter on the prophetic character of psychotherapeutic and humanitarian work. Here *The Brothers Karamazov* (Dostoyevsky, 1992; Frank and Petrusewicz, 2010) will provide most of our illustrations. This chapter makes no claim to completeness as a study of Dostoevskian themes found in Levinas,[3] nor vice versa; it hopes, instead, to contribute to the overall theme of this book.

Life and work[4]

Fyodor Mikhailovich (i.e., son of Mikhail) Dostoevsky (1821–1881) lived, wrote, and died in mid-nineteenth-century Russia. He therefore lived through a period of tremendous change, away from serfdom and toward the immense upheavals that would follow his death into the twentieth century. His contemporaries included such literary giants as Pushkin (a lifelong inspiration for Dostoevsky), Tolstoy, Turgenev, Lermontov, and Gogol. But none of this accounts for the status we accord Dostoevsky today, when he is frequently ranked just after Shakespeare and Dante among those who have conjured the best and worst of the human condition. Even during his lifetime, the Russian satirist Saltykov-Shchedrin wrote of him:

> In depth of thought and in the breadth of tasks of the moral world which he has unfolded, this writer stands absolutely unique among us. He not only acknowledges the legitimacy of those interests which stir contemporary society, but goes even further entering into the realm of previsions and premonitions such as constitute the goal not only of the immediate but of the most distant strivings of mankind.
>
> (Quoted in Jackson, 1993, p. 3)

Who was this Dostoevsky—so earthy in his demands that we attend to the sufferings of the destitute and so insistently *prophetic*, in many senses of the word? Why does he still speak so clearly to so many of us, even through his Slavophilic voice?

Dostoevsky was born in Moscow, the second son of a middle-class doctor, Mikhail, and his wife, Maria Nechayevna. Six more children followed, of whom five survived through childhood. Fyodor remained extremely close to his elder brother Mikhail (also a writer) until the latter's death, and thereafter provided for his family (which exacerbated Fyodor's own financial worries). He lived his first years on the periphery of Moscow, on the grounds of the Mariinsky Hospital for the Poor, where his father worked, and often encountered the children who lived there. Educated at home from the age of three (until he was sent to boarding school at 11), Fyodor was constantly exposed to books by the family's nanny. His mother taught him to read from the Bible at the age of four. His father nightly read the best of Russian and European literature, including Schiller, Goethe, Walter Scott, Homer, and Cervantes, to the whole family.

A physically fragile and sensitive child, Dostoevsky grew into a diminutive adult (he was about five-foot-three) who suffered from epilepsy and various other ailments. He also seems to have suffered under harsh and demanding paternal domination, with no softening influence after Maria Dostoevskaya died in 1837. Mikhail and Fyodor had been sent from the new family home, about 100 miles from Moscow, to study military engineering in St. Petersburg[5] shortly before her death. Both were abandoning serious academic passions to follow their father's instructions. Everyone at the military academy felt that Fyodor was the least military person they had ever met, and noted that he was far more interested in drawing and architecture.

Dostoevsky's father died in 1839, and though he completed his studies at the academy, he gradually found his way into literature. He published his first novel, *Poor Folk*, in 1846, which brought him to the attention of the literary establishment. Three years later, almost by accident, he was arrested in St. Petersburg with other members of the liberal Petrashevsky Circle, imprisoned in the Peter–Paul Fortress, and faced a terrifying mock-execution by firing squad. Instead of being executed, he was condemned to four years of shackled imprisonment and hard labor in Siberia, a punishment that was extended to almost ten years in exile there. In the later years of his exile he read as much European literature as he could find, and, employing his astonishing powers of observation and description, started to write again, using his own suffering as inspiration (Frank and Petrusewicz, 2010). From the nine months in the Peter–Paul Fortress and the first four years in chains in Siberia came *Notes from a Dead House* (Dostoevsky, 2014; Ornstein, 2013), which, in addition to cataloging the subhuman conditions and violent mistreatment, described in psychological detail a kind of conversion. The relatively privileged and well-educated life into which Dostoevsky had been born, miserable as that life had been in its own way, made it a revelation to discover the wretched criminals with whom he lived as fellow human beings.[6]

Subsequently, still in exile, he married and continued with his writing. Finally, in 1859, he returned to Petersburg, where he immersed himself in literary life, interwoven with health, romantic, and financial problems, from which he suffered until the day he died. He sought relief from his epilepsy and financial worries by traveling in Europe, where he repeatedly succumbed to his gambling addiction and was often reduced to begging from friends and fellow writers. He found some stability through his second marriage to his assistant, Anna Grigoryevna Snitkina, in 1867, though they lost their first child and he continued to gamble for several more years. It was in this period that he produced masterpieces like *Crime and Punishment*, *Demons*, and *The Idiot*.

In his final years, after a prolonged exile in Europe seeking cures and avoiding creditors, Fyodor and Anna lived in Russia, dividing their time between St. Petersburg and their summer home in Staraya Russa,[7] where, despite censorship, Dostoevsky produced and wrote for journals while also creating *The Adolescent*, *A Writer's Diary*, and, just before his death in 1881, *The Brothers Karamazov*. By then, he was a national hero, though not without his envious and spiteful critics.

Seeing the poor and suffering

Emmanuel Levinas famously wrote that "ethics is an optics" (Levinas, 1969, p. 29). It concerns seeing, and responding to, the face of the other. As Val Vinokur (2008, p. 47) has observed, this phrase sounds strange from a Jewish phenomenologist known for his Talmudic lectures, for an interpreter of a tradition that proscribes visual images while placing great emphasis on the auditory. "Hear, O Israel . . ." But, Vinokur explains, in midrashic texts, "hearing, strictly speaking, is still pre-ethical—hearing is simply about being open to the other." Reading Russian literature in his father's bookshop— "above all, Dostoevsky!" (Levinas and Robbins, 2001, p. 28)—the young Levinas seems to have learned to regard the capacity to see (without indifference) poverty and misery as the core of ethics. In other words, this kind of seeing demands doing before hearing (*naase ve nishma*),[8] it interprets by responding first, forming a primary source of meaning. Concurrent with his first exposure to Jewish texts, this sensibility preceded Levinas's study of philosophy in Strasbourg at the age of 17.

So what did Dostoevsky see, and allow his readers to see, that so differed from what his literary rivals Tolstoy and Turgenev (giants themselves) left us? What so inspired Levinas that his mantra or slogan—so to speak—comes from Dostoevsky and not from the Torah? In more than half his works, and in almost every interview, Levinas quoted, "each of us is guilty of everything before everyone, and I most of all." Repeatedly, in various forms—in the mouths of various characters in *The Brothers Karamazov*, and in various forms throughout the work of Levinas—we hear these words (Toumayan, 2014). Later in this chapter we return to this hyperbolic responsibility, with its shocking final clause, but for now let us consider how deeply ingrained, how pervasive, how integral is Dostoevsky's way of seeing in Levinasian ethics. Despite profound differences, including Dostoevsky's ever more caustic anti-Semitism, these two men shared an uncompromising refusal to turn away from human misery in all of its forms.[9]

Unlike Levinas, Dostoevsky did not write *about* the need to see human suffering, about the optics. Rather, he tried to convey the force of this suffering in the particular struggles of his characters. Like Charles Dickens and Victor Hugo, enormously admired and thoroughly digested, Dostoevsky could make the reader know destitution. Though Dickens structured his novels to make endings seem inevitable while Dostoevsky never did (Bakhtin, 1973), the former, like Hugo, makes us *see* and feel the misery of the poor, and the indifference of the well-off. Similarly, Dostoevsky learned in prison camp to see his cruel, wretched, and ugly fellow convicts as individual suffering human beings, even if less educated and refined than he. No longer, he discovered, could he use their immorality as an excuse to stand above them, indifferent to their misery. Their faces, equal in value to those considered "important" in society, imposed a command on him. Even as a child, perhaps suffering under the dominance of a despotic father, he had already developed some capacity to perceive suffering in the young patients around him (Frank, 1976). All his stories and novels describe tremendous psychological complexity—even to the point of being plagued by demons and addictions—but part of the complexity results from the struggle not to see, to evade, what one cannot help seeing: human suffering in all its miserable detail.[10] We cannot know for sure whether his own demons and addictions aided his perception of the suffering of others, or resulted from his vulnerability to it. As Robert Louis Jackson (1993, p. 46) puts it, Dostoevsky believed it "the business of man to look" at violence without turning away. Seeing—not physical but moral vision, "optics"—takes on such ethical significance because it means that either we harden our hearts in indifference or we become vulnerable to wretchedness, aware of our endless responsibility, nonindifferent. Like Primo Levi after him, Dostoevsky challenged his readers to see, and to chisel what they had seen into their hearts, or be cursed.

For Levinas, hunger best expressed the contrast between evasion (notseeing) and responsibility in "Secularization and Hunger" (Levinas, 1998), extensively discussed by Robert Bernasconi (2010).[11] But systematized global hunger is hard to see. Vision, on the contrary,

> cuts across the vision of forms and can be stated neither in terms of contemplation nor in terms of practice. It is the face; its revelation is speech. The relation with the Other [primarily the human other, but also the trace of god] alone introduces a dimension of transcendence, and leads us to a relation totally different from experience in the sensible sense of the term, relative and egoist.
>
> (Levinas, 1969, p. 193)

We recall that Russian Christianity focuses on icons, on the face, and that Dostoevsky describes suffering close up. Hunger has faces. Levinas continued:

> The face, still a thing among things, breaks through form that nevertheless delimits it . . . To speak to me is at each moment to surmount what is necessarily plastic in manifestation. To manifest oneself as a face is to *impose oneself* above and beyond the manifested and purely phenomenal form, to present oneself in a mode irreducible to manifestation, the very straightforwardness of the face to face, without the intermediary of any image.
>
> (Levinas, 1969, p. 200; original emphasis)

How do we learn to see? By hearing the misery of others? By contacting our own vulnerability? Remembering, I imagine, the mass of German Lutherans who enthusiastically supported Hitler, and the hordes of European Catholics who did nothing to interfere with Nazi crimes, Levinas claimed that we must accept "the death of a certain god" who makes promises or provides in exchange for granting permission to desecrate the inviolable. Only accepting this loss allows our discovery of the pre-primordial ethical excess, the "I more than the others" of the ethical asymmetry, the utter transcendence of the other's need over my own comfort. He believed that we find this hyperbolic ethical responsibility by means of a kind of retrospection, "the force of transference which goes from the memory of my own hunger to the suffering and responsibility for the hunger of the neighbor" (Banon et al., 1998, p. 11). We gain the holy by rejecting the sacred in favor of the destitute.

Similarly, we might conjecture, Dostoevsky's capacity to feel and express concern for the destitute, his power of ethical vision, relied in part on his own memories of persecution within the family and in Siberia, the affliction of lifelong illness, and economic struggles. The audience to whom this book intends to speak may also share a capacity both to see and to feel the afflictions of others, a capacity developed by familiarity with personal post-traumatic ghosts and demons. These ghosts and demons create black holes in the soul that haunt and obsess with a hunger that only the infinity of the other can fulfill.

Ethical seeing differs from an abstract love for mankind, as the elder Zosima, beloved mentor to young Alyosha Karamazov, explains to an interlocutor who wants easy answers. He reminds her of an old man who told him:

> the more I love mankind in general, the less I love people in particular . . . as soon as someone is there, close to me, his personality oppresses my self-esteem and restricts my freedom. In twenty-four hours I can begin to hate even the best of men: one because he takes too long eating

his dinner, another because he has a cold and keeps blowing his nose. I become the enemy of people the moment they touch me.

(Quoted in Jackson, 1993, p. 57)

Nor can the Grand Inquisitor of elder brother Ivan's famous story, told to Alyosha, really see. The crowd, "numerous as the sands of the sea" (Dostoyevsky, 1992, p. 253), has no human faces to which he responds. Against Jesus, returning to earth as a character in Ivan's story, seeing and responding to the individuals he meets, and to be eliminated anew, the Inquisitor offers not, as he says, "mystery, miracle, and authority", but rather "magic, mystification, and tyranny" (quoted in Jackson, 1993, p. 257). The text does not explain these juxtapositions, but each intends a shift from the compassionate spirit of Jesus to the callous order of the Inquisitor. Each is calculated to keep everyone from seeing misery and extreme injustices for what they are.

Alyosha, who hears and is learning to see, understands that neither the Inquisitor nor his brother Ivan believes in god. But Ivan struggles, no doubt affected by his dialogues with Alyosha, toward the moment, at the novel's end, when he too takes care of a stranger. Both learn that doing precedes hearing; responding precedes understanding and knowing; ethics precedes ontology. Neither Alyosha's faith nor Ivan's skepticism, however, creates a capacity to see; both may prepare, but another kind of engagement actually catalyzes the birth of vision.

We must note with Peter Atterton (2007), however, that Levinas completely agreed with Ivan in rejecting theodicies (justifications of deities in the face of evil). Ivan tells Alyosha about the mother:

She has no right to forgive the torturer for the suffering of her child who was torn to pieces, she dare not forgive the tormentor, even if the child himself were to forgive him![12] And if that is so . . . what becomes of harmony? Is there in the whole world a being who could and would have the right to forgive?

(Dostoyevsky, 1992, p. 245)

Similarly, post-holocaust Levinas writes: "No one, not even God, can substitute himself for the victim. The world in which pardon is all-powerful becomes inhuman" (Levinas, 1990a, p. 20). In this, Ivan's rebellion is both sincere and a necessary rebuke to the excuses religion tends to make for god in the face of injustice.

What, then, does Alyosha learn to see? How does this seeing stand up to Ivan's protestations? Though Dostoevsky often cautioned readers not to mistake him for his characters or his narrators, in this last novel he gave the three brothers the patronymic Fyodorovich, sons of Fyodor, his own name. No psychoanalyst can avoid wondering whether the intellectual and skeptical

Ivan (including his crafty and snarky demon), the impulsive and wounded Mitya (whom Dostoevsky also calls Dmitri), and the apparently innocent and spiritual Alyosha each and all form aspects of their author, with the youngest named after Dostoevsky's recently lost three-year-old Alexei. To me (DMO), Alyosha seems the part of Dostoevsky that he most wanted to be, but he always had to contend with the other parts, much as he wanted to bring them into harmony.[13] Alyosha discovers, and manages to communicate to the egoistic Kolya Krasotkin, in an important subplot of the novel, what the Grand Inquisitor can never see: that the particular human being, no matter how humble, matters.

The conflict between fixation on one's ideals and the value of the particular other comes into stark relief in the character of Kolya, whose name stems from "*krasota*" (beauty). Thought quite handsome, the young teen Kolya thinks his own face hideous, not up to his ideals of beauty. Confronting Ilyusha's suffering, his own role in it, and the futility of his ideals as they crumble in the face of the other's dying, Kolya's heart begins to soften.

Kolya provides a trail marker for Alyosha's complex and sweeping journey to moral vision. In the monastery, Alyosha had listened. He heard the discourses about Christian love, and observed how lovingly his elder treated those who came to him for advice and comfort. He had mystical experiences. But only after he left the monastery, sadly encountering Ivan's elaborate and serious doubt about what kind of god permits the torture of children, did he truly begin to see for himself what he previously could only see through his teacher. First, he found that his attempt to give money to the already humiliated captain shamed him further. The captain almost took the money, but then rejected it on seeing Alyosha's elation. Too much joy in doing good, as Dostoevsky well understood, reverts to a form of egoism or narcissism. Only gradually did Alyosha learn that responding to suffering often meant simple and respectful presence and accompanying. He learned that the sufferer determines what is needed, and that helping means submitting. Ethical seeing means a radical self-emptying (*kenosis*), a preparation to serve without planning ahead for what may be asked. ("Without memory or desire," Bion (1970, p. 41) famously reminded clinicians, but this applies to all humanitarian situations.) What I (DMO) have long called "emotional availability" means also venerating the trace of god by simply and directly welcoming the other. This divinity speaks itself before all and for all, by way of human wretchedness, calling on us to respond *hineni*.

Dostoevsky's reflections from prison had already indicated that ethical vision—as Alyosha learned from Snegyirov, who threw down the proffered and much needed money—means recognizing everyone's incessant hunger for dignity. This broken and humiliated man's surviving sense of his own dignity—so important to Dostoevsky that he ended the novel with Snegyirov's unalloyed ("sneg" means snow) sorrow over losing his son—persisted in asserting itself grotesquely and unforgettably. Dostoevsky wrote:

There are some who think . . . that as long as one feeds a convict [and] looks after him well, does everything according to the law, the matter is at an end. This is a mistaken view. Everyone, whoever he is and however lonely the circumstances in which he has been pushed, demands, albeit instinctively and unconsciously, that respect be shown for his human dignity. The convict knows he is a convict, an outcast, and he knows his place *vis à vis* his superior officer; but no brands, no fetters will ever be able to make him forget that he is a human being . . . *Humane* treatment may make a human being of someone in whom the image of God has faded long ago.

(Dostoevsky, 2014, pp. 111–112; original emphasis)

Even the self-satisfied may be transformed, not by rebuke but by quiet example. When the egoistic Kolya arrives at the dying Ilyusha's bedside to put on an act and make himself the center of attention, Alyosha's quiet presence, having already transformed the other classmates into "gentlemen," gradually changes him too. By the time of the funeral, the 13-year-old Kolya weeps with the rest, and Alyosha can attend to the devastating grief of the bereaved father, Snegyirov.

The radical inversion in ethical vision and sensibility, common to Dostoevsky and Levinas, relentlessly upending egoism, appears clearly in this novel, as recognizing, relating to, affirming the dignity of the other, even when that other no longer identifies with it. Even an "other" like Fyodor Pavlovich, the grotesque father of the Karamazov brothers, feels a sincere disgust for the disingenuousness of the Church that is not entirely inaccurate. This disgust and the pride he takes in the authenticity of his own dissoluteness, his frank depravity, despite his shame in the decadence itself, making of his pride a bravado, still expresses a dignity that has not abandoned him even though he has abandoned it. Though bound by shame beneath it and pride above it, Pavlovich's genuineness expresses an indestructible dimension of dignity. Thus Levinas's frequent allusions to (and quotations of) *The Brothers Karamazov*, and to Dostoevsky generally, should not surprise us.

The refusal of egoism

"*La sortie de soi, la sortie de soi,*" repeated the older Emmanuel Levinas at the end of a video interview: one's exit from ego is the core of the ethical. "The hunger of the other awakens men from their sated drowsing and sobers them up from their self-sufficiency" (Banon et al., 1998, p. 11). Wrapped up in my egoistic worries, concerned for my own self-sufficiency, always seeking my place in the sun,[14] I cannot see the naked and vulnerable face of the other. I protect myself against my own and others' vulnerabilities so thoroughly that I can neither see nor respond "*hineni.*"

As an ethical thinker, Dostoevsky, from beginning to end, in his novels and other writings, caricatured and refuted the rational egoism of Chernyshevsky (see Chernyshevsky and Katz, 1989)—later adopted by Lenin (Lenin and Service, 1988)—with his egoistic antihero the Underground Man (Dostoyevsky, 1993a), whose relatives show up in all the novels. Rakitin (and arguably the Grand Inquisitor) in *The Brothers Karamazov*, shows the utter impossibility and even misery of the completely self-absorbed life. Such a person treats other human beings as things to be managed and used. In the rational egoist's philosophy of materialistic determinism, all turns out for the best when each acts out of self-interest: the philosophy of completely free markets applied to human relations. Ivan Karamazov, who finds no way either to transcend or to be called out from this intellectual trap, ends in apparent madness, though he eventually recovers and helps his brother to escape. His "madness," caused by "brain fever," has roots in his spiritual crisis. Both Mitya and Alyosha are ultimately transformed—though each differently—by loving.

In Ivan's struggle, however, we find the clearest articulation of the problem egoism poses. His case helps us better interpret the exit from its prison—whether Alyosha's, Mitya's, or our own. Ivan exemplifies a necessary refusal—"rebellion" for both Dostoevsky and Levinas: he rejects any provident god who, as a condition of an organized world, permits the abuse and torture of innocent children. To this god's paradise, "I most respectfully return him the ticket" (Dostoyevsky, 1992, p. 245). He thus contributes mightily to Dostoevsky's overall "after the death of a certain god" vision, but does not reveal an ethical way forward. Convinced by Smerdiakov of his fundamental and personal guilt for their father's murder, Ivan descends into madness.

Because the only kind of god available to Ivan—omnipotent, all-good, and provident—makes no sense to him, he remains tormented by an egoist devil who burrows his way into Ivan's imagination. Ivan's conversation with the devil, which evokes myriad dimensions of his ethical struggle, also expresses his belief in his half-brother Smerdiakov's accusation: you taught me that without immortality—the desire of the egoist—everything is permitted, and so you are at least as responsible for our father's murder as I am.

In contrast to Ivan's mighty intellectual flailing, the middle brother Mitya takes the path of expiatory suffering.[15] Once it becomes clear to him that he will be convicted for their father's murder, which he did not commit but which he had wanted to be done, he comes to understand his guilt in another sense: before all and for all. Having learned to love: "I revere her, Alexei, I revere her . . . before was nothing! Before were just her infernal curves that fretted me, but now I've taken her whole soul into my soul. Through her I've become a man!" (Dostoyevsky, 1992, p. 594). Now he would suffer for the world "as a hymn":

What do I care if I spend twenty years pounding out iron ore in the mines, I'm not afraid of that at all, but I'm afraid of something else now: that this risen [in the original Russian "resurrected", brought back from the dead by realizing that all are babes] man not depart from me! Even there, in the mines, underground, you can find a human heart in the convict and murderer standing next to you, and you can be close to him, because there, too, it's possible to live, and love, and suffer! You can revive and resurrect the frozen heart in this convict, you can look after him for years, and finally bring up from the cave into the light a soul that is lofty now, a suffering consciousness, you can revive an angel, resurrect a hero!

(Dostoyevsky, 1992, p. 591)

Dostoevsky had learned this many years before in his own imprisonment. Mitya continues:

And there are many of them, there are hundreds, and we're all guilty for them! Why did I have a dream about a "wee one" at such a moment? "Why is the wee one poor?" It was a prophecy to me at that moment! It's for the "wee one" that I will go. Because everyone is guilty for everyone else. For all the "wee ones," because there are little children and big children. All people are "wee ones." And I'll go for all of them, because there must be someone who will go for all of them. I didn't kill father, but I must go. I accept!

(Dostoyevsky, 1992, pp. 591–592)

Here we find Mitya's, and Dostoevsky's—and Levinas's—answer to Ivan's "I return the ticket!" to a paradise dependent on the torture of children. The failure does not belong to god, but to human beings, to bystanders like Ivan and Alyosha whom Ivan distracts from running to his obligations. Not only are the "wee ones" everywhere, but also, claims Dostoevsky— through Zosima, Alyosha, and Mitya—I (not you) am infinitely responsible for them. Forget arguments about immortality stemming from egoism; forget this provident god who makes evil disappear into harmony. "I will suffer for all of them," Mitya ecstatically promises, making them immortal. Responsibility for the wee ones means infinity and immortality. For Mitya, responsibility becomes what Levinas will later call "substitution":[16] I will go for all of them.

Alyosha, recognizing the validity of his impulsive brother's conversion to an ethic of expiatory suffering, and realizing that Mitya may lack the capacity to sustain this intention, perhaps wondering if he himself could persevere, advises him to reconsider after his trial. Meanwhile, he takes over from the ailing Ivan the planning for Mitya's escape from the 20 years "underground."

Alyosha's conversion from dreamy monastic idealism to practical and realistic goodness is shown not only around Ilyusha's funeral but also in Alyosha's final conversation about escape with Mitya after his condemnation and sentencing:

> "Listen, brother, once and for all," he said, "here are my thoughts about it. And you know very well I won't lie to you. Listen, then: you're not ready, and such a cross is not for you. Moreover, unready as you are, you don't need such a great martyr's cross. If you had killed father, I would regret that you rejected your cross. But you're innocent, and such a cross is too much for you. You wanted to regenerate another man in yourself through suffering; I say just remember that other man always [more difficult and more profound than bearing a cross], all your life, and wherever you escape to—and that is enough for you . . . Heavy burdens are not for everyone, for some they are impossible . . . Of course, bribery is dishonest even in this case, but I wouldn't make myself a judge here for anything, since, as a matter of fact, if Ivan and Katya asked me to take charge of it for you, for example, I know I would go and bribe; I must tell you the whole truth here. And therefore I am no judge of you in how you yourself act. But know, too, that I will never condemn you. And it would be strange, wouldn't it, for me to be your judge in these things? Well, I think I've covered everything."
>
> (Dostoyevsky, 1992, pp. 763–764)

Alyosha relieves his brother of the worry that the person he respects most in the world may judge him—another form of substitution. I suspend judgment and assume that burden, Alyosha implicitly says, much as a good parent holds many worries for young children. Of course, Alyosha realizes that he too had done nothing to protect his father on that fatal night when all three sons knew he was in mortal danger. Therefore, we know that his refusal to judge Mitya is genuine—the exact inverse of the egoist Rakitin, who periodically surfaces throughout the novel as the voice of cold rationality. Alyosha embodies a quiet, unspectacular ethic of substitution: "I before all."

Two forms of guilt: Dostoevsky, Levinas, and responsibility beyond neurosis

At this point in the description of both Dostoevsky's and Levinas's shared ethic of responsible guilt, the reader may begin to wonder if this ethic is too self-involved or aspirational. Mitya's desire to suffer for all the babes might seem histrionic. Alyosha's more radical realization of "I before all," while deeply personal, also makes us wonder if his identification with sainthood betrays some lack of self-awareness. In fact, this suspicion finds support as Alyosha falls into an epileptic fit while his drunken father persists in disparaging Alyosha's mother's memory despite Alyosha's pleas for him to stop. At the very least, this incident reminds us that Alyosha, like many clinicians and humanitarian workers throughout our lives, is much younger than the burdens he has laid upon himself, with the grievous emotional wounds all three brothers carry. Alyosha, Dostoevsky seems to be telling us, carries his vulnerabilities in one of the ways his mother and his author did: through epilepsy.

After all, who can live the level of responsibility to which Alyosha tries to hold himself? Who can expiate for the sins of humanity? Is Levinas's adaptation of this ethic merely the neuroticism of a Jew taking on a morose Russian's over-identification with Christ's sacrifice in order to cope with the trauma of the holocaust? How can one take up this guilt for all without falling into a subtle spiritual egoism? These questions resemble those addressed in the Chapter 3, on moral masochism, but here they assume another reductionistic cast. There, generosity and hospitality were suspected as "nothing but" masochism; here, we suspect Dostoevsky of over-identification with Christ's sacrifice, and Levinas, by proxy, of doing the same.

Before delving into this question of "how," we ought to consider first the "why" more closely. As Ivan keeps asking throughout the novel, why should I be my brother's keeper? Bernstein (2008) places this question in the context of a broad framework for interpreting a primary driving force behind all Levinas's writing: the problem of evil and its full expression in the horrors of the twentieth century. In particular, Bernstein focuses on the landmark essay "Useless Suffering" (Levinas, 1988), in which Levinas zeroes in explicitly on the problem of evil by taking the genocide of Auschwitz, the killing fields of Cambodia, two World Wars, the despotism of Hitler and Stalin, the gulags, and Hiroshima as emblematic examples of the explosion of evil scattered across the span of a century.

We should perhaps pause to note that in its classical formulation the problem of evil confronts the notion of an all-good and omnipotent deity with the existence of evil. If the god is all-good, it must want to prevent evil; if all-powerful, it must be able to. Therefore, the argument concludes, there is no god in any theistic sense. Theodicies respond by defending the believer's god against this argument, either by claiming that evils are needed as contrast in the pattern of the whole (Augustinian theodicy) or by claiming that evil, a "privation," has no reality of its own (medieval theodicy), and thus one's deity is off the hook, free from blame, safe to worship without nightmares.

Auschwitz in particular personally symbolized for Levinas the moral perversion lurking in any attempt to explain away evil as some necessary ingredient of a broader divine plan. It was paradigmatic of gratuitous evil that crystallized its irredeemable uselessness within the consciousness of the time (Levinas, 1988).

In foregrounding this uselessness, Levinas confronts the problem Ivan expresses in his consternation at a god and a religion that expects a mother to forgive her child's torturous murderer: in the name of what, exactly? Similarly, in the name of what, exactly, does the one expiate for the other, no less for all others, even for the Nazi who flipped the switch to start the flow of gas into the chambers at Auschwitz? Why am I guilty before *that* other? Why, more importantly, is this guilt and responsibility infinite and absolute? Or, in other words, why am I my brother's keeper and why is my bond to all fraternal? Above all, how can I hold on to these fraternal ties when evil repeatedly severs them?

Bernstein (2008) finds the solution to this dilemma in a simple insight into what Levinas regards as the root of evil: it has less to do with the perpetrator than with the bystander. Indeed, Levinas locates the source of all evil in this particular sin: "For an ethical sensibility—confirming itself, in the inhumanity of our time, against this inhumanity—the justification of the neighbor's pain is certainly the source of all immorality" (Levinas, 1988, p. 163). After all, compassion for the Jews did not motivate the nations of Europe or elsewhere to oppose Hitler until he became a threat to national security and world order. Saving the Jews from extermination, in itself, was insufficient motivation to fight back.

In seeking to identify a strand of thought that allowed nations to stand by for so long before jumping into action, Levinas (1988) accuses theodicy of a primal failure in the face of the holocaust. Theodicy, Levinas claims, explains away evils, even the worst, by reference to the overall goodness of god, by our need to know good and evil, or by blaming our own sins, whether individual or collective, Jewish or Christian. Since the massacres of the twentieth century, he thought, no one could take theodicy seriously.

The paradigmatic role Levinas (1988) assigns to Auschwitz here acquires the full force of its pathos and condemnation: evil for its own sake. The evil Auschwitz represents is so unconscionable that to blame the sin of the victims, whether original or ancestral, individual or communal, only compounds and extends the work of evil initiated by the Third Reich; as Primo Levi agreed, it deprives the victims of innocence. No matter how theodicy may spin the excuse, when god is let off the hook, the victim invariably receives the blame.

Above all, the denial of these events by those seeking to tear from the pages of history the experiences that tore the victims and survivors of the camps from this world would complete the destruction: "This would be pain in its undisputed malignancy, suffering for nothing. It renders impossible and odious every proposal and every thought which would explain it by the sins of those who have suffered or are dead" (Levinas, 1988, p. 163).

Like Levinas, Ivan Karamazov has no tolerance for theodicy, even in secular form: "Without it [torturing children], they say, man could not even have lived on earth, for he would not have known good and evil. Who wants to know this damned good and evil at such a price?" (Dostoyevsky, 1992, p. 242). Against the egoist, the outraged Ivan rejects a world in which a mother must forgive her child's killer in order for a god to reveal a vision of ultimate harmony to mortal eyes. Like Ivan, Levinas feels no obligation to disprove the possibility of this coherence of sin and virtue in order to feel justified in rejecting it. It offers up a god that Levinas, Ivan, and indeed the co-authors of this chapter would just as well see sacrificed. Therefore, Levinas's polemic against theodicy is not only a visceral rejection but an insistence on a different order of goodness. Indeed, he immediately asks:

> But does not this end of theodicy, which obtrudes itself in the face of this century's inordinate distress, at the same time reveal in a more general way the unjustifiable character in the suffering of the other person, the scandal which would occur by my justifying my neighbor's suffering? So that the very phenomenon of suffering in its uselessness is in principle the pain of the other.
>
> (Levinas, 1988, p. 163)

Here we find a simultaneous articulation of the truth compelling Ivan's passionately youthful revolt right alongside its transcendence toward a more meaningful ethical vision. Without this vision, Ivan merely enacts the moral impotence of Pontius Pilate—in effect washing his hands of the responsibility for human suffering. Ivan's rejection of theodicy ought to throw him back onto his responsibility; instead, he uses it as an excuse for complacency in the face of events that are in his power to affect, of evil that is within his power to counteract.

Again, like the same reinvigorated wave crashing on to an abandoned shore, we hear Levinas's appeal to our own ethical sensibility (Bernstein, 2008). Debating with Ivan precluded Alyosha from seeking out Mitya and interrupting a chain of events that led to the murder of their father. More importantly, this failure also set off a chain reaction of senseless suffering for Mitya, Grushenka, Ivan, Alyosha, and so many others affected by this event. Zosima, moreover, foresaw this event and implored Alyosha to try to intervene by finding Mitya. Instead, Alyosha wasted his time wrestling with Ivan's questions before he was ready to face them. Entrapped in the desperation of Ivan's rebellion against theodicy with only sufficient wisdom to struggle toward some kind of better theodicy, Alyosha turned his back on what he already knew without needing proof. He turned his back, for a crucial moment, on his responsibility to Mitya, to his father, and to the world as a participant in the events that shape it. Instead of honoring that responsibility, for a crucial hour or two, Alyosha fell into a hopeless quest for a barren truth. In the process, for a time, he allowed Ivan's brilliantly hopeless meanderings to seduce him into the position of bystander.

Levinas insists that justifying the suffering of the other person is the epitome of all evil. The example of Ivan implies that even the concern with the question of justice is but a distraction from the just response already commanding us in the face of the other's pain. We will do and we will hear, in that order. Levinas saw only the other's suffering as absolutely meaningless, implying that one's own suffering is potentially meaningful as it teaches us the scandalous shame of every instance in which we turn away from the suffering of the other. Therefore, the evil of all suffering is the evil of failing to respond to the other's pain; useless suffering is all suffering in the other— every instance of my failure to respond to the other's pain. Without bystanders, evil could be rooted out by the simple goodness of people doing for others what they can, whenever they can.

Bernstein (2008) points to Hannah Arendt's recollection of the silence falling over the hall of justice during the Eichmann trial in Jerusalem when the story of Anton Schmidt was told. A German soldier who provided Jewish partisans with forged documents, Schmidt was killed for the assistance he gave the Jews.

Similarly, Goodman (2012) reminds us of the small French town of Le Chambon. During the Second World War, many Chambonnaise opened their homes to shelter, clothe, and feed thousands of Jews; many were raided and executed for their efforts. Goodman records one villager's reaction to being asked what made her help at such peril to herself:

> her big, round eyes stopped sparkling in that happy face, and she said "Look. Look. Who else would have taken care of them if we didn't? They needed our help and they needed it then . . . there are no deeper issues than the issue of people needing help then."
> (Oliner, 1992, quoted in Goodman, 2012, p. 119)

This is the heart of the matter: ethical sensibility is not a theory. Fact more genuine than observation, it already lives in us as not merely beings, but humans (Bernstein, 2008). Already there before the face of the other calls us to respond to its concrete need, it lives in the examples of those who, without deliberation, take care of others in the face of peril. If Auschwitz is paradigmatic of gratuitous evil, then Le Chambon and Anton Schmidt are paradigmatic of the overflowing of goodness in the face of the demon that Auschwitz unleashed onto the earth, and every other demon like it—shabby and mighty alike.

To rephrase the brave, good woman from Le Chambon: there are no issues of greater importance than people needing help when it is in our power to offer it. Their need compels a response. No rationalization, however perfect it may be, absolves us from the responsibility to offer it.

Immediately following the statement above, in which Levinas collapses all the evil of the twentieth century and of all the world's history to the fundamental immorality of justifying the suffering of the other, he adds: "Accusing oneself in suffering is undoubtedly the turning back of the ego to itself" (1988, p. 163). This simple, almost simplistic, statement offers a response adequate to the desperation of Ivan's oh-so-Russianly superlative grievance. Why should the mother not forgive her child's murderer? The answer is not merely that she is also not free from sin. Rather, the refusal to forgive acknowledges limits on goodness; and only a limitless goodness, such as none of us possesses, has the power to redeem her child's senseless death.

Ivan, grieving for this mother and for the child, contemplating the injustice of the world, paralyzed by his resentment, incapable of acting on his own moral impulses, exemplifies the neurotic form of guilt that only perpetuates itself without impelling him toward redeeming action, until all this internal conflict implodes into an epic illness during which he confronts and debates the devil within him in a desperate battle for sanity.

Until then, Ivan is repeatedly irritated by a sense that there is something he is failing to recognize, something he is failing to do, something awry. However, rather than allowing this sense to make him restlessly curious, as Alyosha would to find out the right course of action, Ivan uses it to fuel his disillusionment. As his complacency allows the wound to fester, it finally manifests itself as his half-brother Smerdiakov.

Smerdiakov's genuine surprise at Ivan's outrage at the murderous act echoes the complicity of Ivan's intentional, though not fully conscious, position of bystander. In a dramatic crescendo, Smerdiakov tells Ivan that the latter's philosophy of "everything is permissible" provided the former with the moral justification for killing their father. Ivan's rejection of his own responsibility to try to influence Smerdiakov's actions, together with the assumption that he could philosophize furiously without consequences, created a moral void, a kind of negative space for the lesser demons of Smerdiakov's nature to occupy.

Ivan provides an excellent example of how the failure to be his brother's keeper ends in tragedy. If we do not take on this responsibility, the cruel indifference we see everywhere can consume our humanity. More importantly, all three brothers find their way toward taking responsibility for each other and for those connected to them as the book draws to a close. None exemplifies this better than Alyosha, but even Mitya expresses similar levels of burden (see above). Each in his own way embodies the idea of "giving an onion,"[17] of doing whatever good they can, even in the midst of hellish experiences. It seems like the whole idea comes down to this: a single act of selfless goodness or "active love," as Zosima would state it, disrupts the apparent world order of evil by providing an example of a different possibility.

Were every person to do what good is in their power, then the world would be quite a different place. The import of this idea, which we find repeatedly in the words of Zosima and his brother Markel throughout the text, is that heaven has already dawned on earth. Our failure to recognize its majestic presence blinds us to the goodness in our hearts. This is *why* we are all guilty—the second form, non-neurotic or ethical guilt—for even those who intuitively grasp this truth constantly lapse in their ability to live moment by moment in accordance with it. Accepting the pre-primordial infinite guilt for all the sin of the world, even locally, we can come to terms with all the ways in which we fail to live up to the goodness of non-indifference. In 2015, protest signs on the streets of New York read: "Black Lives Matter!" If this needs to be proclaimed to us, then some of us, many of us, perhaps most of us, are failing in non-indifference to the other. We are standing by. "After the death of a certain god," argued by both Nietzsche and Levinas, we bystanders are the problem of evil.

A responsible subject, thus, does not singlehandedly undo all of the evil in the world, but lives out in full concreteness the possibility of its undoing. Needless to say, this is how the evil of the world becomes undone, and it is reason enough to become my brother's keeper. But, of course, the point of the biblical story, and of Levinas's life work, is that I do not *become* my other's keeper. I am born into that responsibility; I may evade it, but it is always already mine.

Moreover, taking on absolute guilt, the second form, as a responsibility to redeem the world has the added benefit of restoring one's own faith in the world. This can be particularly valuable to the often naturally kind-hearted people who perform humanitarian or psychotherapeutic work. Today's politics of power and money that organize the macro-economy can be so dehumanizing and pervasive as to render Ivan the most sympathetic character in the text. The ultimate ethical accusation, when understood precisely and lived out wholeheartedly, can be a source of unceasing strength and even comfort against the background of seemingly unceasing war, poverty, illness, and corruption.

The reader might still wonder at this point: why not simply try to be decent without these grand notions? The problem is that simply being decent does not undo evil at its root in the heart of the individual. Only the accusation of infinite responsibility, as Levinas (1969) proposes, turns the ego back on to itself. In this "turning back" lies the possibility of untangling the knotted roots of all evil, reversing the evasions of bystandership.

The "how": untangling the ego through self-accusation

In *Totality and Infinity*, Levinas (1969) charts a course in the adventure of the ego[18] as the movement from the consumption of nourishments to labor, possession, and, finally, comprehension—the epitome of the human power to grasp and assimilate ideas, possessions, space, time, and people as modalities of the ego, opposing not only the concrete other but also all otherness. Proximity, both infinitely close to the other so that responsibility cannot be evaded and infinitely distant because the other transcends me utterly, undoes this possessiveness. Now, the other's hunger finds and accuses the ego in its self-complacency, turns the ego from a winding up of possessiveness into the uncoiling of generosity (Livshetz and Goodman, 2015). Initially, Levinas believed, the ego turns to itself, constituted by the enjoyment of its nourishments and the avoidance of its hunger, its suffering. Then, accused, obsessed, tortured, and taken hostage by the suffering of the other, emptied out, no longer an ego, the *moi* turns away from the world of sense objects and looks to what is already in its possession that might satisfy the other's need.

In "The Temptation of Temptation" (1990b), echoing the biblical theme of tasting the knowledge of good and evil, Levinas describes the Western obsession with experience as a desire for knowledge or total comprehension, a temptation ultimately that is unquenchable. Ivan's need to understand the world rather blinds him to the goodness and the urgent needs rattling the gates of his intellectual prison. His very rebellion is predicated, of course, on his own ethical sensibility and his concern with justice. Had he responded to these impulses directly, he might, for instance, have encouraged Alyosha in implementing his good intentions more skillfully. He might have recognized a need in Smerdiakov to be recognized by Ivan—a need that, when unmet, left Smerdiakov with more limited options for recovering the dignity of which their father deprived him from birth. Ivan may have allowed himself to entertain and explore the nature of Smerdiakov's sinister attitude, and attempted to prevent the actions Smerdiakov was both planning and insinuating to Ivan.

Of all three brothers, Ivan is uniquely poised to intervene, for it is only to him that Smerdiakov makes gestures that convey his murderousness. Unfortunately, his very brilliance protects him from emotional and ethical awareness until tragedy has already ensued and he begins to recognize his guilt before the world as the concrete guilt over his father's murder and his brother's false imprisonment. The absolute dimension of this guilt lies in the recognition that Ivan's evil was never that of Smerdiakov. Alyosha's insistence that Ivan is not their father's murderer belies a darker realization that Ivan represents the possibility for all murder in the world. The evil of the bystander teaches us that there are no neutral actions. Even when we abstain from harm, we also abstain from good, and all the while the world cries out for it.

Therefore, Ivan's quest for answers about god's intentions in allowing the suffering of innocent children, important as these are, prevents him from hearing and seeing as Mitya and Alyosha eventually do. There are other choices available to him besides continuing to obsess over answers, but the force of his intellectual passion distracts him from these. By itself, the confrontation with the questions is not in vain, but seeking direct answers to them is precisely the temptation of temptation (Levinas, 1990b). An excuse to be a bystander, the philosophical search for the knowledge of goodness may leave behind a trail of indifference. The temptation of temptation is one way in which ego perpetuates its agenda. Goodness, on the other hand, does not come as a response to an intellectual question, a puzzle, but as a nourishment of a longing, doing before hearing. Alyosha and Mitya learn that it is up to them to respond before they *hear* a call or demand. Their own response, their own active love and pre-emptive acceptance of absolute responsibility, satiates the longing of their souls without perpetuating the agenda of their egos. The ethical response to the other transforms their own useless suffering into the kind of expiation and substitution that redeems the world.

Still, like the other brothers, Ivan influences others while he evolves himself. His complacency does tempt Alyosha to seek answers to impossible questions instead of carrying out the responsibility of which Alyosha, in contrast to Ivan, is aware. However, the naiveté that plagues Alyosha's early attempts at generosity stand in stark contrast to Ivan's maturing wisdom: Mitya rightly should escape his sentence, and Ivan must help him. Organizing the details of the getaway, the same intellect turning Ivan against his responsibility throughout the book turns practical, skillfully living that responsibility. Exasperated by the recognition of its own failures, the same ego that turned toward reason to understand and redeem the existence of evil now becomes the ethical subject, restoring justice in response to injustice. While Alyosha recognizes and obeys the accusation that constitutes his ethical sensibility and even his identity, Ivan responds to Mitya's concrete need and, in the process, helps Alyosha concretely and skillfully respond to the particular other.

However, it is only because Alyosha saves Ivan first[19] and absolves him from the paralysis of guilt for their father's murder that Ivan eventually finds the courage to turn his general moral outrage into concrete action. Alyosha's perseverance in his goodness, despite the crises of faith instigated largely by his conversations with Ivan, eventually helps transform Ivan's moral outrage into just action. Alyosha, in turn, benefits from a confrontation with Ivan's challenges by learning to respond to the need that even such challenges betray, the responsibility for even the responsibility of the other, the completely excessive responsibility for trouble and crimes of the other, which requires not only the awakening of ethical sensibility but a practical wisdom.

Remembering goodness

At the outset, we promised a meditation on remembering goodness, a topic dear to both Levinas and Dostoevsky. Here, shortened for reasons of space, it can be discovered sprinkled throughout this book: gratuitous acts of kindness whose memory nourishes and sustains us every day, as they did for the characters described along our way. As lifesaving as a daily extra bowl of soup in Auschwitz, as unpretentious as a verbal pat on the shoulder for a struggling colleague or patient, such kindnesses merit rehearsing and remembering—another form of spiritual exercise, one that both Dostoevsky and Levinas recommended.

On his way to penal servitude in Omsk in Siberia, Dostoevsky met a number of Decemberists' wives who had followed their husbands into exile, and who routinely met the new caravans of prisoners with whatever small kindnesses they could offer: Bibles with embedded money, kind words. Later, in prison, a kind-hearted doctor took considerable risks to sneak paper and pencils to Dostoevsky so that he could record his experiences for future use. Just as the memory of personal and communal suffering seems necessary for the development of ethical capacity, so do memories of unexpected kindness.[20]

Levinas, too, loved to tell such stories. In his later years, he often referred to one from Vassily Grossman's *Life and Fate* (quoted in Chapter 3). He never forgot that French nuns saved his wife and daughter during the war.

In our darkest hours as clinicians or humanitarian workers, the memories of goodness can sustain us. Alyosha reminds Mitya not to forget his own conversion, and the boys become "gentlemen" to remember Ilyusha's goodness and their own:

> You hear a lot said about your education, yet some such beautiful, sacred memory, preserved from childhood, is perhaps the best education . . . And even if only one good memory remains with us in our hearts, that alone may serve some day for our salvation.
>
> (Dostoyevsky, 1992, p. 774)

For Levinas, such memories conserve for us the sense that goodness and holiness are always possible, even when absent:

> I am not saying that all humans are saints! But it is enough that, at times there have been saints, and especially that holiness always be admired, even by those who seem the most distant from it. This holiness which cedes one's place to the other becomes possible in humanity. And there is something divine in this appearance of the human capable of thinking of another before thinking of himself.
>
> (Levinas and Robbins, 2001, p. 183)

The elder Zosima, described and quoted at length in *The Brothers Karamazov*, functions precisely as the remembered and needed ideal of holiness that Levinas considered crucial. Not by accident did Zosima and Levinas repeat (and hope we would understand), "I am guilty for all and before all, and I more than all the others."

Both Levinas and Dostoevsky, inspiring him, reappear in our next chapter on the prophetic character of clinical and humanitarian work.

Notes

1 It is a particular pleasure to work with Max, whose first language is Russian, and who perceives the Levinasian undertones in *The Brothers Karamazov* as I never could. Maxim Livshetz is a clinical psychologist working out of the Seattle area. He works with people suffering from many forms of psychological pain, often dealing with severe depression, trauma, and domestic violence. A graduate of Middlebury College, he holds a clinical doctorate in psychology from Antioch University, Seattle. His graduate coursework and dissertation focused heavily on the intersections between virtue ethics, hermeneutics, and relational psychoanalysis. Currently, his scholarship focuses on the practical ways in which the meeting points between various theoretical strands take on concrete forms in the healing relationship.

2 Dostoevsky is sometimes spelled either "Dostoyevsky" or "Dostoevskii," depending on the original source.

3 More extensive treatment can be found in Atterton (2007).

4 In English, Joseph Frank has provided a magnificent five-volume biography, running to thousands of pages, and a hefty one-volume condensation (Frank and Petrusewicz, 2010).

5 In Russian literature, the "St." is usually omitted, leaving only "Petersburg." In casual conversation it may be shortened even further, to "Peter."

6 "Even in penal servitude, among thieves and bandits, in the course of four years I finally succeeded in discovering human beings . . . among them there are deep, strong, magnificent characters, and cheering [them] was to find gold under the fire" (Dostoevsky quoted in Roos, 1982, p. 16). *Notes from a Dead House*, sometimes considered a novel, collects Dostoevsky's memories, impressions, and reflections from his four years in penal servitude.

7 This resort town, with a name that translates as "Old Russia," has salt/mud baths and is home to one of the oldest offices of the Russian Orthodox Church. So it is fitting that Dostoevsky wrote *The Brothers Karamazov*, a theological treatise as well as a novel, there.

8 One of Levinas's earliest Talmudic lectures (Levinas, 1990b), begins with this text from the Torah, also translated as "we will do and we will hear," and goes on to its Talmudic commentaries. Like William James in *The Will to Believe* (James et al., 1979), Levinas meditates at length on the necessity of commitment before understanding, ethics preceding ontology (see also Levinas, 1969).

9 Some speculate that Dostoevsky's famous Judeophobia, rarely obvious in his novels but often evident in his notebooks and in *A Writer's Diary* (Dostoyevsky, 1993b), was a reaction against aspects of himself that he felt were Jewish (Vinokur, 2008), and that Levinas, partly because of his immersion in Russian literature, absorbed a Christian sensibility very young.

10 ML: This reveals a dialectic tension in Levinas's work between his critique of vision and image and the ethical impossibility of turning away. To be present responsibly is also a refusal to turn away that involves seeing.

11 One of the few places in his properly philosophical works where Levinas quotes Talmudic sources concerns this topic: "'To leave men without food is a fault that no circumstance attenuates; the distinction between the voluntary and the involuntary does not apply here' says Rabbi Yochanan" (Levinas, 1969, p. 201).

12 DMO: To consider fully the topic of forgiveness here would take us too far afield, but thinking back to Primo Levi, and the many lost to genocide, we may remember the words F. Scott Fitzgerald jotted in a notebook: "Forgotten is forgiven" (quoted in Tufte, 2006, p. 64). In brief, with Levinas and Dostoevsky, I feel it is beyond my jurisdiction to pardon crimes done to others.

13 ML: He had trouble trusting that purity in himself and had to make Alyosha naive, but the dialogue between these parts of Dostoevsky's soul actually strengthen Alyosha over time.

14 After Dostoevsky's "I am guilty before all and for all," Levinas most frequently quoted Blaise Pascal: "that is my place in the sun. Here is the beginning and the image of the usurpation of all the earth" (Pascal and Ariew, 2005, p. 295).

15 To "expiate" is to repay within a theology of sin that resembles an economy of debts. I may repay debts I never personally incurred.

16 Substitution, alluded to in Chapter 2, which forms the conceptual heart of Levinas's second masterpiece, *Otherwise than Being* (Levinas, 1981), embodies responsibility and obsession with the other, from simple courtesy to placing one's life at risk in extreme situations for an other. The *possibility* of such non-indifference, proven by the actuality of sacrifice, makes evasion and bystander behavior reminiscent of Cain: "Am I my brother's keeper?" (see Bernasconi, 2002).

17 "Giving an onion" refers to a story that Grushenka, lover of both Mitya and the father Fyodor Pavlovich, told to Alyosha:

> Once upon a time there was woman, and she was wicked as wicked could be, and she died. And not one good deed was left behind her. The devils took her and threw her into the lake of fire. And her guardian angel stood thinking: what good deed of hers can I remember to tell God? Then he remembered and said to God: once she pulled up an onion and gave it to a beggar woman. And God answered: now take that same onion, hold it out to her in the lake, let her take hold of it, and pull, and if you pull her out of the lake, she can go to paradise, but if the onion breaks, she can stay where she is. The angel ran to the woman and held out the onion to her: here, woman, he said, take hold of it and I'll pull. And he began pulling carefully, and had almost pulled her all the way out when other sinners in the lake saw her being pulled out and all began holding on to her so as to be pulled out with her. But the woman was wicked as wicked could be, and she began to kick them with her feet: it's me who's getting pulled out, not you; it's my onion, not yours. No sooner did she say it than the onion broke. And the woman fell back into the lake and is burning there to this day.
>
> (Dostoyevsky, 1992, p. 352)

Grushenka went on to say that in her whole life she had given only one little onion.

18 By "ego" Levinas does not mean the self-organizing center and possibility of stable and integrated experience and responsible maturity and relatedness described by various psychoanalytic schools. His usage, instead, resembles that common in social contract ethics, in the contrast between egoism and altruism, and the like. "Ego," for Levinas, names a moral preference for oneself and one's own concerns, with a corresponding indifference toward the suffering of the other.

19 For readers who perhaps read *The Brothers Karamazov* long ago, we recommend a rereading of at least its final 20 pages. A full reading might be an enormously rewarding treat.

20 ML: I think this speaks to the "how" of taking on the accusative. Remembering goodness happens by itself. Therefore, remembering is already the practice of goodness—it orients the subject to experience in such a way that the possibilities for benefiting a situation become spontaneously apparent. DMO: My clinical experience leads me to believe, instead, that many people need ritual, and

witness, to help them internalize and use memories of goodness; traumatic memory, shocking and disorganizing as it can be, disables this capacity, while many, whose developmental situation lacked the good-enough, never formed it. But I agree that remembering goodness enables the accusative, passive, vulnerability that characterizes the ethical. ("The accusative" in Levinas is a *double entendre*. It refers to the grammatical shift from the nominative *je* (I) to the accusative *moi* (me). It also refers to my capacity to receive, to be accused by, the need, the misery, the destitution of the face of the other. I am guilty for all.)

References

Atterton, P. (2007). Art, Religion, and Ethics *Post Mortem Dei*: Levinas and Dostoevsky. *Levinas Studies*, 2, 105–132.

Bakhtin, M. M. (1973). *Problems of Dostoevsky's Poetics*. Ann Arbor, MI: Ardis.

Banon, D., Levinas, E., and Ricoeur, P. (1998). *Emmanuel Lévinas: philosophe et pédagogue*. Paris: Editions du Nadir de l'Alliance israélite universelle.

Bernasconi, R. (2002). What is the Question to which "Substitution" is the Answer? In S. Critchley and R. Bernasconi (Eds.), *The Cambridge Companion to Levinas* (pp. 234–251). Cambridge: Cambridge University Press.

Bernasconi, R. (2010). Globalization and World Hunger: Kant and Levinas. In P. Atterton and M. Calarco (Eds.), *Radicalizing Levinas* (pp. 69–86). Albany, NY: State University of New York Press.

Bernstein, R. (2008). Evil and the Temptation of Theodicy. In S. Critchley and R. Bernasconi (Eds.), *The Cambridge Companion to Levinas* (pp. 249–264). Cambridge: Cambridge University Press.

Bion, W. (1970). *Attention and Interpretation: A Scientific Approach to Insight in Psycho-Analysis and Groups*. New York: Basic Books.

Chernyshevsky, N. G., and Katz, M. R. (1989). *What Is to Be Done?* Ithaca, NY: Cornell University Press.

Cox, R. (1969). *Between Earth and Heaven: Shakespeare, Dostoevsky, and the Meaning of Christian Tragedy*. New York: Holt.

Dostoevsky, F. (2014). *Notes from a Dead House*. Translated by R. Pevear and L. Volokhonsky. New York: Pantheon.

Dostoyevsky, F. (1992). *The Brothers Karamazov: A Novel in Four Parts with Epilogue*. Translated by R. Pevear and L. Volokhonsky. London: Vintage.

Dostoyevsky, F. (1993a). *Notes from Underground*. Translated by R. Pevear and L. Volokhonsky. New York: Alfred A. Knopf.

Dostoyevsky, F. (1993b). *A Writer's Diary*. Edited by G. S. Morson. Translated by K. A. Lantz. Evanston, IL: Northwestern University Press.

Frank, J. (1976). *Dostoevsky: The Seeds of Revolt, 1821–1849*. Princeton, NJ: Princeton University Press.

Frank, J. (2002). *Dostoevsky: The Mantle of the Prophet, 1871–1881*. Princeton, NJ: Princeton University Press.

Frank, J., and Petrusewicz, M. (2010). *Dostoevsky: A Writer in His Time*. Princeton, NJ: Princeton University Press.

Goodman, D. M. (2012). *The Demanded Self: Levinasian Ethics and Identity in Psychology*. Pittsburgh, PA: Duquesne University Press.

Jackson, R. L. (1993). *Dialogues with Dostoevsky: The Overwhelming Questions.* Stanford, CA: Stanford University Press.

James, W., Burkhardt, F., Bowers, F., and Skrupskelis, I. K. (1979). *The Will to Believe and Other Essays in Popular Philosophy.* Cambridge, MA: Harvard University Press.

Lenin, V. I., and Service, R. (1988). *What Is to Be Done?* London and New York: Penguin.

Levinas, E. (1969). *Totality and Infinity: An Essay on Exteriority.* Pittsburgh, PA: Duquesne University Press.

Levinas, E. (1981). *Otherwise than Being, or, Beyond Essence.* The Hague and Boston Hingham, MA: M. Nijhoff and Kluwer Boston.

Levinas, E. (1988). Useless Suffering. In R. Bernasconi and D. Wood (Eds.), *The Provocation of Levinas: Rethinking the Other* (pp. 156–167). New York: Routledge.

Levinas, E. (1990a). *Difficult Freedom: Essays on Judaism.* Baltimore, MD: Johns Hopkins University Press.

Levinas, E. (1990b). *Nine Talmudic Readings.* Bloomington, IN: Indiana University Press.

Levinas, E. (1998 [French original 1976]). Secularization and Hunger. *Graduate Faculty Philosophy Journal*, 20, 3–12.

Levinas, E., and Robbins, J. (2001). *Is It Righteous to Be? Interviews with Emmanuel Lévinas.* Stanford, CA: Stanford University Press.

Livshetz, M., and Goodman, D. M. (2015). Honoring the Sensate Bond between Disparate Subjectivities in Psychotherapy. *Humanistic Psychologist*, 43, 177–193.

Malka, S. (2006). *Emmanuel Levinas: His Life and Legacy.* Pittsburgh, PA: Duquesne University Press.

Oliner, P. M. (1992). *Embracing the Other: Philosophical, Psychological, and Historical Perspectives on Altruism.* New York: New York University Press.

Ornstein, P. (2013). Dostoevsky's Autobiographic Novel *The House of the Dead*: His Survival and Recovery from His Siberian Penal Servitude. Unpublished manuscript.

Pascal, B., and Ariew, R. (2005). *Pensées.* Indianapolis, IN: Hackett.

Roos, P. (1982). Dostoyevsky's "Crime and Punishment". *Scandinavian Psychoanalytic Review*, 5, 75–89.

Scanlan, J. P. (2002). *Dostoevsky the Thinker.* Ithaca, NY, and London: Cornell University Press.

Terras, V. (1981). *A Karamazov Companion: Commentary on the Genesis, Language, and Style of Dostoevsky's Novel.* Madison, WI: University of Wisconsin Press.

Toumayan, A. (2004). "I More than the Others": Dostoevsky and Levinas. *Yale French Studies*, 104, 55–66.

Tufte, V. (2006). *Artful Sentences: Syntax as Style.* Cheshire, CN: Graphics Press.

Vinokur, V. (2008). *The Trace of Judaism: Dostoevsky, Babel, Mandelstam, Levinas.* Evanston, IL: Northwestern University Press.

Chapter 8

Clinical and humanitarian work as prophetic word

> Since it is difficult to distinguish true prophets from false, it is as well to regard all prophets with suspicion.
>
> (Levi, 1986a, p. 229)

Prophets disturb us. They cry out against injustice, shaking us out of our comfort zones, requiring us to respond or to exile them. We may even diagnose them so that we will not have to deal with their sometimes violent-sounding voices, or with the challenge of their lived example. And yet, paradoxically, often quiet and gentle souls by nature, they do not want this vocation,[1] begging that someone else be chosen because they know the hatred and banishment that await them. Still, as humanitarian workers—including psychotherapists, doctors without borders, nurses, teachers, caregivers, and many other unrecognized and underpaid servants of us all—these prophetic pragmatists feel themselves responding to a call they cannot avoid.

In his final years Dostoevsky often recited Pushkin's famous and terrifying poem "The Prophet" (Pushkin, 1825). Indeed, Joseph Frank (2002) entitled the fifth and final volume of his Dostoevsky biography *The Mantle of the Prophet*. Clearly Dostoevsky identified with this biblical role, as Primo Levi did not, no matter how exactly his "Shemà" (see Chapter 5) takes exactly the prophetic biblical tone. Nelson Mandela, on his inauguration, said that he began his term "not as a prophet, but as your humble servant." Similarly, Emmanuel Levinas, I believe, would have rejected the role and title of prophet for himself, but clearly understood his message as prophetic, even though philosophically articulated.[2] The problem, as Marc Ellis (2007) notes, is that prophecy tends to indict the very communities from which the prophetic word originates, calling out their own injustices.

My four main questions—intended to pull together many themes in this book—are the following:

1 What is the prophetic—ancient and contemporary—and how do we recognize it?

2 Can a concept of prophetic action help us to see psychoanalysis and humanistic approaches to psychotherapy as forms of humanitarian work, and humanitarian work as implicitly therapeutic?

3 How does the discourse of human dignity relate to the prophetic?

4 Can we understand Levinasian "holiness" in terms of the prophetic?

We address these questions by way of a journey, sketchy to be sure, through ancient biblical prophecy and Levinasian ethics, psychoanalytic enactment theory, and human dignity discourse, before finally returning by considering the Levinasian talk of holiness.

Prophecy—ancient and contemporary

I could not begin a meditation on the prophetic qualities of clinical and humanitarian work without studying Abraham J. Heschel's monumental *The Prophets* (1962).[3] Having begun as a philosophy student at the University of Berlin, precisely in the heyday of phenomenology, reading Husserl and Heidegger, and having found this study excessively abstract, Heschel turned to work on the Hebrew prophets, to whom he brought phenomenology's emphasis on lived experience, while rejecting both what he viewed as overly theological, excessively neutral and uninvolved, and what he viewed as reductionistically psychological (e.g., Cohen, 1962) approaches, and attempted to understand the consciousness of the prophet himself. He described, most centrally, the "sympathy" of the prophet with the "divine pathos"—that is, with god's fury, disappointment, love, and compassion with and for "his"[4] people. In this sense, the prophet—Heschel studied in particular Amos, Hosea, Isaiah, Micah, Jeremiah, Habakkuk, and Second Isaiah[5]—heard god's word, saw as "he" saw, and spoke with "his" voice. Thus saith the Lord!

Why such fury and disappointment? "Ah, sinful nation, a people laden with iniquity, offspring of evildoers, sons who deal corruptly! They have forsaken the Lord, they have despised the Holy one of Israel, They are utterly estranged" (Isaiah 1:4).[6] In what does this iniquitous evildoing consist? It involves corrupt dealing for sure, and we also know about syncretism (worship of the local idols along with their own god), but several prophets reserve the greatest rage for the rich who cannot seem to see the poor upon whose backs they are living (remember Dostoevsky!):

> Hear this, you who trample upon the needy,
> And bring the poor of the land to an end,
> Saying: When will the new moon be over,
> That we may sell grain?
> And the Sabbath,
> That we may offer wheat for sale,

That we may make the ephah small and the shekel great,
And deal deceitfully with false balances,
That we may buy the poor for silver,
And the needy for a pair of sandals,
And sell the refuse of the wheat?

(Amos 8:4–6)

The shepherd Amos called out the rich and powerful, so they told him to go away and stop prophesying. Imagine what response his words would bring now, when so many are homeless and invisible after the "great recession" while the wealthy become ever richer and retreat into their gated palaces. Their splendid houses and apartments, costing countless millions, would start Habakkuk talking:

Woe to him who heaps up what is not his own . . .
Woe to him who gets evil gain for his house . . .
For the stone will cry out from the wall,
And the beam from the woodwork respond
Woe to him who builds a town with blood,
And founds a city on iniquity!
(Habakkuk 2:6, 9, 11–12)

Conventional ideas of beauty, wisdom, common sense, and reckoning turn upside down. God becomes clearly identified with the poor; the rich need serious conversion and repentance.[7] The prophet delivers judgment upon them, then goes back to god to plead for mercy on "his" people, not to destroy everyone, but at least to make some distinctions. Heschel (1962, p. 108) comments that "it is the moral corruption of the leaders that has shattered God's relationship to his people." Despite Isaiah's pleading with god, the judgment comes:

Behold the day of the Lord comes,
Cruel, with wrath and fierce anger,
To make the earth a desolation,
And to destroy its sinners from it . . .
I will punish the world for its evil,
And the wicked for their iniquity;
I will put an end to the pride of the arrogant,
And lay low the haughtiness of the ruthless.
(Isaiah 13:9, 11)

This passage addresses not just Israel but the entire world, reminding me strongly of Philip Cushman's "burning world" (Cushman, 2007; see also West, 2004), ever hotter, where the world's poor suffer ever more each year from the developed world's indifference to the effects of our "lifestyle" choices.

What happened to the compassion and love in the prophets' message? Clearly it returns in the image of god's love for "his" sinful people, in the extension of this prophetic care to the Ninevites despite Jonah's evasion (Shulman, 2008), but even more in the kind of repentance required. But not everyone will return: "Their deeds do not permit them to return to their God. For the spirit of harlotry is within them and they know not the Lord" (Hosea 5:4).

Should we return from sin, we must embrace not only sackcloth and ashes but also an ongoing conversion. Remember why god is enraged:

> The Lord shall enter into judgment
> With elders and princes of his people:
> It is you who have devoured the vineyard;
> The spoil of the poor is in your homes.
> What do you mean by crushing my people,
> By grinding the face of the poor?
>   (Isaiah 3:14–15)

Repentance means seeing that the riches in my home crush the poor, and doing something about it. How, in a world of ever more extreme economic inequalities and unnecessary miseries, can these ancient prophets not reproach us today? But, again, what do they require: religious observance in whatever faith or tradition to which we adhere? Clearly not. Repentance means a life of utter humility, simplicity, justice, and *chesed* (loving-kindness):

> With what shall I come before the Lord,
> And bow myself before God on high?
> Shall I come before Him with burnt offerings,
> With calves a year old?
> Will the Lord be pleased with thousands of rams,
> With ten thousands of rivers of oil?
> Shall I give my first-born for my transgressions,
> The fruit of my body for the sin of my soul?
> He has showed you, O man, what is good;
> And what does the Lord require of you
> But to do justice, and to love kindness,
> And to walk humbly with your God?
>   (Micah 6:6–8)

Irrespective of whether we agree with Heschel (1962, p. xxix) that "prophecy ceased," his view that "the prophets endure and can only be ignored at the risk of our own despair" would be hard to dispute. A few more recent voices on inequality and climate change clearly belong to this tradition, while others argue only on economic and pragmatic grounds. Organized psychoanalysis, unfortunately, has, in the name of survival and the movement above all else, mostly excluded its more prophetic voices, such as Sandor Ferenczi and Erich Fromm (Wolstein, 1992), hidden and minimized them (Mann, 2000), or seen them as marginal at best (Aron and Starr, 2012; Cortina and Maccoby, 1996; Roazen, 2001).

Though he did not see himself as a prophet, having studied the biblical prophets too carefully to be confused about this, Levinas often spoke and wrote in a prophetic tonality, as many have observed, and understood the life of responsibility as prophetic. Let us consider what this could mean. True, the biblical prophet deals primarily in words, but these words teach us to see differently, with different optics, to watch ourselves oppressing the poor, to see that we are responsible and must change our hearts and our way of life. Levinas (1998b) referred to prophecy most extensively in *Otherwise than Being*. Because readers may find the Levinasian text difficult, I offer clarifications in square brackets:

> We call prophecy this reverting[8] in which the perception of an order coincides with the signification of this order given to him that obeys it. [Hearing the call or demand, seeing the face of the suffering other coincides with the meaning as demand on me—the prophetic provides no space for deliberation.]
>
> Prophecy would thus be the very psyche in the soul: the other in the same [the irreducible individual suddenly presents herself from what has been reduced to a totality or a category in the same], and all of man's spirituality would be prophetic [for the other]. Infinity is not announced in the witness given as a theme [a said, a generality].
>
> In the sign given to the other, by which I find myself torn up from the secrecy of Gyges [where I hide and evade responsibility, as in Plato's story], "taken by the hair" [Ezekiel 8:3] from the bottom of my obscurity in the saying without the said[9] of sincerity, in my "here I am" [*hineni*], from the first present in the accusative [a play on words: I am accused by the other, infinitely guilty and responsible, and also my subjectivity is a very humble accusative *moi* in the grammatical sense, the done to, demanded of, an non-agentic presence], I bear witness [a word Levinas uses almost interchangeably with "prophecy"] to the Infinite . . .
>
> This recurrence [response to the other, constituting ethical subjectivity] is quite the opposite of return upon oneself, self-consciousness. It is sincerity, effusion of oneself, "extraditing" of the self to the neighbor. Witness is humility and admission; it is made before all theology [another form of reductionism, totalizing, the said]; it is kerygma [message] and prayer, glorification and recognition . . .
>
> The transcendence of the revelation lies in the fact that the "epiphany" comes in the saying of him that received it [there is no revelation without response]. The order that orders me does not leave me any possibility of setting things right side up again with impunity [once

inverted, this asymmetrical order where the other transcends me utterly can never be evaded].

(Levinas, 1998b, p. 149)

A phenomenologist, Levinas describes the prophetic experience. The demand, addressed to me alone, forms the only valid individuating principle and makes me irreplaceable (Ciaramelli, 1991). There is no going back. One who hears the cry of the other, and sees the face of the other, can never set things right side up again. But responsibility comes first, anarchically, as Levinas often said, before all beginnings, before the other arrives:

An obedience preceding the hearing of the order, the anachronism [prophecy predicts backwards, *nachträglich*, explaining that the response implied a preoriginal command] of inspiration or of prophecy[10] is, for the recuperable time of reminiscence, more paradoxical than the prediction of the future by an oracle [the popular, not the biblical, use of "prophetic"]. "Before they call, I will answer" [Isaiah 65:24], the formula is to be understood literally. In approaching the other I am always late for the meeting [the other always precedes me, whether I realize it or not].

(Levinas, 1998b, p. 150)

But have we now re-installed the ethical in some kind of universalizing theology? Does connecting ethics to the biblical history of prophecy ("Thus saith the Lord!") not overcommit us in terms of faith? It depends, as I have often told philosophy students who asked me whether I believed in god, on what kind of god they have in mind. Levinas (1998b, p. 152) continued:

By reason of these ambiguities [especially with respect to theological language tending to treat the other and the idea of god as information], prophecy is not the makeshift of a clumsy revelation. They [these ambiguities] belong to the glory of the Infinite [the more-than-can-be-thought, the excess, non-reciprocity, asymmetry of the ethical relation] . . .

Transcendence owes it to itself to interrupt its own demonstration. Its voice [the voice of demonstration and theodicy, I think] has to be silent as soon as one listens for its message. It is necessary that its pretension be exposed to derision and refutation,[11] to the point of suspecting in the "here I am" [*hineni*] that attests to it a cry or a slip of a sick subjectivity. But of a subjectivity responsible for the other! There is an enigmatic ambivalence, and an alternating of meaning in it. In its [prophecy's] saying, the said and being are stated, but also a witness, an inspiration of the same by the other, beyond essence.

The biblical *hineni* (*me voici*, here I am, but without I or me[12]), the paradigmatic Saying, appears repeatedly in Genesis, spoken by Noah and Abraham. In *Otherwise than Being*, Levinas (1998b) refers to Isaiah 58:6–9,[13] clearly indicating his desire to link this pivotal response of the ethical subject to social justice. Even more surprising, reversing his emphasis in the earlier *Totality and Infinity* (Levinas, 1969), he uses a text that places *hineni* in the mouth of god: "You shall cry, and he will say, Here I am [*hineni*]" (Isaiah 58:9). In responding to the cries of the naked and hungry poor, we treat them mercifully, with holiness, as speaking with the voice of the infinite, now infinitely close as well as transcendent. Levinas (1969, p. 74) commented:

> It is not a gift of the heart, but of the bread from one's mouth, of one's own mouthful of bread. It is the opening not only of one's pocketbook, but of the doors of one's home, a "sharing of your bread with famished," "a welcoming of the wretched into your house" (Isaiah 58).

Hospitality, both gentle in the "bonjour" and extreme in substitution, shows itself here as an indispensable prophetic theme.[14]

We who try to do justice, we shall cry too. We both suffer and are commanded to respond to the suffering of others. In a crucial footnote, Levinas (1998b, p. 199, n11) quoted Isaiah's response to his prophetic vocation: "Here I am! Send me" (Isaiah 6:8). Levinas commented that "Here I am!" means "send me." According to Claire Elise Katz (2013), Levinas relied on Isaiah for the meaning of *hineni* because he wanted to disrupt our complacency, to remove us from bystanding. Though Levinas always insisted on asymmetry, he also echoed the prophet who assures us that we will hear *hineni* when our turn comes to cry.

I believe, with Adriaan Peperzak, that Levinas attached his radically ethical Saying to the prophetic precisely because he wanted to show how it includes a discourse of social justice. The prophets, writes Peperzak,

> were the protagonists of a justice that extends itself to the whole of humankind. The nakedness of the other symbolizes also the other's being unprotected, exiled, and dissociated as a stranger who still must be served as the presence of the infinite.
>
> (Peperzak and Levinas, 1993, p. 175)

Nevertheless, we will next consider how the quiet, daily work of clinicians and other humanitarian workers (nurses, doctors without borders, teachers who work with the poor even in developed countries, aid workers, and the like) may well belong in the area of the prophetic.

Enactment: prophetic word and action in clinical work

Dabar, "the word" in Hebrew,[15] was so effective that it could not be taken back. Words, even if spoken just once, have the power to create, to sustain, and to murder. The speech-act of twentieth-century British philosophy (Austin, 1967)—including its relative, the performative utterance—finds no stronger exemplar than the *Shemà* (whose echoes we hear, of course, in Levi's):

> Hear, O Israel: The LORD our God is one LORD; and you shall love the LORD your God with all your heart, and with all your soul, and with all your might. And these words which I command you this day shall be upon your heart; and you shall teach them diligently to your children, and shall talk of them when you sit in your house, and when you walk by the way, and when you lie down, and when you rise. And you shall bind them as a sign upon your hand, and they shall be as frontlets between your eyes. And you shall write them on the doorposts of your house and on your gates.
>
> (Deuteronomy 6:4–9)

These words, like the prophetic, affect the people who hear them and repeat them to themselves and to their children, wearing them on their hands and foreheads, placing them on the doorposts of their dwellings. Such words, repeated, studied, and treasured, change us.

Similarly, contemporary psychoanalysis[16] has rediscovered the inter-changeability of word and deed under the rubric of "enactment." Of course, our primary means of engagement in psychoanalysis, whether classical, self-psychological, or contemporary relational, has always been verbal. We listen and speak. By listening—partially deaf as we may be—we mean that we allow the emotional life of the other to affect us, to resonate in us, to engage us. We hope that our speaking will respond to and engage the emotional life of the other so that this dialogic process continues, grows, and deepens. If this occurs, both people find themselves changed by their encounter in ways that they did not expect.

But speaking is more. Even as children we knew that "words will never hurt you" was a reassuring lie; instead "sticks and stones may break your bones, but words may break your heart." Freud, buttressed by the whole tradition of Western philosophy, taught us that words could bring under-standing that changed something more than superficially. In addition, he understood—though this is frequently overlooked—that healing words often occurred in a ritual situation, and always within the relationship that he called transference. We now value the non-verbal, preverbal, situational, and relational aspects of psychotherapy more fully—though still probably not adequately, and in some respects perhaps not as much as Freud himself did. In any case, our patients speak to us in many ways besides the literally lexical (the kinds of words that can be written on a page), and we to them. (I pause only to mention a vast literature on preverbal infant communication and on metaphor (Beebe and Lachmann, 2001; Lakoff and Johnson, 2003; Stern, 1977).)

Enactment, a concept very dear to most contemporary relational psychoanalysts (Davies, 1997; Harris, 2002; Hirsch, 1998; Maroda, 1998; Spezzano, 1998; Stern, 2009), stretches the "talking cure" even further. It implies that psychoanalysis works through a dramatic process in which patient and analyst both inevitably play their parts. Inevitably, yes, but enactment has retained something of a bad reputation: one catches oneself or a supervisee in an enactment with a patient. Often we find this same ambivalent attitude toward countertransference generally: of course, everyone has it and no understanding arrives without it. On the other hand, both Freud and Kohut warned us to clean our eyeglasses, see our patients clearly, without countertransference, without the biases imported by our own history and emotional experience. Bion similarly counseled us to listen without memory or desire; in other words, to listen without past or future as if we could make a fully innocent, pre-traumatic space for them, a welcoming place. So we have this same problem with enactment: is it the human condition, the analytic condition, or something about which we should feel ashamed?

Probably both and neither. But before we can solve this conundrum, we need to study some history of the concept of enactment in psychoanalysis. (I shall leave aside its important history in family and group therapies for now.) Probably this concept, less familiar to many of us not trained in the interpersonal school, can bear some genealogy here. Surely we need not revisit the infamous "acting out" with which psychotherapists, unfortunately influenced by obsolete psychoanalytic vocabulary, still disparage their struggling patients. "Enacting," to generalize somewhat, bears a closer look for its reference to drama and history. Chosen historically almost as frequently as "acting out," its usage represents a subtle shift toward an attempt to understand a developmental narrative. Theorized by contemporary Freudians as "countertransference enactment" (Jacobs, 1986, 1997, 1999, 2001) or simply "enactment" (McLaughlin, 1987, 1991), the term highlights the awareness of embodied communication needed to fill out the "talking cure." James McLaughlin's graceful prose is worth quoting at some length:

> Enactment in a broad sense can be construed in all the behaviors of both parties in the analytic relationship. This is so because of the enormous intensification of the appeal or manipulative intent of our words and silences, normally present to some degree in all dialogue. The intensification takes place in the analytic situation for both parties because ordinary actions are forsworn and visual communication is curtailed.

Given the potential for regression in both parties induced by the deprivations inherent in the analytic situation, it is expectable that words, as the word "enactment" itself informs us, become acts, things— sticks and stones, hugs and holdings. This secondary process, which we cherish for its linearity and logic, becomes loaded with affective appeal and coercion, to be experienced by either or both parties as significant acts or incitement to action.

These charged words of the analytic dialogue are themselves embedded in and surcharged by a steady clamor of nonverbal communication between the pair, much of which is registered and processed, at times subliminally, by both parties.

Each had learned from infancy, long before the words were there for the saying, how to appeal, coerce, clarify, and dissimulate through the signals of body language, gestures, facial expression, and vocal qualities. And both went on to add to, not relinquish, these wordless capacities to influence and be influenced as they also gradually learned the supple power and diplomacy of words.

(McLaughlin, 1991, p. 598)

I cherish this *locus classicus* for the concept of enactment for several reasons. First, McLaughlin calls attention to both sides: actions speak and words act. Without collapsing the distinction between words and actions, his writing, here and elsewhere, constantly explores both embodied communication and the effective power of the word.[17] Second, he presumes full mutuality of participation everywhere. Both parties register, process, appeal, coerce, clarify, and dissemble. No appeal here to equality or to a reciprocity of responsibility (Rozmarin, 2007); on the contrary, his position accords easily with the mutuality plus responsibility described by Lewis Aron (1996), where the analyst remains asymmetrically responsible. Third, I find in McLaughlin's account of enactment no shame, blame, or "gotcha." Even when he uses words like "manipulative," he normalizes them. Enactment, for him, simply communicates, as humans are prone to do. We patients and analysts are humans. So we play out what we are trying to tell each other and to work out. It's a simple syllogism. Fourth, and important for my argument, his entire description of enactment presumes what self-psychologists often call "developmental striving" (Fosshage, 1988) and what I try to interpret generously and hospitably. Within a hermeneutics of trust, I try to presume that both my patient and I are doing our best to tell a story and to work out something (probably something terrible) as best we can.

The New York Relational School,[18] especially under the influence of Philip Bromberg, adds the claim that dissociation produces enactment. Looking closely, we can see that the enactment concept itself changes with this feature added:

when the feared perceptual experience is embodied, the trauma is to some degree *relived*, not just talked *about*. This often (but not always) pulls patient and therapist into an *enactment* of the trauma in the here and now, as a part of which the therapist is dissociatively experienced by his patient as a contemporary version of an abusive, uncaring, or neglectful other, and because he is in a dissociative state of his own, he *contributes* to the patient's perception of him. That is, the dissociative enactment is a joint "cocoon" that continues to hold them in thrall *while* the therapist is consciously engaged in doing the work with another part of his patient—a part who may, at least for a while, appear to be collaborating splendidly and is seeming very attached to the therapist; perhaps a bit "too" attached.

(Bromberg, 2003, p. 709; original emphasis)

Suppose, to resolve the difficulty, we consider enactment as developmental process engaged or resumed. Estelle Shane (2006, p. 299), paraphrasing ideas from Malcolm Slavin, coined almost in passing the expression "developmental enactment" "that forms around the patient's wanting the analyst to go where she [presumably the analyst] wouldn't go in another relationship." But it also poses the question, too long delayed now, about how to understand the word "developmental," since my whole argument hinges on it.[19]

Calling enactment "developmental" means understanding that the patient, the suffering neighbor (i.e., the sufferer who seeks my help; *patior* = to suffer, to undergo) calls on me, requires of me, unpremeditated by either of us, an enactment not initiated by me but one that responds to the age of the patient in the transference (Winnicott, 1975), in psychoanalytic language, or to the naked suffering of another human being, in ethical language. I do not choose agentically to respond from my position of sovereign autonomy, or egoistic narcissism, but allow myself to be taken hostage, traumatized by the other, drawn into a role, perhaps of primary maternal preoccupation or of the grandfather of an adolescent (Pizer, 2008), that I would never have chosen but in which I find myself, in responsibility to the patient's needs. Something produces itself in me, a subjection to the developmental enactment, so that both of us are changed, for the sake of the patient (Davoine and Gaudillière, 2004). My patient's desperate need— "Donna, say something to me!"—ruptures my arrogant and complacent self-satisfaction, and forces me to find a response so that she or he may not die alone. This amounts to a subjectivity incapable, as Levinas (1998a) would say, of shutting itself in and the other out.

Such a process would have all the embodied and relationally intricate entanglement that McLaughlin described and that any nonlinear systems or complexity theorist could cherish. It could delight the heart of every infant researcher who believes the psychoanalyst meets and holds what was poorly, disastrously, or never met or held. But, thinking intersubjectively, it also turns the lens on the developmental troubles of the analyst or therapist, and on the painful interlocking of these with those of the person who comes for help. In self-psychological language, the selfobject needs of both people become engaged. Viewing enactment as a continuous mutual developmental process makes it clear how crucial is the analyst's readiness or unreadiness to change and to be changed in every treatment, in every hour. A developmental and prophetic view of enactment accords seamlessly with the major developments in contemporary self-psychology: with the engaged clinical attitudes of Lichtenberg, Lachmann, and Fosshage (1996) and of Teicholz (1999); with the intersubjective systems theory of my collaborators Stolorow, Brandchaft, and Atwood (1987); with Bacal's (2006) specificity; with Coburn's (2014) complexity. Each theory suggests that in every clinical moment the other's particular lived and embodied trouble calls on me and commands me to empty myself, holding my theories and biases lightly, so that you may become liberated to become you.

Ready to change means ready to hear your challenges, ready to imagine that I may be trapping and imprisoning you in my expectations. Ready to change means watching you look away or seem to lose vitality. Ready to change means being prepared to abandon my metaphor for yours. Prepared to change may even mean taking an interest in some art, or sport, or area of the news or history of which I have known little or nothing, because you and I need that common ground right now. Developmental enactment means not only being drawn in, unconsciously, but also joining you in creating an "optimal entanglement" (Galatzer-Levy, 2011, p. 148) where old wounds may be at least partially understood, witnessed, and healed, and psychological development may resume. As Mary-Joan Gerson (1996) believes, developmental enactments expand or loosen a system. They may also, of course, engage our egoistic tendencies, and, so to speak, develop backwards toward evil and violence. Once again, everything hinges on how we understand "developmental." Developmental enactments, in the sense I prefer, will produce generosity, inclusion, and peace. Prophetically, they implicitly, and sometimes explicitly, protest while they nourish the other, speaking a word of welcome.

Finally, having directed this book as a support and challenge to clinicians and humanitarian workers, I need to say clearly that seeing words as actions and actions as words makes them belong to each other. Practitioners of the "talking cure," clinicians practice a prophetic action of challenge to those who would give up on the most wretched and devastated. Every time we see and respond to a human face that others might throw away, might relegate to the "takers," to the impossible borderlines or psychotics, we are working in the world of the prophetic. Humanitarian workers practice, often in the most desperate and isolated circumstances, their belief in the word that every single human being matters—perhaps the central prophetic claim. They are therapists and clinicians in the best senses of these words.

Human dignity

Primo Levi, arguably the central and most challenging character in this book, refused "the mantle of the prophet," and, due to his understated demeanor and devotion to "the facts," actively tried to avoid it. Nevertheless, he relentlessly refused to soften his story, or to stop asking how humanity could be so lost and so methodically destroyed. His precise and logical mind ruled:

> When the unspoken dogma [every stranger is an enemy[20]] becomes the major premise in a syllogism, then, at the end of the chain, there is the *Lager* [Levi's word for the Nazi concentration and death camps]. Here is the product of a conception of the world carried to its logical conclusion.
>
> (Levi, 1986b, p. 9)

What seems to have galled him most, what no postmodernist or constructivist evasion could ever dim, was the memory of the deliberate, cynical, and systematic reduction of human beings to empty shells with numbers on their arms. The *Lager* systematically destroyed language and understanding, reducing human beings to sub-human *bruti* (brutes), interested in nothing but mere survival. Antoine Philippe (2004, p. 130) writes:

> destroying humanity entailed more than killing men; it required destroying the very life of living men, transforming them into *Muselmänner*, into men between life and death, into men whose lives were so dim that they fell below animal life down to the level of vegetative life, where nothing matters anymore except eating and surviving. This means that since the Nazis tried to destroy ethics in humanity, surviving was in itself an ethical act; saving oneself as a potentially ethical being was paramount to saving the possibility of ethics, paramount to saving humanity.

Educated in the humanistic traditions of Western Europe as well as in a non-observant Judaism, having memorized large sections of Dante, Levi had clearly internalized the fundamental respect for human dignity inhering in both the Jewish and the Christian traditions, along with the sense of what constituted sin within these traditions—what conduct, as Joseph Farrell (2011, p. 88) writes, "is incompatible with humanity." From the moment he regained his voice on leaving Auschwitz, his entire corpus, stretching over more than 40 years, constituted a meditation on human dignity and its violations, joining him decisively to my internal chorus. He believed, with the bulk of the Western tradition, that a distinct and meaningful difference split humans from other species, and that this difference mattered: "you were not made to live like brutes or beasts, but to pursue virtue and knowledge" (Dante Alighieri, 2000, p. 485); "Consider if this is a woman . . . womb cold as a frog in winter" (Levi et al., 1992, p. 9). Not only were victims reduced to animal levels, but perpetrators behaved like brutes. Despite all the brutality—note another reference to brutes—Levi had endured, and despite postmodernist scorn for the humanism he cherished, this distinction, derived from Western literature and philosophy, served him constantly. In an interview almost 40 years after his liberation, he noted:

> It is curious how this animal-like condition would repeat itself in language: in German there are two words for eating. One is *essen* and it refers to people, and the other is *fressen*, referring to animals. We say a horse *frisst*, for example, or a cat. In the *Lager*, without anyone having decided that it should be so, the verb for eating was *fressen*. As if the perception of the animalesque regression was clear to all.
>
> (Levi, 1983)

Representing the descent to the subhuman, to the empty shell, the figure of the *musselmano* (in his Italian)[21] haunted Levi. Preventing oneself from so descending became the first priority. A fellow inmate, Steinlauf, explaining his strategy of keeping himself clean, advised Levi, "we must not become beasts." Levi, understanding the seriousness of the warning, watching the rapid destruction and emptying out of humanity all around him, developed his own methods: reciting Dante; judging the conduct of others as brutish; working as a chemist; taking care to remember everything so that, should he return home, he could report what he had seen, despite the Nazis' determination to cover their tracks. The mason Lorenzo, whose extra soup and courage saved Levi, saved his own dignity by doing his work well: "with well staggered bricks and as much mortar as was required, not in deference to orders but out of professional dignity" (Levi, 1989, p. 122). He, like others, defined for himself what counted as resistance. Indeed, as Levi noted repeatedly, it seemed crucial to the Nazis not just to eliminate their victims, but first to destroy their humanity. Some managed to salvage traces, remnants, scraps of this humanity.

In later years, Levi wrote that whereas war comes from anger, "in Auschwitz there is no anger. Auschwitz is not in us, it is not an archetype, it is outside of man" (Levi et al., 2005, p. 28). What could he have meant? Probably Joseph Farrell has it right when he conjectures:

> Levi's assertion is not only a valiantly defiant reassertion of his fundamental trusting the human being but also a consequent dismissal,

as not appertaining to humanity, of those capable of crimes whose nefariousness is beyond comprehension. Auschwitz belongs in that realm not of the inhumane but of the nonhuman.

(Farrell, 2011, p. 97)

Levi always worried that the next Auschwitz lurked just around the corner. Evasion of responsibility alarmed him just as it did Dostoevsky, Bonhoeffer, and Levinas. All repeat that the world of "*laggiù*"—"down there", as if in Dante's *Inferno* itself—must not be allowed to stand as a human possibility; goodness, or in terms congenial to Dostoevsky and Levinas, holiness, constitutes the evidence for human dignity. None of these writers— Dostoevsky with his Ivan Karamazov, Bonhoeffer with his "cheap grace," Levi with his allergy to providence combined with reverence for the human, or Levinas, for whom divinity can be found only in the face of the other who commands, "You may not kill me"—permits escape through religion. Levi's challenge stands, insistently prophetic:

> It [the Auschwitz Monument] must be a warning dedicated by humanity to itself, which can bear witness and repeat a message not new to history, but all too often forgotten: that man is, and must be sacred to, man, everywhere and forever.
>
> (Levi et al., 2005, p. 7)

Before turning to goodness and holiness in the prophetic voice, let us consider a woman who is well known to those of us who have worked with people devastated by war, political violence, and sexual abuse—Judith Lewis Herman, founder of Victims of Violence. The daughter of Helen Block Lewis, who turned our clinical attention to shame and taught her daughter how to stand up by her courageous behavior when called before the notorious McCarthy committee, Herman (1992; Herman and Hirschman, 1981) pioneered the understanding that the "shell-shocked" and the sexually abused were suffering from the same thing: what came to be called "posttraumatic stress." Unpretentious yet insistent, teaching yet always learning, collaborator yet a lonely truth-seeker, Herman models for me the quiet version of the prophet. Like Mandela, she keeps saying, "That's not right," and also like him she counsels picking one's activist battles, so that one focuses on where one can make some difference. During a long clinical life, she has taught many clinicians, including myself, a pragmatic devotion to human dignity, lived out in community with others who support each other as they respond to the most vulnerable.[22] Levi described the *Häftling*, the concentration camp inmate, as "desperately and ferociously alone" (Levi, 1989, p. 134); Herman understands the restoration of dignity as intricately connected to reestablishment of human connections, of community, as far as possible for the destroyed. Recently, she has been teaching us to understand complex post-traumatic stress (a compassionate way to think about "dissociative disorders") and post-traumatic suffering generally in terms of shame (Herman, 2011). Her determination to find a way to restore human dignity to those brutally robbed of it, her own quiet dignity in the face of professional marginalization, her unassuming style: all these attributes place her among my favorite prophets, and, yes, always among my internal voices.

And yet, as Tzvetan Todorov (1996) reminds us, my own dignity is only a relative value; concern for the dignity and need of the other ranks much higher. In the best prophetic tradition, Herman's and Levi's understated style keeps the ethical focus on the human dignity of the devastated other.

Holiness[23]

Levinas, as we have seen, distinguished between useless and useful suffering, the kind demanded of us for the sake of the other, in which a kind of substitution occurs. One for the other. In his last years he loved to repeat stories illustrating what he called "holiness," where unexpected response to the other occurs—unexpected by the recipient and by the giver. It seems to come, like the prophetic word, from elsewhere, from before the situation, from an-archical responsibility, as both Dostoevsky and Levinas believed. Vasily Grossman's *Life and Fate* provided Levinas with a favorite story we have already included in Chapter 3 to illustrate unexpected goodness; Ivan Karamazov finds himself caring for a stranger whom he would earlier have ignored. But other thinkers have also refused to believe that massive, radical evil means that human beings have become incapable of surprising goodness. Dori Laub, psychoanalyst and interviewer of holocaust survivors, writes:

> As a teenager during the war, she [one of Laub's informants] had lost most of her family and witnessed many awesome events. Among them was the choking to death of a small baby who had cried too loudly, as well as the burning alive of several of her close relatives. These relatives had been put into a boarded-up wooden shack that was set afire. Toward the end of the war, she participated as a partisan in the hunting down and killing of local collaborators. During this period, her fellow partisans captured and turned over a seventeen-year-old German youth to her. She was given free hand to take revenge. After all that she had witnessed and lived through, this woman bandaged the German's wounds and turned him over to the POW camp. When asked why she had done this, she replied, "How could I kill him—he looked into my face and I looked into his."
>
> (Laub, 1992, p. 80)

This story invites a Levinasian reflection on the demand created by the face of the other. Of course, many might have done otherwise. Why do some respond? We can only speculate in particular instances. Why did Lorenzo risk his life repeatedly to sustain Primo Levi's life? Why did the teenager in Laub's story save the German youth? Why did the Russian woman give bread to the German soldier? I imagine something like what Winnicott (1965, p. 73) called "the development of the capacity for concern," where good-enough environmental provision facilitates the development of a child capable of genuine care and concern for others, even in extreme circumstances.

Todorov (1996, pp. 201–202) relates another tale, from Auschwitz:

> An SS guard there named Viktor Pestek approaches various inmates with an offer to help them escape. He has a plan: he will get hold of another officer's uniform and the two of them will leave the camp together, as if everything were perfectly normal. The inmates are wary of the offer, suspecting a trap. Finally, one of them, a man called Lederer, accepts, and the escape succeeds. Later, Pestek returns to Auschwitz to arrange more such escapes, but this time he is caught and executed. Why did he take such risks? It seems that while fighting on the Russian front he had taken part in a punitive action against a village suspected of concealing resistance fighters. Pestek was wounded during the attack and left behind by his comrades. The following day several members of a Russian family found him hiding in their barn. Pestek was thirsty; instead of finishing him off, they led him to the stream.

So, in addition to developmental explanations, we have memory: *remembering goodness* can support the ethical seeing, the vulnerability to others' suffering, the reluctance to turn away that produce these moments of holiness, that engender heroes who never consider themselves heroic. Never forget. This mantra, warning us always to remember the worst, to carve these words into our hearts, also reminds us to hold the stories of uncommon and unexpected goodness.

Hermann Langbein (1972), another Auschwitz survivor, collected rare stories like those of Viktor Pestek. Scientific observer that he ever remained, Primo Levi, determined to recount the exceptions to every horrifying generalization, wrote:

> And right here, as a breath of fresh air and to prove how alien I am to global judgments, I would like to recount an episode: it was exceptional, and yet it happened:
>   In November 1944 we were at work in Auschwitz. Together with two companions I was in the chemical laboratory I have described elsewhere. The air raid sounded and immediately the bombers were visible: there were hundreds, the raid promised to be monstrous. In the camp there were several large bunkers, but they were for the Germans and off limits to us. We had to make do with the fallow grounds, by now already

covered with snow, within the enclosure. All of us, prisoners and civilians, ran down the stairs, headed for our respective destinations, but the head of the laboratory, a German technician, held us *Häftlinge* chemists back: "You three come with me." Astonished, we followed him at a run toward the bunker, but at the entrance stood a guard with a swastika on his armband. He said, "You can go in; the others beat it." The head of the laboratory answered: "They are with me; it's either everyone or no one," and tried to force his way inside: a boxing match ensued. The guard, who was a strong fellow, certainly would have won, but fortunately for everyone the all-clear sounded: the raid was not for us, the planes had continued north . . . if anomalous Germans, capable of such modest courage, had been more numerous, that time's history and today's geography would be different.

(Levi, 1989, p. 169)

For Levi, this man showed "modest courage," but of course he might well have been shot for what he did. For our purposes, we notice that this incident stayed with Levi, along with the kindnesses and courage of fellow prisoners, to the end of his life.

Many examples of what Levinas called "*sainteté*" (holiness), unexpected goodness, response to the other, occur without much notice. A neighbor in my suburban New Jersey town recently overheard a German couple in the local pharmacy as they were refused desperately needed medication because they had no US identification. He followed them to the door of the store where he found them in tears, told them to wait, and bought them the medication. He regarded the strangers as his neighbors, and took the trouble. Granted, all the people involved in this story had white skin and spoke good-enough English, but I see similar occurrences in New York among people who do not share either language or skin color almost every day. I believe we need to notice, to remember, to create an inner "ground bass" or *continuo* for our internal chorus, to reassure ourselves continually that the ethical life is real and therefore possible.

Postscript

Harsh and demanding, prophets remind us that remaining faithful, responding with non-indifference to injustice, working to restore dignity, has its hazards. Socrates, internal chorister for most philosophers, spoke at his trial:

Now I want to prophesy to those who convicted me, for I am at the point when men prophesy most, when they are about to die. I say gentlemen, to those who voted to kill me, that vengeance will come upon you immediately after my death, a vengeance much harder to bear than that which you took in killing me. You did this in the belief that you would avoid giving an account of your life, but I maintain that quite the opposite will happen to you. There will be more people to test you, whom I now held back, but you did not notice it. They will be more difficult to deal with as they will be younger and you will resent them more. You are wrong if you believe that by killing people you will prevent anyone from reproaching you for not living in the right way. To escape such tests is neither possible nor good, but it is best and easiest not to discredit others but to prepare oneself to be as good as possible. With this prophecy to you who convicted me, I part from you.

(Plato, 1997, *Apology*, 39c–d)

Speaking truth to power, our contemporary cliché for prophesying, has deep roots in Hebrew and Greek traditions, with strong resonances among all the courageous voices in this book, even those who might have preferred a quieter path.

Notes

1 In 1934, Dietrich Bonhoeffer, watching the Nazis take power and rearm Germany, preached:

> Jeremiah was not eager to become a prophet of God . . . he resisted, he tried to get away. But as he was running away, he was seized by the word, by the call. Now he cannot get away anymore . . . He was accused of fantasizing, being stubborn, disturbing the peace and being an enemy of the people as of those in every age even up to the present day who were seized and possessed by God . . . O Lord, you have enticed me, and I was enticed . . . I had no idea what was coming when you seized me . . . How could we know that your love hurts so much, that your grace is so stern? . . . God, why are you so terrifyingly near us?

> (Quoted in Schlingensiepen, 2010, p. 154)

2 After drafting this chapter, I found and read two extraordinary treatments of prophecy in Levinas by Claire Elise Katz (2013), who begins, as I have done, with Heschel, and by Oona Ajzenstat (2001), who emphasizes the Levinasian transformation of obedience into command. We do not simply discuss matters of social justice; rather, hearing the prophetic call, experienced in the encounter with the other, changes us into speakers, protesters, critics, prophets.

3 An astute reader may notice the Hebrew prophets as my primary reference points. I am also well aware that in the history of Islam, the Prophet Muhammad had the same role: insisting that god is one, and calling out the rich and powerful on behalf of the poor. Unfortunately, I am not much educated in the history of Islam.

4 In this era, common to Jews like Heschel and Levinas as well as to Christians, masculine pronouns—"he" or "*il*"—were used when referring to the deity. Others had to face them with the implications of their own prophetic social justice.

5 Biblical scholars now regard the Book of Isaiah as having at least two major authors, with Chapters 40–55 ascribed to a nameless writer from the exile period.

6 Heschel quoted from the Revised Standard Version of the Bible in *The Prophets*, so I shall do likewise.
7 This spirit continues into the Second Testament: Jesus embodies the prophetic hatred of poverty and love for the poor.
8 Reverting and reversal express the countercultural quality of both ancient and Levinasian prophecy:

> One can call prophecy this reversal whereby the perception of the *order* coincides with the meaning of this order, made up by the one who obeys it. Thus prophecy would be the very psychism of the soul: the other within the same; and all of man's spirituality would thereby be prophetic.
> ("Truth of Disclosure and Truth of Testimony" in Levinas et al., 1996, p. 105; original emphasis)

9 The reader will find some oversimplified explanation of Levinas's use of "the saying" and "the said" in Chapter 2, note 6.
10 Ciaramelli (1991) quotes in this connection the extraordinary words of Levinas's friend Maurice Blanchot: "one must manage somehow to understand the immediate in the past tense" (Blanchot and Smock, 1995, p. 24).
11 Some of Levinas's harshest words, as well as Primo Levi's and Ivan Karamazov's, are reserved for theodicy, the defense of an omnipotent, all-good, and provident God who permits the death and torture of innocent people (see Bernstein, 2002).
12 See Chapter 3, note 2.
13

> Is not this the fast that I choose:
> to loose the bonds of wickedness,
> to undo the thongs of the yoke,
> to let the oppressed go free, and to break every yoke?
> Is it not to share your bread with the hungry,
> and bring the homeless poor into your house;
> when you see the naked, to cover him,
> and not to hide yourself from your own flesh?
> (Isaiah 58:6–7)
>
> Then you shall call, and LORD will answer;
> You shall cry, and he will say, Here I am [*hineni*].
> (Isaiah 58:9)

14 Earlier, distinguishing totality from infinity, Levinas (1969, pp. 22–23; original emphasis) had written of prophetic eschatology:

> a relationship with *a surplus always exterior to the totality*, as though the objective totality did not fill out the true measure of being, as though another concept, the concept of infinity, were needed to express this transcendence with regard to totality, non-encompassable within a totality."

15 James Muilenburg (1961, p. 32): "The word has both noetic content and dynamic force, the content of knowledge and the power and drive of the speaking self."
16 Levinas repeatedly accused psychoanalysis of totalizing, of reducing everything and everyone to an idea or concept (e.g., Levinas, 1990).
17 To my knowledge, McLaughlin never referred to the Hebrew *dabar*, the effective word that cannot simply be deleted because it has already acted. The Christian text (John 1:1–3)—"In the beginning was the Word"—gives a Greek slant to

the Hebrew *dabar*, reading it as *logos*. (Many thanks to Donald Braue for providing this insight.) It seems to me that McLaughlin restored the richer implication of *dabar*.

18 According to Terry Marks-Tarlow (2011, p. 118), the New York Relational School has a saying: "That which gets dissociated is bound to be enacted."

19 Indeed, my primary sense of the particular contribution of psychoanalysis to the psychotherapeutic project involves its developmental sensibility. All my most beloved teachers in psychoanalysis—Ferenczi, Winnicott, Kohut, and Loewald—have shared a belief in psychoanalytic psychotherapy as a developmental project, as an opportunity for a new beginning.

20 Note the Levinasian inversion of this logic: the widow, the orphan, and the stranger are the ones to whom I am pre-primoridially responsible, non-indifferent.

21 Perhaps this extreme pejorative indicates how desperate inmates were to separate themselves from those who had given up, naming them contemptuously, intolerantly, as if to assure their exclusion from the humanity to which each one clung so precariously.

22 Herman's humanity and passion for the restoration of dignity are also obvious whenever she offers advice to clinicians and students.

23 A theologian, which I emphatically am not, would approach this section with a discussion of Rudolph Otto's classic *The Idea of the Holy* (1958). While Otto and Levinas agreed on emphasizing utter transcendence and separation, Levinas further distinguished the holy (the infinite met in the human) from the sacred, which he characterized as pagan because excessively concrete.

References

Ajzenstat, O. (2001). *Driven Back to the Text: The Premodern Sources of Levinas' Postmodernism*. Pittsburgh, PA: Duquesne University Press.

Aron, L. (1996). *A Meeting of Minds: Mutuality in Psychoanalysis*. Hillsdale, NJ: The Analytic Press.

Aron, L., and Starr, K. (2012). *A Psychotherapy for the People: Toward a Progressive Psychoanalysis*. New York: Routledge.

Austin, J. L. (1967). *How to Do Things with Words*. Cambridge, MA: Harvard University Press.

Bacal, H. (2006). Specificity Theory: Conceptualizing a Personal and Professional Quest for Therapeutic Possibility. *International Journal of Psychoanalytic Self Psychology*; 1, 133–155.

Beebe, B., and Lachmann, F. M. (2001). *Infant Research and Adult Treatment: A Dyadic Systems Approach*. Hillsdale, NJ: The Analytic Press.

Bernstein, R. J. (2002). *Radical Evil: A Philosophical Interrogation*. Cambridge and Malden, MA: Polity Press and Blackwell.

Blanchot, M., and Smock, A. (1995). *The Writing of the Disaster*. Lincoln, NE: University of Nebraska Press.

Bromberg, P. (2003). On Being One's Dream: Some Reflections on Robert Bosnak's "Embodied Imagination". *Contemporary Psychoanalysis*, 39, 697–710.

Ciaramelli, F. (1991). Levinas's Ethical Discourse between Individuation and Universality. In R. Bernasconi and S. Critchley (Eds.), *Re-reading Levinas* (pp. 83–105). Bloomington, IN: Indiana University Press.

Coburn, W. (2014). *Psychoanalytic Complexity: Clinical Attitudes for Therapeutic Change*. New York: Routledge.

Cohen, S. (1962). The Ontogenesis of Prophetic Behavior: A Study in Creative Conscience Formation. *Psychoanalytic Review*, 49A, 100–122.

Cortina, M., and Maccoby, M. (1996). *A Prophetic Analyst: Erich Fromm's Contribution to Psychoanalysis*. Northvale, NJ: Jason Aronson.

Cushman, P. (2007). A Burning World, an Absent God: Midrash, Hermeneutics, and Relational Psychoanalysis. *Contemporary Psychoanalysis*, 43, 47–88.

Dante Alighieri (2000). *Inferno*. Translated by R. Hollander and J. Hollander. New York: Doubleday.

Davies, J. (1997). Dissociation, Therapeutic Enactment, and Transference–Countertransference Processes. *Gender and Psychoanalysis*, 2, 241–257.

Davoine, F., and Gaudillière, J.-M. (2004). *History Beyond Trauma: Whereof One Cannot Speak, Thereof One Cannot Stay Silent*. New York: Other Press.

Ellis, M. (2007). *Reading the Torah Out Loud: A Journey of Lament and Hope*. Minneapolis, MN: Fortress Press.

Farrell, J. (2011). The Humanity and Humanism of Primo Levi. In S. Pugliese (Ed.), *Answering Auschwitz: Primo Levi's Science and Humanism after the Fall* (pp. 87–102). New York: Fordham University Press.

Fosshage, J. (1988). Chapter 8 Dream Interpretation Revisited. *Progress Self Psychology*, 3, 161–175.

Frank, J. (2002). *Dostoevsky: The Mantle of the Prophet, 1871–1881*. Princeton, NJ: Princeton University Press.

Galatzer-Levy, R. (2011). Commentary on Paper by Terry Marks-Tarlow. *Psychoanalytic Dialogues*, 21, 140–151.

Gerson, M.-J. (1996). *The Embedded Self: A Psychoanalytic Guide to Family Therapy*. Hillsdale, NJ: The Analytic Press.

Harris, A. (2002). Multiplicity as a Form of Enactment. *Psychoanalytic Dialogues*, 12, 827–835.

Herman, J. (1992). *Trauma and Recovery*. New York: Basic Books.

Herman, J. (2011). Posttraumatic Stress Disorder as a Shame Disorder. In R. Dearing and J. Tangney (Eds.), *Shame in the Therapy Hour* (pp. 261–276). Washington, DC: American Psychological Association.

Herman, J., and Hirschman, L. (1981). *Father–Daughter Incest*. Cambridge, MA: Harvard University Press.

Heschel, A. J. (1962). *The Prophets*. New York: Harper & Row.

Hirsch, I. (1998). The Concept of Enactment and Theoretical Convergence. *Psychoanalytic Quarterly*, 67, 78–101.

Jacobs, T. (1986). On Countertransference Enactments. *Journal of the American Psychoanalytic Association*, 34, 289–307.

Jacobs, T. (1997). In Search of the Mind of the Analyst: A Progress Report. *Journal of the American Psychoanalytic Association*, 45, 1035–1059.

Jacobs, T. (1999). Countertransference Past and Present. *International Journal of Psychoanalysis*, 80, 575–594.

Jacobs, T. (2001). On Unconscious Communications and Covert Enactments. *Psychoanalytic Inquiry*, 21, 4–23.

Katz, C. (2013). *Levinas and the Crisis of Humanism*. Bloomington, IN: Indiana University Press.

Lakoff, G., and Johnson, M. (2003). *Metaphors We Live By*. Chicago, IL: University of Chicago Press.

Langbein, H. (1972). *Menschen in Auschwitz*. Wien: Europaverl.

Laub, D. (1992). An Event without a Witness: Truth, Testimony and Survival. In S. Felman and D. Laub (Eds.), *Testimony: Crises of Witnessing in Literature, Psychoanalysis, and History* (pp. 75–92). New York: Routledge.

Levi, P. (1983) *Sorgenti di vita* [television interview]. RAI, March 25.

Levi, P. (1986a). *The Reawakening*. New York: Macmillan.

Levi, P. (1986b). *Survival in Auschwitz and The Reawakening: Two Memoirs*. New York: Summit Books.

Levi, P. (1989). *The Drowned and the Saved*. New York: Vintage International.

Levi, P., Belpoliti, M., and Wood, S. (2005). *The Black Hole of Auschwitz*. Cambridge and Malden, MA: Polity.

Levi, P., Feldman, R., and Swann, B. (1992). *Collected Poems* (new edn.). London and Boston, MA: Faber & Faber.

Levinas, E. (1969). *Totality and Infinity: An Essay on Exteriority*. Pittsburgh, PA: Duquesne University Press.

Levinas, E. (1990). *Difficult Freedom: Essays on Judaism*. Baltimore, MD: Johns Hopkins University Press.

Levinas, E. (1998a). *Collected Philosophical Papers*. Pittsburgh, PA: Duquesne University Press.

Levinas, E. (1998b). *Otherwise than Being, or, Beyond Essence*. Pittsburgh, PA: Duquesne University Press.

Levinas, E., Peperzak, A. T., Critchley, S., and Bernasconi, R. (1996). *Emmanuel Levinas: Basic Philosophical Writings*. Bloomington, IN: Indiana University Press.

Lichtenberg, J. D., Lachmann, F. M., and Fosshage, J. L. (1996). *The Clinical Exchange: Techniques Derived from Self and Motivational Systems*. Hillsdale, NJ: The Analytic Press.

McLaughlin, J. (1987). The Play of Transference: Some Reflections on Enactment in the Psychoanalytic Situation. *Journal of the American Psychoanalytic Association*, 35, 557–582.

McLaughlin, J. (1991). Clinical and Theoretical Aspects of Enactment. *Journal of the American Psychoanalytic Association*, 39, 595–614.

Mann, C. (2000). Fromm's Impact on Interpersonal Psychoanalysis. *International Forum of Psychoanalysis*, 9, 199–205.

Marks-Tarlow, T. (2011). Merging and Emerging: A Nonlinear Portrait of Inter-subjectivity during Psychotherapy. *Psychoanalytic Dialogues*, 21, 110–127.

Maroda, K. J. (1998). Enactment. *Psychoanalytic Psychology*, 15, 517–535.

Muilenburg, J. (1961). *The Way of Israel*. New York: Harper.

Otto, R. (1958). *The Idea of the Holy: An Inquiry into the Non-Rational Factor in the Idea of the Divine and Its Relation to the Rational*. New York: Oxford University Press.

Peperzak, A., and Levinas, E. (1993). *To the Other: An Introduction to the Philosophy of Emmanuel Levinas*. West Lafayette, IN: Purdue University Press.

Philippe, A. (2004). The Drowned as Saviors of Humanity: The Anthropological Value of *Se questo e un uomo*. In S. Pugliese (Ed.), *The Legacy of Primo Levi* (pp. 125–131). London: Palgrave Macmillan.

Pizer, S. (2008). The Shock of Recognition: What My Grandfather Taught Me about Psychoanalytic Process. *International Journal of Psychoanalytic Self Psychology*, 3, 287–303.

Plato (1997). *Complete Works*. Edited by J. M. Cooper; associate editor D. S. Hutchinson. Indianapolis, IN: Hackett.

Pushkin, A. (1825). The Prophet. Retrieved from http://poemsintranslation.blogspot. com/2011/09/pushkin-prophet-from-russian.html (accessed August 27, 2015).

Roazen, P. (2001). The Exclusion of Erich Fromm from the IPA. *Contemporary Psychoanalysis*, 37, 5–42.

Rozmarin, E. (2007). An Other in Psychoanalysis. *Contemporary Psychoanalysis*, 43, 327–360.

Schlingensiepen, F. (2010). *Dietrich Bonhoeffer, 1906–1945: Martyr, Thinker, Man of Resistance*. London and New York: T. & T. Clark.

Shane, E. (2006). Editor's Epilogue. *Psychoanalytic Inquiry*, 26, 295–304.

Shulman, D. (2008). Jonah: His Story, Our Story; His Struggle, Our Struggle: Commentary on Paper by Avivah Gottlieb Zornberg. *Psychoanalytic Dialogues*, 18, 329–364.

Spezzano, C. (1998). Listening and Interpreting: How Relational Analysts Kill Time between Disclosures and Enactments: Commentary on Papers by Bromberg and by Greenberg. *Psychoanalytic Dialogues*, 8, 237–246.

Stern, D. B. (2009). *Partners in Thought: Working with Unformulated Experience, Dissociation, and Enactment*. New York: Routledge.

Stern, D. N. (1977). *The First Relationship: Mother and Infant*. Cambridge, MA: Harvard University Press.

Stolorow, R. D., Brandchaft, B., and Afwood, G. E. (1987). *Psychoanalytic Treatment: An Intersubjective Approach*. Hillsdale, NJ: The Analytic Press.

Teicholz, J. G. (1999). *Kohut, Loewald, and the Postmoderns: A Comparative Study of Self and Relationship*. Hillsdale, NJ: The Analytic Press.

Todorov, T. (1996). *Facing the Extreme: Moral Life in the Concentration Camps* (1st US edn.). New York: Metropolitan Books.

West, C. (2004). *Democracy Matters: Winning the Fight against Imperialism*. New York: Penguin Press.

Winnicott, D. (1965). *The Maturational Processes and the Facilitating Environment*. New York: International Universities Press.

Winnicott, D. (1975). *Through Paediatrics to Psycho-Analysis*. London: Hogarth Press.

Wolstein, B. (1992). Resistance Interlocked with Countertransference: R. N. and Ferenczi, and American Interpersonal Relations. *Contemporary Psychoanalysis*, 28, 172–189.

Chapter 9

From contrite fallibilism to humility

Clinical, personal, and humanitarian

In its persecution, the ego returns to the self, not to reflect on the self but to denude itself in the absolute simplicity of identity.

(Levinas et al., 1996, p. 88)

Not all that a person desires does he or she obtain: the winds blow without regard for the wishes of the ships.[1]

(al-Mutanabbī, 1967)

What we cannot do, we must now simply let go of and limit ourselves to what we can and should do.

(Bonhoeffer and Bethge, 1971, p. 32)

The injury cannot be healed.

(Levi, 1989, p. 23)

Like the prophets, philosophers—in their gadfly role—also disturb us. Unlike the self-absorbed and self-satisfied puritans described by the historian of philosophy Francis Cornford (1960),[2] they may speak and act on behalf of those who have no voice. Cornford wrote of the puritan

holding to the tradition of Socrates' cheerful indifference to bodily pleasures, but disposed to mistake this indifference for a rather grim and graceless asceticism. He can see no distinction between trust in providence and submission to fate. He marches, *in the filthy rags of righteousness*, with face set towards a peak of infallible wisdom and virtue, which even the small company of the elect have little or no hope to claim.

(Cornford, 1960, p. 108; emphasis added)

By contrast, we shall consider both the intellectually humble pragmatist and the clinical humanitarian, having learned her limitations from long and painful experience, like the Stoics and other more recent writers we have considered, as interior resources. None of these makes asceticism a goal.

Instead, we hold our theories fallibilistically so that we can keep learning, and hold ourselves unobstrusively to live for the other.

Pragmatic fallibilism

When philosophers do their prophetic work, they disturb themselves and others. Recently asked to comment on a favorite passage from U.S. philosopher Charles Sanders Peirce (for Thellefsen, 2014),[3] I chose:

> no matter how far science goes, those inferences which are uppermost in the mind of the investigator are very uncertain. They are on probation. They must have a fair trial and not be condemned till proved false beyond all reasonable doubt; and the moment that proof is reached, the investigator must be ready to abandon them without the slightest tenderness toward them. Thus, the scientific inquirer has to be always ready at a moment to abandon summarily all the theories to the study of which he has been devoting perhaps many years.
>
> (Peirce et al., 1992, Vol. 2, p. 25)[4]

I commented that, for Peirce, fallibilism constituted more than a logical or scientific procedure; it was an ethical attitude, implying responsibility.

But let us look back. First, we must notice that what Peirce came to call "fallibilism" named both a principle—with spreading roots and ramifications throughout his philosophy—and an attitude, reflected in the quotation above, but extending far beyond it. Of this attitude, he famously wrote that "out of a contrite fallibilism, combined with a high faith in the reality of knowledge, and an intense desire to find things out, all my philosophy has always seemed to me to grow" (Peirce, 1931, Vol. 1, para. 14). While rebuking both theologians and book-scientists (as contrasted with "laboratory men"), he resorted to religious language—contrition, faith—to express the humble devotion to truth required when surprising facts confront our preconceived ideas. Never block the road of inquiry. Faithfulness to scientific inquiry and evolutionary-love ethics converged for him, becoming close to a religious duty.

As a principle, Peircean fallibilism most importantly links to the theory of abduction or hypothesis as the working scientist's everyday method,[5] together with his phenomenologically understood categories. So, for example, he wrote:

> perceptual judgments are to be regarded as an extreme case of abductive inferences, from which they differ in being absolutely beyond criticism. The abductive suggestion [the hunch] comes to us like a flash. It is an act of insight, though of extremely fallible insight.
>
> (Peirce, 1931, Vol. 5, para. 181)

So the qualitative/perceptual first, together with the impact of the unyielding second or fact, is already fallibly if rudimentarily interpreted. But what has happened here? The percept "absolutely beyond criticism," with its immediate claims imposed by firstness or perception and secondness or fact, has already sneaked into the realm of thirdness or generality, judgment, as Carl Hausman (Anderson and Hausman, 2012) explains. Somewhere between first and second arrives the flash of abductive suggestion or hypothesis, the hunch, to be regarded as tentative. Along with fallibility enter the only absolutes in science: the requirement of humility, and the need for the community of scholars.

Humility aside for the moment, the community of scholars is intrinsic to fallibilism itself. Unless the flash of insight is brought to the community for consideration, testing, improvement, or possible discard—that is, unless we hold theory lightly—science (be it physical or human science) becomes a sham, a form of ideology. Because the community of scholars, the beloved community, is indispensable to the growth of science, of knowledge, of truth, every member of the community, as well as the community as a whole, "has to be always ready at a moment to abandon summarily all the theories to the study of which he has been devoting perhaps many years." As equally fallible, for us clinicians and humanitarian workers, we must regard our convictions and methods, learned in school or from mentors held in reverence. If not, we injure each other and our patients, imposing our prejudgments, leaping into diagnoses, falling into contempt for those with whom we disagree. We need contrite fallibilism. We must not block the path of inquiry.

What Peirce would not question was the very conception of inquiry as fallible. We could say that a moral infallibilism lay beneath his scientific fallibilism, and we might not be far wrong. Years before he coined the word "fallibilism," he told us not to doubt on paper (like Descartes) what we do not doubt in our hearts. And later, "Do you call it doubting to write down on a piece of paper that you doubt? If so, doubt has nothing to do with any serious business" (Peirce, 1931, Vol. 5, para. 416). He did not fault Pope Pius IX for proclaiming, "Thou shalt not kill," but for making *himself* the arbiter of infallible truth.[6] He invented the word "fallibilism" from his outrage that the pope should claim infallibility.

"Critical common-sensism" and the "contrite" scientific fallibilism went together for Peirce (Misak, 2004), and they require each other. The critical common-sensist takes for granted a background of everyday beliefs, while working to keep one's abductive hypotheses—"mere conjectures," says Misak (2004, p. 163)—held lightly. Traumatic shock shatters precisely this background of everyday beliefs, as working clinicians recognize. But normally we need to assume such everyday beliefs: the sun will rise tomorrow, the floor will hold me up, even "I will do as I say I will." Thus one remains prepared for more surprising facts. Judith Lewis Herman says repeatedly that exactly at the moment when she believes she has heard the worst things human beings can do to each other, she hears something newly shocking and unthinkable. We must remain ready to learn from colleagues—often patients or refugees—within the community of scholars. Peirce called it "walking on a bog":

> After a while, as Science progresses, it comes upon more solid ground. It is now entitled to reflect: this ground has held a long time without showing signs of yielding. I may hope that it will continue to hold for a great while longer.
>
> (Peirce, 1931, Vol. 5, para. 589)

Sandra Rosenthal calls this achieved ground "pragmatic certainty": "The product of interpretive activity," she writes, "is about a 'taken' rather than a 'given'" (Rosenthal, 2004, p. 202).

Contemporary logic of science speaks more often of "corrigibilism," suggesting that fallibilism means that all beliefs and theoretical tenets simply require testing in the fire of facts. Verificationism and non-falsifiability are familiar mid-twentieth-century versions of this view. It seems clear, not only from Peirce's expostulations but also from examining the web of his own beliefs, that his own understanding was far more complex, profound, and ethical than most of the views that go under the heading of "fallibilism" today. He would surely have made up a name for it, "ugly enough to be safe from kidnappers" (Peirce, 1931, Vol. 5, para. 414). That said, let us look at some of the complexity, even beyond noting fallibilism's embeddedness in abductive inference and in his phenomenology.

One source of this complexity, which might have endeared Peirce to today's systems, chaos, and complexity theorists, is that, like them, he believed in real possibility and chance (his term for this was "tychism")—that is, in a non-necessitarian universe. A universe actually developing, involving actual novelty, requires not only abductive reasoning but ongoing receptiveness to the unexpected. Peirce taught us to expect surprising facts every so often. Like William James (1902), he thought *variety* the "most marked and obtrusive character of nature" (Peirce, 1931, Vol. 1, para. 159). Though Peirce might not have welcomed the name "chaos" for his cosmology, he might have found congenial as tychistic (theory of chance) contemporary complexity and general systems theories. Insisting on novelty, the ever emergent, and irreducibles (Coburn, 2002; Galatzer-Levy, 1995), these theories attempt to keep the road of inquiry open in contemporary studies of psychological development and therapeutic systems (Coburn, 2009; Ghent, 2002; Thelen and Smith, 1994).

Indeed, Peirce's theory of continuity (his term for this was "synechism"), which was closely linked to his fallibilism (Peirce, 1931, Vol. 1, paras. 141–179: "Fallibilism, Continuity, and Evolution"), made any insistence on dogmatism and absolute certainty in science or religion ridiculous.

He understood that people could also ridicule fallibilism, which claims only that

> people cannot attain absolute certainty concerning questions of fact . . . But to say that *if* there are two persons and each person has two eyes there *will be* four eyes is not a statement of a fact, but a statement about the system of number which is our own creation.
>
> (Peirce, 1931, Vol. 1, para. 149; original emphasis)

But much more important, he went on to say, was the presupposition of continuity—that is, of infinity. We must *suppose* that everything—time, for example—is infinitesimally joined, he thought; we cannot really *know*. We must therefore be fallibilists.

Now let us return to the quote with which we began. What is the status of fallibilism itself? Is it an inference to be thrown into the trash-bin without regret or tenderness when it fails us? In what would such failure consist? First we must note that Peirce distinguished between absolute and practical fallibility: "But though nothing else is *absolutely* infallible, many propositions are *practically* infallible; such as the dicta of conscience" (Peirce, 1931, Vol. 2, para. 75; original emphasis). It seems to me that both his connecting of fallibilism to his presumption of a holistic universe and his insistence on intellectual humility within a community of scholars suggest that fallibilism was not, for Peirce, an inference but itself an ethical attitude. It selects for the trash-bin, but cannot go there itself. The quasi-religious language of contrition and faith supports my guess.

Peirce himself, I believe, would have said that fallibilism is a required logical attitude consisting of several aspects. One aspect senses the limits of one's own knowledge, and of that of the scientific community so far. This means a disciplined recognition that one might always be mistaken, that one is fallible, and, moreover, that one is likely to be mistaken insofar as one takes one's own opinion to be the whole, final, and absolute truth. It does not mean a flippant, "Oh, I could always be wrong," but rather describes the attitude of someone who always and genuinely wants to learn more. In Peirce's words:

> For years . . . I used for myself to collect my ideas under the designation *fallibilism*; and indeed the first step toward *finding out* is to acknowledge you do not satisfactorily know already; so that no blight can so surely arrest all intellectual growth as the blight of cocksureness; and ninety-nine out of every hundred good heads are reduced to impotence by that malady—of whose inroads they are most strangely unaware!
>
> Indeed, out of a contrite fallibilism, combined with a high faith in the reality of knowledge, and an intense desire to find things out, all my philosophy has always seemed to me to grow.
>
> (Peirce, 1931, Vol. 1, paras. 13–14; original emphasis)

Here we see that Peirce's fallibilism resembles the contriteness required by Wittgenstein to avoid the temptations toward logical sin. We can easily see the moral and religious tone of the recommended fallibilism when we notice the contrast with another attitude—that of cocksureness. Fallibilism here amounts to intellectual humility.

Fallibilism for working clinicians

Why should Peircean fallibilism matter to psychoanalysts, to relational psychoanalysts, or to psychotherapists and humanitarian workers generally? Have we not already relinquished Freud's claim that psychoanalysis is a science? Have we not already moved to a more dialogic and less authoritarian approach to our work? Are we not constantly revising our general and clinical theories in the face of new evidence from infant research, from attachment studies, finding ourselves inspired by less mechanistic and reductionist, more pluralistic and emergent, human studies?

In the first place, we cannot overstate our profession's dogmatic and authoritarian power heritage. Freud's propensity to excommunicate those who disagreed with him—Jung, Adler, Rank, Tausk, and finally Ferenczi, to name only the most famous—is well known. The so-called "controversial discussions" in the British Society read more like a war than a dialogue, while both the International and the American Psychoanalytic Associations have exercised tight control over membership, evidently requiring orthodoxy in doctrine and practice, and excluding creative voices like Erich Fromm and Wilhelm Reich, not to mention non-medical practitioners and anyone suspected of being "less than" fully heterosexual. In many countries today, revenge is still practiced against groups who start psychoanalytic training programs not sanctioned by these organizations. So, on an institutional level, it might be fair to say that organized psychoanalysis has been more devoted to preserving its legacy than to the search for more adequate beliefs that take into account differing perspectives and new research. Laboratory science or no, our discipline requires for its development, in theory and practice, a Peircean "contrite fallibilism."

Second, the authoritarian dogmatism in organized psychoanalysis—the tradition I know best, but others may become inflexible too—can seep into any of us so that we pass it on, via a dogmatic tone or a dismissive attitude toward heterodox ideas. Our students (in psychoanalysis, called candidates and supervisees) may learn neither to think for themselves nor to voice their doubts about the received opinions.[7] We may unwittingly perpetuate a climate in which beliefs or even hypotheses are described as unpsychoanalytic. It seems to me that we who write and teach in psychoanalytic institutes have a particular responsibility to exemplify a fallibilistic attitude, willing always to submit our own beliefs to the tests of dialogue and praxis:

> The elements of every concept enter into logical thought at the gate of perception and make their exit at the gate of purposive action; and whatever cannot show its passports at both of those two gates is to be arrested as unauthorized by reason.
>
> (Peirce, 1931, Vol. 5, para. 212)

This means we must take our students' questions seriously, and thereby refuse to block the road of inquiry. Our need for admiration, common to most in the teaching profession, as Professor of Writing Emeritus Carl Klaus (1999) writes, often prevents our adjusting to a diminished sense of importance in retirement, our embracing the new possibilities it may provide, and accepting the possibility that the world will likely get on very well without us. These very natural needs, for me, have also impeded conversion from infallibilism, privileged attitudes, and being a *Besserwisser* toward taking the ethical turn as the guiding condition of my life.

Most important is a fallibilistic attitude in our daily practice. Though clinical examples are not common in philosophical discussion, among pragmatists they may be useful to illustrate the practical import of fallibilism itself. Here is a short clinical tale, first cited in an earlier book (Stolorow et al., 2002, p. 103):

> "I have been so upset," my long-time patient begins. "I can't get out of my head that you called me a borderline. I can't stop thinking that that is what I really am and that that is how you see me." "Oh, no," I think, "it's not possible. I have a poor memory, but I couldn't have. I don't even believe in the borderline concept and cannot remember ever having called anyone by that name." So the analyst says to her patient that this is terrible what she has done to him, and asks him to tell her when it happened, and what they had been talking about. She acknowledges that his memory is generally much better than hers.

This story—which critics have labeled inauthentic, while also violently and widely criticizing me as a liar with pants on fire—illustrates not only contrite fallibilism but also the hospitable fallibilism that is needed when working with very fragile patients. Granted, it would have been wise to provide more context. But knowing or not knowing that this patient had been recently hospitalized, and might not have benefited from the confrontation they recommended, my critics generally seemed to assume:

1   that we have infallible access to the literal "whole truth and nothing but the truth"; and
2   that inflicting our truth on patients, no matter how robust or terrified, would always be an ethical or wise choice.

Precisely because my internal dialogue—in this instance, shared with readers—remains always fallible, I chose to respond to a fragile patient as a parent reassures a frightened child, even when the parent may also be afraid.

A long clinical life has taught me to recognize that many such statements by patients diminish our treasured sense of our professional self, leading to instant narcissistic injury, and that we may thus be too readily inclined reactively to pathologize the patient's perspective. We have learned to wonder about the meanings the accusation, thrown at us or by patients at themselves, could have for patients, now and here, then and elsewhere. Still, we analysts also seem to participate in a common human propensity to see one's own perspective as the measure of truth, and rather automatically to judge those with whom we disagree as unrealistic and misguided. We thus miss what Peirce would have recognized as the surprising facts, thereby failing to notice available openings in the road of inquiry.

For a fallibilist, however, there will be no arguments about reality. Reality is whatever it is, but as analyst my task is to hold my own perspective as lightly as I can so that the other's words can speak to me. It is really not important whether I used the word "borderline" or not. That was my patient's way of pointing to his realization—surprising, to me at least—that something had gone very wrong between us; and my instant denial— verbally expressed or not—would have signaled my unawareness that anything had happened. A fallibilistic attitude could now help me to attend to, to maximize truth-as-possible-understanding (Frank, 1999), emergent truth in Peirce's ultimate long-run sense, and minimize truth as cor- respondence to fact. Whatever the facts may be, we must find ways to converse about the meanings, and relegate arguments about reality to philosophy and politics.

The associated dogmatic and authoritarian insistence that the patient must recognize the analyst's perspective is usually the quickest exit from the search for understanding. Our own convictions, by the way, may deafen us to the way even subtle insistence feels to a patient. In this instance, in our previous session this patient had found me reductive (classifying) and demeaning of his experience. I had to recognize that I had been carried away in an I-am-so-smart-and-I-can-tell-you-what-the-trouble-is moment, and had blocked the road of inquiry. Since he had grown up in a home where the DSM (psychiatry's diagnostic and statistical manual) was the family dictionary, the story came out in these words. But this was not important. What helped was for me to acknowledge that I had set myself in a know-it- all position vis-à-vis my patient, and that this had caused actual—if perhaps only temporary—harm to our connection and to our joint search for emotional understanding.

Now let us turn from intellectual humility or fallibilism, theory held lightly, to the personal humility engendered and needed in a long clinical life.

Humility

Personal weaknesses, professional boundaries, and crimes against humanity bring us down. Still, the two words "psychoanalytic" and "humility" rarely appear together. In the earliest instance I have been able to find, Lawrence Kubie (1954, p. 187) wrote that the "fundamental" distinction between normality and neurosis

> implies neither that an obsessional, introspective self-consciousness is a prerequisite for normality, nor that the well-analyzed initiate is entitled to look down his well-analyzed nose at the rest of the world from Olympian heights, with a preposterous assumption that he has full insight into his every motivation at every moment. It implies rather an analytic humility, based upon a full acknowledgment of the impossibility of knowing one's own unconscious to such an extent.

Freud, of course, had recognized that his "discovery" of the unconscious, dethroning pretensions at conscious self-knowledge and control, struck a terrible blow at human narcissism. Still, he went on to exclude from official psychoanalysis everyone who did not see and propound his discovery just as he did. Fallibilistic in his own process of discovery, always revising, he was dogmatic and undialogical in relation to others. So we need to learn humility elsewhere.

Though later references to analytic humility come, as we might expect, from the relational school (inclusively conceived), attitudes like fallibilism, modesty, and resistance to arrogance have characterized many great psychoanalysts before and beyond relational psychoanalysis. When analysts actually speak in these terms, as in the only two English-language references I have found, they often show up in discussions of complexity (Davies, 1999)[8] or complexity theory (Galatzer-Levy, 2011). Clearly the tremendous and irreducible intricacy of our joint situation in every clinical process has begun to affect our attitudes. Inspired by Ferenczi's unpretentious fallibilism and emotional availability, taught by Winnicott's devotion and warmth (Roazen, 2001), stretched by our patients of race, culture, gender, and sexual orientation different from our own, analysts have begun to write of working "unobtrusively" (Grossmark, 2012) or recognizing that the work we therapists do is a gift we receive with gratitude for the honor of being welcomed into the most intimate places of another's life (Shabad, 2010). This kind of humility counters the everyday talk of "my patient" or "my client," carrying, sometimes, a kind of arrogance. Once I heard Orna Guralnik say: "Our patients are not ours to have."[9] Scholars who work in this non-possessive spirit have no time to worry about priority of discovery or who said what first (Ogden, 2003); instead, they recognize, with Winnicott, that we all plagiarize unconsciously, giving credit as much as we can, grateful to be working in a community of scholars.[10]

Unfortunately, "analytic humility" can be and has been misunderstood, and thus discarded, in the same ways as empathy has been. Here is an unfortunate example from a relational thinker whose work I generally admire, Owen Renik:

> If an analyst communicates a feeling of being able to offer interpretations concerning the patient's psychic reality *not as that reality appears to the analyst through the lens of his or her own constructions, but from the patient's vantage point*, then the patient and analyst together become susceptible to colluding in a disavowal of the distinction between developing one's own meanings and accepting the meanings implicitly communicated by another. The analytic work relationship may be experienced like the relationship between mother and infant, in which giving meaning encourages development. So the analyst, like the good mother of early infancy, "understands" perfectly. While this is perhaps a necessary and useful illusion for a time in some treatments, if it persists the patient's autonomy is coopted in the name of empathy or analytic humility.
>
> (Renik, 1993, p. 568; original emphasis)

Empathy, though not my topic here, remains a difficult and contested theme in contemporary psychoanalysis, treasured by some, reviled by others, in part because the word has no single meaning or context (Poland, 2007). To equate it with an attitude of analytic humility, however, seems to me a serious mistake. It could even be argued that some patients' autonomy actually emerges in the context of the empathy Renik disparages. One can surely agree with Renik that we have no privileged access to the experience of the patient; rather, subjectivity consists precisely in what-it-is-like-to-be-you (Nagel, 1974). This position itself begins the attitude of analytic humility, in a more relational form, toward which Kubie gestured so many years ago.

According to my thesis, as an antidote to crippling shame, we need humility as a fundamental attitude to practice truly relational psychoanalysis, or any kind of good psychoanalysis, psychotherapy, or humanitarian service. Before going on to elaborate this thesis, in a spirit of full disclosure: I am not very good at this lifelong project. That said, why work so hard at it? Because, as Simon Critchley (2007, p. 57; original emphasis) writes, "the Levinasian subject is constituted through an act of approval to a demand to which it is fundamentally *inadequate*." I relate myself, he goes on, to what exceeds my relational capacity. I persevere, knowing that I will often be defeated, but continuing to accept excessive relational demands, consenting to excess.

In an extraordinary look at the philosophical problem of evil (if there is a good god, how can "he" allow evil?; if there is an all-powerful god, why does "he" not prevent it?), Levinas (1987) re-imagines, as I read him, the last judgment for each of us. Each of us, in the face of the excessive suffering of others, would be asked, "Where were you?" In other places he has led us to meditate on the words "Am I my brother's keeper?" We can only hang our heads in shame and guilt, both pre-originary and personal.

Our defeats come with abject shame, perhaps because the humanitarian clinician has already endured too long; perhaps because the other's needs grate too hard on the worker's own wounds; perhaps because the therapist humanitarian harbored a secret *hubris*, or just a desire to meet the devastated stranger; perhaps because one dreamed of creating something enduring (Buechler, 2015);[11] perhaps because this particular work simply outstripped the worker's capacities. In my last years working as a clinician, perhaps deluded by my capabilities for helping the devastated in the past, I accepted work that truly exceeded my capacities. I came—with the steady help of a trusted supervisor—to comprehend that I needed to turn this work over to others, but some patients could not accept this. I humbly had to realize that I had done harm by not insisting that certain patients concurrently attend a trauma group as a condition of working with me. I reread and responded to Judith Lewis Herman (1997) too late. Indeed, it was surely a mistake to begin working with seriously traumatized patients as I was approaching retirement. I fell into the trap when they insisted that only I could help them, imagining that giving them something, even for a few months or years, would be better than sending them to others. None of us is exempt from doing harm while intending to do good; this is humbling. To accept my failures with more acceptance and compassion for my own human and professional limitations has meant working on, and now entering retirement from clinical practice, less paralyzed by shame.[12]

Intending good,[13] without a robust sense of one's own limitations, can be the worst temptation to hubris and overreaching. Still, it is a familiar story to those of us who receive patients from disappointing or disastrous previous treatments. Perhaps the patient says, "I need someone who isn't afraid to hear the full horror of my story, who doesn't turn away, who can stay with me and not tell me to get over it, who can hear my pain a thousand times." Or perhaps the patient asks, directly or implicitly, "Will you too turn into Mr. Hyde unexpectedly and throw me into the trash-can as my previous therapist did?" Especially if the previous therapist came from a different tradition—classical, Kleinian, Jungian, gestalt, self-psychological, cognitive behavioral—we may be convinced that we will do better. Whatever the challenge in that first session, we want to be the healer of the suffering person before us, even if we do not yet, or for a long time, imagine the measure of the task. But our therapeutic and ethical being responds, and we begin. Before long, we find ourselves in the grip of our theories, an important way in which we clinicians organize our countertransferences and manage our anxieties. By then, our unconscious know-it-all (*Besserwisser*) has taken over.

Why does holding theory lightly come so hard to us clinicians? First, to contextualize a little, let us note that holding theory lightly (Peirce's advice) comes easily to no one. Peirce thought that every scientific classroom and laboratory should contain a large sign: "Do not block the road of inquiry." He recommended, as we saw above, an attitude of scientific humility that he called "contrite fallibilism": the understanding that one can always be mistaken, that one is always learning within a community of scholars—the viewpoint with which we began this chapter.

Remembering his words, without any specific allusion to psychoanalysis or to clinical work, we can see why holding theory lightly might prove so hard to achieve. Our theories become like family to us. To throw our cherished convictions away on pragmatic grounds, because they prevent us from hearing and helping those we serve, to jettison them like excess baggage without the slightest tenderness, to abandon them, do we hear this emotional language?

Perhaps our theories possess selfobject—to use the Kohutian lexicon for a moment—functions for us. Perhaps, extending Kohut's original idea only a little, they come to stabilize us, organize and consolidate our self-experience when we feel fragile and lost in our clinical work. We do not easily abandon what holds us together. Or, in Winnicott's language, our theories live in the transitional space of play and creativity. If we can keep them there, instead of treating them like treasured antiques, anchors in the storm, or, in Bernard Brandchaft's words, the dictates of antiquity (Brandchaft et al., 2010), we may be more able to hold them lightly. Or they may, for those of us who write, come to mean even more: our fame, our legacy, our ego, and our place in the sun. Who wants to loosen a grip on all of that in the face of a terrified patient who implicitly says he cannot do it my way? For each of us, theories take on meanings that keep us gripping tightly.

Often, to concede some ground, to approach a more relational or dialogical attitude, we attempt to overcome the "binary" in which, for example, I am either perfect or an utter failure. We try to work "dialectically." The problem for me when I try to hold both sides of a clinical impasse, as many contemporary theorists would have us do, is that the patient perceives my impatience, my point of view and my unconscious judgments, even when I do not. "You must hate hearing this from me over and over," they say. Or I appear in their dreams as a poisonous orange snake, trying to kill them. They see my efforts, while understanding that I am not really with them.

Fortunately, we have in the self-psychology tradition a famous text on the topic of clinical humility that always bears repeating:

> If there is one lesson that I have learned during my life as an analyst, it is the lesson that what my patients tell me is likely to be true—that many times when I believed that I was right and my patients were wrong, it

turned out, though often only after a prolonged search, that *my* rightness was superficial whereas *their* rightness was profound.

(Kohut et al., 1984, pp. 93–94; original emphasis)

Or, as Jacques Derrida put it at the graveside of Emmanuel Levinas: "the relation to the other is deference" (Derrida, 1999, p. 46).

"Comfort ye," the tenor sings in Handel's music to the words of the prophet; only after a prolonged search do the best of us surrender to the patient's rightness, and learn to hold our theories lightly. For myself, consultation and returning to my best role models and cultural resources have often helped. But the rewards of clinical humility in the face of the naked and perhaps rebellious face of the other who says "I cannot do it your way" arrive unannounced and unpretentious. The trumpet may not sound, but we shall be changed.

A profound "yes" to our limitations constitutes the most important advantage of humility, both personal and professional. Knowing this, and working with colleagues and supervisors at every stage of our work, protects us from ethical transgressions, and from various failures. Humility keeps our courage from being brash, hubristic, and overconfident. Recently a colleague consulted with me about a prospective new patient with a complex trauma history and a tendency toward impulsive behavior. The colleague reported nightmares after her first session with this patient. I asked about the makeup of the rest of her practice. It turned out that she had three other patients whom she was barely keeping from hospitalization. Having learned my own lessons in humility, I recommended that she refer the new patient to a clinic where several people would be involved in her care: an individual therapist, a psychiatrist, and a group therapist. My grateful colleague had needed reassurance to accept her own limitations, and to heed the warnings from her own dreams.

Of course, we cannot always avail ourselves of such an "easy" solution. What then? In addition to the internal resources this book has been assembling, humanitarian workers, including psychoanalysts and humanistic psychotherapists, need each other for continuous consultation and support. Humility needs the beloved community, *in vivo* and in our literature. An early humanistic voice from the contemporary Freudians, James McLaughlin, described his own struggles to hear his patient and himself:

A fresh gesture now took center stage as she lived out her episodes of fury. She would clutch, white-knuckled, her necklace or pendant, a brooch, or the collar of her blouse as she cried out her outrage either that I was ignoring her misery or that I did not understand her at all. From my side, I became aware, during my too-vigilant listening, of painful tension in my hands and neck . . . Often I had small hand-twinges while she was quiet and ruminating, or silent just after I had intervened. Some of these twinges happened just before an outburst or before I was consciously aware that we were headed for a blow-up. In after-hours pondering on these strenuous sessions, I ruefully likened these hand signals to the whispering baskets the Sioux Indians carried on their heads. Dangling from the rims were small silver-tipped thongs that tinkled softly as the Sioux walked their plains and woodlands. The lore has it that these Indians had learned to be hyperalert for attack when suddenly aware that the familiar tinkle had stopped: their neck tension that quieted the small sound was a response to ominous sights and sounds they had not yet consciously registered. This sortie into cross-cultural anthropology was small comfort, to be sure. That Mrs. T. did not carry out her threats, however, was reassuring. Meanwhile I had grown aware that I was being spooked into excessive helpfulness by my anger and need to deny it.

(McLaughlin, 1987, p. 571)

McLaughlin taught us to heed subtle warnings. In more extreme moments it helps to hear both Judith Lewis Herman's (1997) hopeful and determined voice, reminding us to pick our battles, to stay focused on human dignity, and to rely on community, and Leanh Nguyen's tormented acceptance:

What they [torture victims] know too much, too well, too irretrievably, is that there exists a dimension in this life where there is no meaning, no intentionality, no mutuality, where embracing death is the way to keep living, where shutting down one's mind and turning blind to the other's mind is the best way to survive. It is this knowledge, not the amputated limb or the torn vagina, which is the deadly blow.
    At the end of the day, I am confronted with the knowledge that some lives cannot be repaired. Through moments of connection, I hold out for my patients the hope of something wondrous, but I am also the portent of renewed pain. "I can't bear to be alive," said one patient. And though I grieve for what has happened to him I know in that moment that we are different, and how I am more human than he.[14] For I, and you who have seen the traumatized but have not been touched by trauma, can bear being alive, being in love, giving birth, preparing for death, even though we have been shown the dead . . .
    And so maybe we look into traumatized lives in order to figure out how to work out the way to remain intact in this traumatized, and traumatizing, culture. We look into that which has been de-formed and de-humanized in order to find our way to remaining human. We listen to these patients who embody what we may resist know- ing about ourselves: That we in this modern technological culture are being gradually de-humanized, and are de-humanizing others; that we

are being impoverished in our meaning-making capacity and our narratives of life; that we are ignorant, even negligent, in our dealings with psychic pain, with death and dying; that we are more and more alienated from the relevance and the ambiguity-laden task of human connection.

(Nguyen, 2007, p. 66)

Collectively and personally, we struggle to remain emotionally available to accompany those whom we serve (Orange, 2006, 2009): the biblical widow, orphan, and stranger become the lost soul, refugee, and torture-victim at our door. Humbly, we admit that we often lose the battle to keep our ethical eyes open, our ears attuned, our hearts and doors open.

Why be humble?

Uriah Heep, Charles Dickens's caricature in *David Copperfield* of everything he admired, has given humility a bad name by hiding insincerity and obsequiousness:

> "I am well aware that I am the umblest person going," said Uriah Heep, modestly; "let the other be where he may. My mother is likewise a very umble person. We live in a numble abode, Master Copperfield, but have much to be thankful for. My father's former calling was umble. He was a sexton."

(Dickens, 2004, p. 244)

False humility can take many forms, of course. Further, modesty and fallibilism can be mistaken for masochism, itself mistaken for a desire to suffer, as we saw in Chapter 3. Above all, in a land that has long idealized the rags-to-riches achiever, the unpretentious humanitarian who lives to serve others is seldom a cultural ideal.

Truly humble people, I suspect, never describe themselves as such; rather, they worry about their own pride, arrogance, and hubris. Uneasy about the inherited privilege they take for granted and enjoy even as they serve, they wonder about their own motivations. Discomforted by the magnitude of human needs, and the complexity of the problems they face, they wonder whether their efforts matter. They find no time to boast about their contributions, or, much less, about their humility.

When the folksinging activist Pete Seeger died in 2013, a story came to light illustrating what I mean. Like many clinicians and humanitarian workers, he worried for years about a person he failed to save. In 1976, on his way to catch the train to his home in upstate New York, he met Phil Ochs (also a folk singer and a good friend). Ochs was depressed and very much wanted to talk, but Seeger chose to jump onto his train. Ochs hanged himself that night. Seeger, at the age of 94, still haunted by wishing he had done something to stop his friend, related the story to Neil Young after 37 years. Young, who had had a similar experience with Kurt Cobain, advised him, much as wise clinicians do with each other in such circumstances: "Don't try to take it with you. Leave it where it happened ... You can't carry it with you" (Wegman, 2014). We must humbly accept.

Nevertheless, because we fail often, because our understanding is so severely limited, because complexity renders inadequate our attempts to help, because, as the Stoics taught and as Glen Gabbard (2009) reminds us, we have so little control over our patients' choices, because the demands and responsibilities that face us so exceed our finite capacities, we need something like humility. Lacking a good definition, we might say that humility is *something like*:

- the contrite fallibilism discussed above, which keeps us holding our theories lightly;
- the vulnerability, susceptibility, and passivity embodied in Levinasian substitution, also discussed previously;
- the reversal of the "inopportune ... as if a strange weakness caused presence or being-in-act [*l'être en acte*] to shiver and topple" (Levinas and Poller, 2003, p. 6);
- in other words, the priority of weakness;[15]
- nameless identity: "the other man commands by his face, which is not confined in the form of its appearance; naked, stripped of its form, denuded of its very presence, which would mask it like its own portrait" (Levinas and Poller, 2003, p. 7);[16]
- understanding our work as service (Poland, 2000, 2006);
- the strong association between ethical subjectivity and vulnerability, discussed in Dostoevsky and Levinas; and, above all,
- Uriah Heep notwithstanding, sincerity.

Of sincerity—never to be confused with Heideggerian authenticity—Emmanuel Levinas wrote:

> it suggests, in the primary suffering, in suffering as suffering, a hard unbearable consent that animates passivity, strangely animates it in spite of itself, whereas passivity as such has neither force nor intention, neither like it or not. The impotence or humility of "to suffer" is beneath the passivity of submission [not masochism, but surrender; see Chapter 3]. Here the word *sincerity* takes on all its sense; to discover oneself totally defenseless, to be surrendered. Intellectual sincerity, veracity [i.e., fallibilism], already refers to vulnerability, is founded in it.
> (Levinas and Poller, 2003, p. 64; original emphasis)

Sincerity thus characterizes this search for ethical humility. Quiet (except when injustice demands protest), modest (except when accepting praise supports community), simple (except when complexity protects dignity), sincerity fits with trustworthiness and reliability, hospitality and inclusion, warmth and care. Self-reflective, personal and communal, sincerity keeps us humble, making us wonder if our middle- and upper-middle-class lifestyles befit those who serve the poorest. What comforts do we truly need—surely we need some?—to sustain our lives of service? Timothy Zeddies provides a slightly aslant definition of "unconsciousness," addressing such questions: "a complex, historically woven tapestry of moral and ethical values, beliefs, and assumptions that shape and give accent to the unfolding of human history in a broad sense and the individual lives we lead more particularly" (Zeddies, 2002, p. 235). When, by way of dialogue, we become aware of what we take for granted, we may come to an unpretententious awareness that "psychoanalysis is simply neither as special nor unique as many of its practitioners believe it to be" (Zeddies, 2002, p. 236). This sensibility in hand, we analysts can begin to learn from other psychotherapeutic traditions, including some of those founded by practitioners whom Freud cast out, as well as from other devoted and nameless humanitarian workers worldwide.

Despite the lonesome-cowboy messages of North American culture, despite the shame inculcated by our training (Buechler, 1997), preventing our asking each other for help, despite the internal voices calling us "stupid" and "good-for-nothing," humility keeps us communitarians. The troubles we attempt to address are too big and we are too little, but small acts of kindness from one colleague to another can make a difference. Supporting colleagues who present clinical work can replace a *Besserwisser* attitude that belittles and shames. My supervisees, I find, learn much more easily from me after they have first perceived my respect and care for them; moreover, I learn from them.[17] Recognizing clinical complexity develops empathic understanding both for patients and for the treating clinician. One colleague said to me of a patient, "He wouldn't be so selfish if he didn't have to be," an apt paraphrase of my hermeneutics-of-trust discourse (Orange, 2011). Treating each other as if we can learn from the other cultivates an ambience of respect and hospitality in our professional homes.

Returning to the *Besserwisser*, this word literally translates as "better-knower." The needs of the other, on the contrary, belong to the other, not mine to know. As we saw in the study of Dostoevsky, "we will do and we will hear" means responding before understanding in its knowing sense. At least initially, and within my capacities to respond, I must allow others to speak for themselves. True, my doctor may tell me that I need surgery, drugs, physical therapy, or a dietary change, but this expert opinion should follow, and return to, a careful listening to the patient. Even if I rely on expert advice, I do not relinquish my voice as a human being, irreducible and irreplaceable. Even if I hate the advice or reject it, my doctor may treat me with care and respect.

We clinicians and humanitarian workers, likewise, serve the other to the best of our abilities, continuing to learn when the other says "no." Otherwise we may dominate by a form of liberal politics and ethics containing a subtle egoism. Without going to the extremes of Raskolnikov in *Crime and Punishment*, such utilitarians—even radicals—dominate by knowing. What do they know? *Besserwissers*, they know what the other needs. Instead of listening to the other in true liberality, realizing that the other remains both close and infinitely distant from his or her own experience, the "liberal," political, clinical, missionary tells the other, "You need . . ." In the end, the message is usually that the other "needs" to think, feel, and behave like us, to strive for what we strive for, to value what we value, to enjoy what we enjoy. The others—the widows, the orphans, and the strangers—are not allowed to speak of their own needs, or to place us in the position of passive hostage, of the persecuted, of responsibility. The "liberal" may presume to define the stranger's need. No argument for fundamentalism or conservatism here, of course; rather, we need a thoughtful and humble other-wise liberality.

Let me say something here about mistakes. Even if a therapist cultivates the attitude that Martin Buber called "inclusion" (or, to use my term, "clinical hospitality"), we will make thousands of mistakes, committing what many theorists call "microaggressions" (see www.microaggressions.com). This term, coined by Chester Pierce in 1970 in the context of racial microaggressions, refers to "subtle, stunning, often automatic, and non-verbal exchanges which are 'put downs'" (Pierce et al., 1978, p. 66). The term, common in the literature of cultural sensitivity, is defined by Sue (Sue et al., 2007, p. 273) as "brief and commonplace daily verbal, behavioral, or environmental indignities, whether intentional or unintentional, that communicate hostile, derogatory, or negative racial slights and insults toward people of other races." If we allow ourselves to be taught, we can begin to hear our own racist, sexist, and other microaggressions, but we will never be free of them. Always situated within culture, we cannot hear the way we sound to the other.

For years, in the New York area, I have worked with many patients from China, India, and other places whose cultures I scarcely know. I have learned, sometimes, to ask patients to say important things in their own language, and then to translate for me. I have learned to ask them to correct me as often as possible when I misunderstand or hurt them, and to teach me the most needed things about their own respective cultures. The same goes for African American, Latino, Native American, and LBGTQ cultures and subcultures. I say to the other: "I need your help, and I will try to keep learning and changing." It is not always possible to make a referral to a therapist who already understands. In a spirit of hospitality, it is up to me to stretch.

Aging humbles us too. Whether considered in Levinasian terms as uniquely individualizing because inescapably assigned to me as constitutive of subjectivity, as traumatized temporality (Levinas, 1998, p. 52), whether denied by every means available to technology and medicine, whether accepted grudgingly or gracefully, aging humbles. Even humanitarians, even psychoanalysts whose role models "died in harness," even positive-thinking optimists, all succumb to aging and death. Ultimate vulnerability in aging requires, demands, exacts, extorts humility as compassion for oneself received from community, with dependency on the other received and given simultaneously as grace. Where Uriah Heep's "umble" leaves us ridiculous, true humility brings integrity, dignity, and ongoing care for the other:

> To suffer by the other is to take care of him, bear him, be in his place, consume oneself by him . . . a responsibility that I did not assume at any moment, in any present. Nothing is more passive than this challenge prior to my freedom, the pre-original challenge, this sincerity . . . passivity of the vulnerable, condition (or incondition) by which being shows itself creature.
>
> (Levinas and Poller, 2003, p. 64)

In conclusion

Levinasian radical responsibility is hyperbolic,[18] not extreme. Often gentle and humble, it throws the money-changers out of the Temple and also binds up their wounds. Our responsibility is infinite but we are not. Often we will not be able to do it all any more, as we once pretended we could to others and ourselves. As elders, we serve as we can, and yield to others the tasks we can no longer carry. One of my inner choristers, Marcus Aurelius, counsels: "Not to live as if you had endless years ahead of you. Death overshadows you. While you're alive and able, be good" (Marcus Aurelius, 2002, 4.17).

Perhaps part of our problem loving and serving is that we talk too easily of surviving trauma. Primo Levi used a different term in Italian, something like straggling back: "*i rediti*" (those who returned). Maybe those of us who work with the traumatized are also among the returned, and we too may go down, like Ferenczi, like Winnicott, like Levi. We should not be ashamed, but humbled, to be in their company. In Dietrich Bonhoeffer's words, "a clearer and more sober estimate of our own limitations and possibilities . . . makes it possible for us genuinely to love our neighbor" (Bonhoeffer and Bethge, 1971, p. 276).

Notes

1 I prefer this recent translation to the more well known: "A man does not attain everything that he desires; the winds convey whither the ships do not list" (al-Mutanabbī, 1967, p. 12).

2 Unfortunately, Cornford identified this attitude with Stoicism. Neither Pierre Hadot nor I shares this view of the ancient Stoic philosophers. See Chapter 4.

3 My philosophy dissertation, and first book, concerned Peirce's theism. Though I have not written for philosophical journals for many years, Peirce scholars invited me to contribute to *Charles Sanders Peirce in His Own Words: 100 Years of Semiotics, Communcation and Cognition* a century after his death. In this section I make use of parts of what I contributed to that book.

4 This extract is from a manuscript entitled "Of Reasoning in General," which was not included in the 1931 edition of Peirce's *Collected Papers.*

5 In abduction, which differs from deductive and inductive thinking, a thinker generates, often in a moment of insight or intuition, a hypothesis to be tested.

6 The doctrine of papal infallibility in matters of faith and morals became official Roman Catholic dogma in the First Vatican Council of 1869–1870. It has also long been understood to extend to the Magisterium (council of bishops). Most recently, the Congregation of Faith, under Cardinal Josef Ratzinger, proclaimed that restriction of priestly ordination to men belongs infallibly to "the deposit of faith." Peirce first used the word "fallibilism" in the 1870s.

7 Not having learned this culture when I entered psychoanalysis from philosophy, I asked too many questions of Martin Bergmann (1913–2014) in our Freud course, and was informed emphatically, in his wonderful Austrian accent, "I am here to teach you, not to argue with you!"

8

> The patient's response resonates with so many different parts of us that we are never in a position to objectively evaluate any one particular intervention from any one point in the treatment situation. We are confronted with a model of mind based on a loose organization of multiple experiencing and reacting centers, and a new psychoanalytic humility born of the need to acknowledge that we can never be quite sure, at any given moment, who within the patient is listening and who within the analyst is speaking.
>
> (Davies, 1999, p. 198)

9 In an IARPP online colloquium on boundary violations, 2013.

10 Ironically, the writer of a book like this one currently spends several weeks searching out copyright owners, writing permission letters, and paying for the permissions. Community runs up against intellectual property law.

11 Buechler's meditation on the Henry James short story "The Middle Years" (Oates, 2013, pp. 171–190), among stunning stories by other authors she considers within her chapter on aging, expands my reflections on personal and clinical humility.

12 Rabbi and psychoanalyst Dennis Shulman (2008) writes of the Talmudic study of repentance, including awareness, confession, resolution, and restitution, all components of clinical humility.

13 The following paragraphs are adapted from my response to Steven Stern's plenary presentation at the International Conference on the Psychology of the Self, Chicago, 2013.

14 A few years later she seems less sure (Nguyen, 2012). She notes that she cannot name her own history while accompanying the others.

15 Blessed are the poor in spirit; blessed are they who mourn; blessed are the meek . . .

16 Actually, we have in the psychoanalytic literature a similar idea: "One may say in this regard [transference] the analyst intentionally functions as a cipher, a nonentity to be invested with meaning by the patient" (Loewald, 2000, p. 490, n2).

17 Goethe: "We learn only from people we love" (Goethe and Eckermann, 1984, p. 115).
18 For studies of comparable Second Testament usage, see Douglas (1925, 1931).

References

al-Mutanabbī (1967). *Poems of al-Mutanabbī*. Selected and edited by A. J. Arberry. Cambridge: Cambridge University Press.
Anderson, D., and Hausman, C. (2012). *Conversations on Peirce: Reals and Ideals*. New York: Fordham University Press.
Bonhoeffer, D., and Bethge, E. (1971). *Letters and Papers from Prison* (enlarged edn.). London: SCM Press.
Brandchaft, B., Doctors, S., and Sorter, D. (2010). *Toward an Emancipatory Psychoanalysis: Brandchaft's Intersubjective Vision*. New York: Routledge.
Buechler, S. (1997). The Right Stuff. *Contemporary Psychoanalysis*, 33, 295–306.
Buechler, S. (2015). *Understanding and Treating Patients in Clinical Psychoanalysis: Lessons from Literature*. New York and London: Routledge.
Coburn, W. (2002). A World of Systems. *Psychoanalytic Inquiry*, 22, 655–677.
Coburn, W. (2009). Attitudes in Psychoanalytic Complexity. In R. Frie and D. Orange (Eds.), *Beyond Postmodernism: New Dimensions in Clinical Theory and Practice* (pp. 183–200). New York: Routledge.
Cornford, F. (1960). *Before and after Socrates*. Cambridge: Cambridge University Press.
Critchley, S. (2007). *Infinitely Demanding: Ethics of Commitment, Politics of Resistance*. London and New York: Verso.
Davies, J. (1999). Getting Cold Feet, Defining "Safe-Enough" Borders: Dissociation, Multiplicity, and Integration in the Analyst's Experience. *Psychoanalytic Quarterly*, 68, 184–208.
Derrida, J. (1999). *Adieu to Emmanuel Levinas*. Stanford, CA: Stanford University Press.
Dickens, C. (2004). *David Copperfield* (rev. edn.). Introduction and notes by J. Tambling. London and New York: Penguin.
Douglas, C. (1925). *The Use of Hyperbole in the New Testament*. N.p.
Douglas, C. (1931). *Overstatement in the New Testament*. New York: H. Holt & Company.
Frank, M. (1999). Style in Philosophy, Part I. *Metaphilosophy*, 30, 145–167.
Gabbard, G. (2009). What is a "Good Enough" Termination? *Journal of the American Psychoanalytic Association*, 57, 575–594.
Galatzer-Levy, R. (1995). Psychoanalysis and Dynamical Systems Theory: Prediction and Self Similarity. *Journal of the American Psychoanalytic Association*, 43, 1085–1113.
Galatzer-Levy, R. (2011). Commentary on Paper by Terry Marks-Tarlow. *Psychoanalytic Dialogues*, 21, 140–151.
Ghent, E. (2002). The Emergent Ego: Complexity and Coevolution in the Psychoanalytic Process. *Journal of the American Psychoanalytic Association*, 50, 352–356.
Goethe, J., and Eckermann, J. (1984). *Conversations with Eckermann, 1823–1832*. San Francisco, CA: North Point Press.

Grossmark, R. (2012). The Unobtrusive Relational Analyst. *Psychoanalytic Dialogues*, 22, 629–646.

Herman, J. (1997). *Trauma and Recovery* (rev. edn.). New York: Basic Books.

James, W. (1902). *The Varieties of Religious Experience: A Study in Human Nature*. New York: Longmans, Green, & Co.

Klaus, C. (1999). *Taking Retirement: A Beginner's Diary*. Boston, MA: Beacon Press.

Kohut, H., Goldberg, A., and Stepansky, P. E. (1984). *How Does Analysis Cure?* Chicago, IL: University of Chicago Press.

Kubie, L. (1954). The Fundamental Nature of the Distinction between Normality and Neurosis. *Psychoanalytic Quarterly*, 23, 167–204.

Levi, P. (1989). *The Drowned and the Saved*. New York: Vintage International.

Levinas, E. (1987). *Collected Philosophical Papers*. Dordrecht and Boston Hingham, MA: Nijhoff and Kluwer Academic.

Levinas, E. (1998). *Otherwise than Being, or, Beyond Essence*. Pittsburgh, PA: Duquesne University Press.

Levinas, E., and Poller, N. (2003). *Humanism of the Other*. Urbana and Chicago, IL: University of Illinois Press.

Levinas, E., Peperzak, A., Critchley, S., and Bernasconi, R. (1996). *Emmanuel Levinas: Basic Philosophical Writings*. Bloomington, IN: Indiana University Press.

Loewald, H. W. (2000). *The Essential Loewald: Collected Papers and Monographs*. Hagerstown, MD: University Publishing Group.

McLaughlin, J. (1987). The Play of Transference: Some Reflections on Enactment in the Psychoanalytic Situation. *Journal of the American Psychoanalytic Association*, 35, 557–582.

Marcus Aurelius (2002). *Meditations*. Translated by G. Hays. New York: Modern Library.

Misak, C. (2004). *The Cambridge Companion to Peirce*. Cambridge: Cambridge University Press.

Nagel, T. (1974). What Is It Like to Be a Bat? *Philosophical Review*, 83, 435–450.

Nguyen, L. (2007). The Question of Survival: The Death of Desire and the Weight of Life. *American Journal of Psychoanalysis*, 67, 53–67.

Nguyen, L. (2012). Psychoanalytic Activism: Finding the Human, Staying Human. *Psychoanalytic Psychology*, 29, 308–317.

Oates, J. (2013). *The Oxford Book of American Short Stories* (2nd edn.). New York: Oxford University Press.

Ogden, T. (2003). What's True and Whose Idea Was It? *International Journal of Psychoanalysis*, 84, 593–606.

Orange, D. (2006). For Whom the Bell Tolls: Context, Complexity, and Compassion in Psychoanalysis. *International Journal of Psychoanalytic Self Psychology*, 1, 5–21.

Orange, D. (2009). Kohut Memorial Lecture: Attitudes, Values and Intersubjective Vulnerability. *International Journal of Psychoanalytic Self Psychology*, 4, 235–253.

Orange, D. (2011). *The Suffering Stranger: Hermeneutics for Everyday Clinical Practice*. New York: Routledge.

Peirce, C. (1931). *Collected Papers of Charles Sanders Peirce*. Cambridge, MA: Harvard University Press.

Peirce, C. S., Houser, N., Kloesel, C. J. W., and the Peirce Edition Project (1992). *The Essential Peirce: Selected Philosophical Writings*. Bloomington, IN: Indiana University Press.

Pierce, C., Carew, J., Pierce-Gonzalez, D., and Wills, D. (1978). An Expert in Racism: TV Commercials. In C. Pierce (Ed.), *Television and Education* (pp. 62–88). Beverly Hills, CA: Sage.

Poland, W. (2000). Commentary. *Journal of the American Psychoanalytic Association*, 48, 80–93.

Poland, W. (2006). The Analyst's Fears. *American Imago*, 63, 201–217.

Poland, W. (2007). The Limits of Empathy. *American Imago*, 64, 87–89.

Renik, O. (1993). Analytic Interaction: Conceptualizing Technique in Light of the Analyst's Irreducible Subjectivity. *Psychoanalytic Quarterly*, 62, 553–571.

Roazen, P. (2001). *The Historiography of Psychoanalysis*. New Brunswick, NJ: Transaction.

Rosenthal, S. (2004). Peirce's Pragmatic Account of Perception: Issues and Implications. In C. Misak (Ed.), *The Cambridge Companion to Peirce* (pp. 193–213). Cambridge: Cambridge University Press.

Shabad, P. (2010). The Suffering of Passion: Metamorphoses and the Embrace of the Stranger. *Psychoanalytic Dialogues*, 20, 710–729.

Shulman, D. (2008). Jonah: His Story, Our Story; His Struggle, Our Struggle: Commentary on Paper by Avivah Gottlieb Zornberg. *Psychoanalytic Dialogues*, 18, 329–364.

Stolorow, R., Atwood, G., and Orange, D. (2002). *Worlds of Experience: Interweaving Philosophical and Clinical Dimensions in Psychoanalysis*. New York: Basic Books.

Sue, D. W., Capodilupo, C. M., Torino, G. C., Bucceri, J. M., Holder, A. M. B., Nadal, K. L., and Esquilin M. (2007). Racial Microaggressions in Everyday Life. *American Psychologist*, 62, 271–286.

Thelen, E., and Smith, L. (1994). *A Dynamic Systems Approach to the Development of Cognition and Action*. Cambridge, MA: MIT Press.

Thellefsen, T. (2014). *Charles Sanders Peirce in His Own Words: 100 Years of Semiotics, Communcation and Cognition*. Berlin: Walter de Gruyter.

Wegman, J. (2014). Pete Seeger, Neil Young and the Importance of Letting Go. *New York Times*, January 28. Retrieved from www.nytimes.com/2014/01/29/opinion/pete-seeger-neil-young-and-the-importance-of-letting-go.html?_r=2 (accessed August 28, 2015).

Zeddies, T. J. (2002). Historicity, Humility, and the Analytic Exercise: Reply to Commentaries by Drs. Palombo and Horner. *Journal of the American Academy of Psychoanalysis*, 30, 235–240.

Index

Note: Page numbers followed by 'n' refer to notes.